C0-BZG-107

FAITH AND THE · PROFESSIONS ·

FAITH AND THE PROFESSIONS

THOMAS L. SHAFFER

BRIGHAM YOUNG UNIVERSITY

For Nancy

Library of Congress Cataloging in Publication Data
Shaffer, Thomas L., 1934–
Faith and the professions.

Bibliography: p. 311
Includes indexes.
1. Medical ethics—United States. 2. Legal ethics—United States.
I. Title.
R724.S45 1987 174′.2 87-863 ISBN 0-88706-561-9

Brigham Young University, Provo, Utah

Printed in the United States of America

Distributed by State University of New York Press, State University Plaza, Albany, New York 12246-0001

Rabban Gamaliel, the son of Rabbi Judah ha-Nasi, said: Let all who work for the community do so from a spiritual motive, for then the merit of their fathers will sustain them, and their righteousness will endure forever. "I credit you with great reward [God says] as if you had accomplished it all."

—The Ethics of the Fathers

Books by Thomas L. Shaffer

Death, Property, and Lawyers (1970)

The Planning and Drafting of Wills and Trusts (1972, 1979)

Legal Interviewing and Counseling (1976; second edition, co-author with James R. Elkins; 1987)

The Mentally Retarded Citizen and the Law (co-editor with Michael Kindred, Julius Cohen, and David Penrose; 1976)

Lawyers, Law Students, and People (co-author with Robert S. Redmount; 1980)

Legal Interviewing and Counseling Cases (co-editor with Robert S. Redmount; 1980)

On Being a Christian and a Lawyer (1981)

American Legal Ethics (1985)

Faith and the Professions (1987)

Contents

Chapter One

· § ·

STORIES

Stories . . . are not told to explain as a theory explains, but to involve the agent in a way of life. A theory is meant to help you know the world without changing the world yourself; a story is to help you deal with the world by changing it through changing yourself.

—Stanley Hauerwas

THE morals of an American professional person—a doctor or a lawyer—begin long before professional practice begins. Morals begin, I think, in stories. And so, if this project of mine is to be a search for the morals of doctors and lawyers, it had best begin in an ordinary way, in the stories we grew up hearing and that we continue to hear.

This beginning is still a search, but it is the search that begins in places where we have found things before. I have three or four places where I expect to find my reading glasses. My reading glasses aren't really lost when I can look in those places and find them; but, still, my looking for them is a search.

Augie March, growing up a Jewish boy in Chicago, located his morals the way I locate my reading glasses. "All the influences were lined up waiting for me," he said. "I was born and there they were to form me, which is why I tell you more of them than of myself."

Augie's heart led him to the influences, made him want them. "I know I longed very much, but I didn't understand for what. . . . Friends, human pals, men and brethren, there is no brief, digest, or shorthand way to say where it leads. Crusoe, alone with nature, under heaven, had a busy, complicated time of it with the unhuman itself."

"And I," Augie said, "am in a crowd that yields results with much more difficulty and reluctance and am part of it myself."

Search is an attractive metaphor in talking about the morals of lawyers and doctors in America, though, if only because so much of what is said in professional societies and taught in professional schools is manifestly aimless. There must be more to it than *that*! And so I look around, as Augie did, as if to find my reading glasses, to see if I can find what it is. And, like where my reading glasses are, or Augie March's "influences," what I find is not new. The roots and sustenance of the morals of doctors and lawyers in America have more to be noticed than to be found.

And so, the first and last place to look for influences will be in doctor and lawyer stories. There rather than in the deliberations of medical societies or bar associations, or in the decisions of courts and committees, or even the sources of moral principles that we are all familiar with—the Bible, the great thinkers, the wisdom of rabbis and sages.

To look for professional ethics in America in stories involves, though, biases and choices. I should make those clear, at the beginning. My agenda in this chapter is partly introductory because my biases and my choices should be described and defended before I begin to thresh around among the deeper and more difficult implications of professional morality.

I think of medical or legal ethics as ethical subjects rather than as medical or legal subjects. When it comes to "professional responsibility," which is the name given to the required course I teach in university law schools, I am more interested in morals than I am in law. I agree with my friend Monroe Freedman, who said, in a lecture dedicated to the memory of Pope John XXIII, that the question that interests him is whether a good person can be a lawyer. For Freedman, I think, and for me, the interesting question has to do with the goodness of being a lawyer. But to say that is also to make the claim, which Freedman and I do, that moral questions can be talked about with the analytical rigor we lawyers are thought to bring to questions about justice, and doctors are thought to bring to questions about health. And to claim intellectual rigor for ethics in professional discourse is to disapprove of the way people in schools usually go about dealing with moral subjects. I see four positions here.

1. *Moral subjects are relevant to the formation of doctors and lawyers, who, in professional school and beyond, are in fact being formed.* I part company with the law teacher of a colleague of mine who countered a student's objection by saying, "Ethics, shmethics! Ethics is for Episcopalians."

2. *The attempt to separate science or law from morals, in order to better study medicine or law, is corrupting.* It is fatuous to make this attempt when the discussion has to do with health or with justice, when the topic is a philosophy of what sickness or civil discord are. Both professions had tedious flirtations with this attempt in the nineteenth century. The legal experiment failed, early, and American jurisprudence declined into the somber positivism most of us American lawyers meet in law school: The law is what the judge says it is; law is power. The medical experiment, the claim that healing is science, lasted longer, of course, and had more promise, but story words, moral words, seem now to carry more hope than scientific words do. One set of examples is in Eric Cassell's distinction between sickness (an interpersonal and a social condition) and disease, and between healing and cure (healing is possible where cure is not). Those distinctions carry in them the memory of stories; and by that I mean they suggest that stories are where the distinctions come from. That is even more clearly the case in Cassell's characterization of the founders of medical ethics. The Hippocratic School describes the physician as "calm and effective, humane and observant, prompt and cautious, at once learned and willing to learn, pure in mind and body, and fearing lest he fail to serve." I think not of Hippocrates but of Donald Westfall of "St. Elsewhere."

When the discussion is about ethics (and by "ethics" I mean the processes and theories with which morals are discussed), the attempt to separate law from morals, or healing from the images and memories that gave rise to Cassell's distinctions and Hippocrates' description of the doctor, is untruthful. It is like Augie March trying to account for himself without mentioning the influences that were lined up waiting for him. These attempts are, because untruthful, also corrupting. The attempts corrupt—have corrupted—doctors and lawyers. To say, as the Harvard law professor of fable did, "If you want to study justice you should go to divinity school," is erroneous in substance and corrosive in moral effect. Part of the corrosion is the exclusion of morals from the category of subjects that can be explicated, explored, analyzed, and evaluated in school and in the organized professions.

3. *The attempt to isolate law or healing from morals is one of the explanations for the fact that lawyers and doctors say professional school was and is an inhuman place, that people there were not and are not treated well.* The exclusion of morals as an intellectually interesting subject does not mean that there is no moral formation in school; it means that there is bad moral formation in school. Socrates told Thrasymachus that the two of them could learn about justice *from one another* by what they said to one another and by the way they treated one another. Socrates was talking about the *virtue* of justice. When virtue is excluded from discussion, as it is in the misnamed and perennial model of "Socratic" law teaching, the discussers learn how to *mistreat* one another. When life and health are treated separately (the lesson, perhaps, in Rembrandt's painting *The Anatomy Lesson*), the discussers learn how not to talk about what health is.

· § ·

These three claims might have led me to argue that ethics in the professions should be analyzed as science or philosophy or law usually is, in terms of tentative and abstract statements of principle. Legal and medical ethics are sets of fraternal principles. This is the way American doctors and lawyers learned to talk about the subject after the fathers of Anglo-American professional ethics spoke—Sir Thomas Percival in medical ethics, in 1791, and David Hoffman in legal ethics, in 1817. Hoffman's efforts, most notably his "Fifty Resolutions on Professional Deportment" of 1836, along with George Sharswood's 1854 essay on legal ethics were not codes, but they were later translated into official consensus statements from bar associations, courts, and legislatures. The codal form was followed by the American Bar Association in its 1908 *Canons,* its 1969 *Code,* and its 1983 proposed *Rules.*

Percival used the codal form from the beginning for medical ethics (which seems to prove that nonlawyers are more likely to be legalistic than lawyers are). And all the subsequent formulations of the American Medical Association have been codal. In all these cases, abstract principle is the form of ethical statement. This is as true of the proposed ABA *Rules* and the 1980 AMA *Principles* as it was of the nineteenth-century codal formulations, although the modern statements stridently avoid such words as "moral," "ethical," or "conscience." There are, of course, some statements of *law* in these documents; for example, certain behavior is described as subject to penal sanction. However, all these documents, to the extent they are devoted to moral admonition at all, are stated abstractly, as principle. This brings me to a fourth position:

4. *Moral principles are not an adequate way to state, to analyze, or to study ethics in the professions.* Not, at least, if we are to stay with the question that is interesting for ethics: Is it possible to be a good person and a doctor or a lawyer?

The most persistently useful textbook I have used in teaching legal ethics is Harper Lee's novel *To Kill a Mockingbird* (1960). I have learned through my undeserved success to respect Miss Lee's lawyer, Atticus Finch, and to wonder why he is such an effective teacher. It seems superficial, if not impossible, to use moral *principles* as a way to analyze (a) Finch's being defense counsel for Tom Robinson, a black man, falsely accused of rape; or (b) Finch's insistence on speaking the unspeakable truth in Robinson's trial. (The unspeakable truth was that the alleged victim of rape attempted to seduce Tom Robinson, and failed, and cried rape in frustration and guilt.)

It is possible, of course, to say that a lawyer has a responsibility to see to it that every person accused of crime has the effective assistance of counsel and that a lawyer must do the best job she or he can for the client, let the chips fall where they may. Atticus Finch seems to have obeyed those principles. He would have nodded if someone had spoken them out loud. (No one did.) The problem is that such principles didn't say much about the moral substance of the case.

The moral substance of the case included what "effective" can mean in a situation in which the only way to have saved the not-guilty Robinson would have been to help him become a fugitive; a fugitive, as they say, from justice. But, if analysis is going to stay with the facts, we should admit that Atticus Finch did not understand the case, the "issues," or the moral substance as a situation involving the effective assistance of counsel.

To state the case as turning on these professional principles is not the best way to understand Atticus Finch because it is not the way he understood himself. The way *he* saw the case has to do not so much with his having been a lawyer alert to what the bar association gave as the ethical principles of his calling as with his having been a rural Southerner and a Christian gentleman. This is not to say that Atticus Finch was unprincipled. To the extent that he announces principles (e.g., he cannot be one person in town and another person at home; he cannot go to church and worship God unless he helps Tom Robinson; he must tell the truth about Robinson and the alleged victim, Mayella Ewell, in court; and it is a sin to kill a mockingbird), his principles are not bad principles. That is, they are not, on analysis, illogical or irrational. Those principles do not, however, answer the question we want to answer: Can a good person be a lawyer? Or, rather, as Harper Lee saw it, how did Atticus, a good person, go about being a lawyer?

Finch's principles only make the question more difficult because the usual sources of moral principle, for examples, Atticus Finch's church (the white Baptist and Methodist congregations in Maycomb), and the organized bar, gave him no support in what he did. Atticus did not *help* Tom Robinson when he did the things lawyers in court usually do to help people; if any tactic held promise for Tom Robinson's acquittal, it was *not* telling the truth. "Don't kill mockingbirds" is only another way to say "do good and avoid evil." As a *principle* it is an unexamined place to begin to talk about ethics; it says nothing about how a good person goes about the practice of a profession. Yet, Atticus Finch is a *good person,* and he is a *lawyer,* and he knows *how* to be both at the same time. He provides useful guidance on our questions, but the statement and analysis of his principles is not the way to learn from him.

Character

One thing you could say about Atticus is that he had *character*. You could say that as well of physicians in our popular stories—from Dr. Gillespie to Anthony Trollope's Dr. Thorne, to the three aging doctors in "St. Elsewhere." And we all have our personal examples of teachers who have character. The creator of Atticus Finch said that the story was the story of "his view of life," of his conscience. The fact that Atticus is a favorite among American readers and moviegoers says to me that we have learned from him about character. There is a relationship between what a person is and what he seems to have decided to do. We call that relationship character.

The advantage in analyzing Atticus in terms of character, rather than in terms of principles, is that it begins to tell us a little about where he comes from, about his motives, and about who he is. This is to say that his moral decisions come from who he is and help to determine who he is. The point is even more elementary. Because of who he is, Atticus understands a situation as moral when someone else would see it as political or economic or not a "problem" at all.

In being the person he is, Atticus is able to do what he does, and in doing what he does he forms and reforms the person he is. We say that a good person has character, but we do not mean to say only that he believes in discernible moral principles and, under those principles, makes good decisions. We mean also to say something about who he is and to relate who he is to his good decisions. When discussion proceeds in this way, principles need not even be explicit. We can say, "How would Atticus *see* this situation?" or "What would Atticus do?" rather than, "What principles apply?"

We arrive at a sense of who a person is when we learn about his grief, his joy, and his irrationality, more about him than about his decisions. Most of the time we don't search for character. We recognize it because of skills we have learned from our parents and teachers and the people we know in our towns and religious congregations, which is to say that character is culture. Atticus Finch is popular among readers and moviegoers; I find that law students are more familiar with him than they are with the Bible. We say that he teaches us about character. That is true, but it is true because Atticus and his story are the influences that are lined up waiting for *us*, too. We don't *find* Atticus; we notice him.

But sometimes our learning about character is a shock, even if it is also a gradual acculturation. An example is Dolphus Raymond, the odd old fellow who sits outside the courthouse in Atticus Finch's Maycomb and drinks from a bottle in a paper sack. He appears to the town to be an old drunk but he does not drink moonshine whiskey; he drinks Coca-Cola. And who does he let know what he is drinking? Not the community, which thinks Dolphus is drinking moonshine. Instead, he tells three children who are learning to weep over what people in the community do to one another in the name of the law. Dolphus is not an old drunk; he is a tragic figure, a teacher, a moral critic, a prophet.

Another example in the Finch story is Mrs. Dubose, who is dying and, as she dies, is overcoming morphine addiction—cold turkey. When we first know about what is going on with her, as Jem reads to her from *Ivanhoe,* we know about the meaning of caring for old people, and about Atticus, and about the formation of a gentleman.

The Dubose story illustrates what Cassell means when he talks about healing. Illness, he says, is cultural. He tells of a patient of his who was in danger of a heart attack and who had to be pointed to, and to decide on, a place for treatment. The critical fact in the case turned out to be that the man had come to the city without his wife; the important thing, from the standpoint of illness, was for him to be treated near her. Mrs. Dubose had a terminal disease; it made good sense—or, at least, customary medical sense—to treat her with morphine, to allay her pain as she died. She was also ill, and her illness was not the same thing as her disease. In fact, her illness was her morphine addiction; she was ill with morphine. She accepted her death, but she wanted to die free from morphine addiction.

The Dubose story also illustrates the way the principles of professional ethics work and don't work. Mrs. Dubose was a cranky old bigot. She called from her porch to the Finch children, and when she got their attention, insulted the children's father. The substance of her insults was that Atticus Finch, to use what Faulkner called "that ancient subterrene atavistic ethnic fear," was a "nigger lover." It was after such an attack from Mrs. Dubose that Jem Finch stormed into her flower garden and beheaded all her camellias. The result of the attack was that Atticus sent Jem and Scout to Mrs. Dubose's house, to read to her, every afternoon, from *Ivanhoe.*

Atticus knew about the addiction; he had learned about that from Mrs. Dubose when he interviewed her so that he could draft her will. He knew that the pain of withdrawal from morphine came to her most severely in the afternoon, at about the time of the sessions with *Ivanhoe.* He probably also knew that the pain of hearing *Ivanhoe* read out loud was enough to distract a person from the pain of withdrawal from morphine addiction. But he did not tell the children about the medical reason for their visits to Mrs. Dubose's house; they went there, as they thought, for punishment and to learn how to treat old people in the neighborhood. Most children in my generation got such lessons. If children no longer get them, or no longer get them in this neighborly way, I would be sorry to know it.

And then Mrs. Dubose died. Atticus brought Jem a deathbed gift from her, a white box. "Inside, surrounded by wads of damp cotton, was a white, waxy, perfect camellia. It was a Snow-on-the-Mountain." Atticus told his children about the morphine addiction. He told them partly, I suppose, because it was unjust for them to grow into adulthood thinking that Mrs. Dubose was, as Jem put it, an "old hell-devil." But that is not what Atticus said; nor did he say he wanted them to learn how a good person takes care of the old. "I wanted you to see something about her," Atticus said. "I wanted you to see what real courage is, instead of getting the idea that courage is a man with a gun in his hand. It's when you know you're licked before you begin but you begin anyway and you see it through no matter what. You rarely win, but sometimes you do. Mrs. Dubose won, all ninety-eight pounds of her. According to her views, she died beholden to nothing and nobody. She was the bravest person I ever knew."

Atticus's act in telling the children was a violation of the Code of Ethics of the Alabama Bar Association. "Communications and confidence between client and attorney are the property and secrets of the client, and cannot be divulged, except at his instance; even the death of the client does not absolve the attorney from his obligation of secrecy." I mention it to show that the principles of professional ethics and the influences that are lined up waiting for us are not the same, not in the way we cope with them, nor in their substance. As a result of events such as this one in Jem's life, he came to the day when he looked at his father (a dull, bookish, controlled man) and said, "Atticus is a gentleman, just like me!" I don't know if Jem ever did learn anything about the code of legal ethics.

Knowing character is not primarily a matter of having a principled explanation for a person's *acts*. For example, why did Atticus take the Robinson case? He was not a criminal-defense lawyer; in fact, he usually lost his criminal cases. "His first two clients were the last two persons hanged in the Maycomb County jail," Scout says. "Atticus had urged them to accept the state's generosity in allowing them to plead guilty to second-degree murder and escape with their lives, but they were Haverfords, in Maycomb County a name synonymous with jackass. The Haverfords had dispatched Maycomb's leading blacksmith in a misunderstanding arising from the alleged wrongful detention of a mare, were imprudent enough to do it in the presence of three witnesses, and insisted that the-son-of-a-bitch-had-it-coming-to-him was a good enough defense for anybody. They persisted in pleading Not Guilty to first-degree murder, so there was nothing much Atticus could do for his clients except be present at their departure, an occasion that was probably the beginning of my father's profound distaste for the practice of criminal law."

We think we know something, though, about why Atticus nonetheless took Robinson's case (for no fee) when Judge John Taylor asked him to. We think we know something about that even if what Atticus did was not exactly a decision (the novel doesn't even describe it, whatever it was). Atticus says a lot about why he represents Robinson as he does, but nothing about why he agreed to represent him in the first place. It is not a decision he is shown making; it is not an act. If there is a principle to explain it, it is not a principle Atticus bothers to mention. Probably every reader will say, by the time he finishes the book, that it is, after all, the sort of thing Atticus would do. It is like a mother who looks at her new baby and loves the baby (James McClendon's example). Does she *decide* to love the baby? Is the most significant thing her *act* in loving the baby, or does it have more to do with something not understood primarily as a matter of decisions or acts? It is significant to know that she loves her baby, but what we then know is not knowledge about a principle or a decision or an act.

Many morally significant facts in professional life are not decisions or acts, or do not seem to be. Atticus, for example, gets angry at white business people who take advantage of black customers. He says, in his anger, that such people are trash. But he does not seem to have *decided* to call them trash. Much of what Atticus does is a matter less of decision, or of act, than of disposition. One could use other words for it. Conviction, for instance, explains much of it. Some old-fashioned words for it are virtue or habit, or, if the disposition is evil, vice. Those words turn on the particularity of a person, on who he is, on his integrity or lack of integrity, and on how we come to know about him. They cause us to say, "Well, that's the way he is." We say that of the people who show us what our morals are, and, when we do, we of course say something about ourselves, too. That is Augie March's point: He was a part of the crowd from which he sought moral answers.

Disposition, virtue, and habit are character words, that is, words about traits of character. They are stronger, more telling words than, say, the word *opinion.* If I were to trust Atticus or Mark Craig of "St. Elsewhere" or one of my teachers with a matter of great importance to me, it would be because I had some idea of how she or he would behave on my behalf. It would not be because of his opinions, or because of the moral decisions I could predict he would make, or even the acts I imagined to flow from my turning to him, but it would be because I trusted his character.

Harper Lee does not begin *To Kill a Mockingbird* with a statement of Atticus's principles, and by the time she finishes telling us about Atticus such a statement would be distracting. Instead, she acquaints us with the character of Atticus Finch in an ordinary way.

She tells us a story. We come to know him as we came to know our parents, our aunts and uncles, our family doctors, our playmates, and our favorite teachers. We know his family; we know the people he admires; we know his neighbors, and we know him as they know him; and we know his enemies. We know something too, about his views on politics and religion, but there our knowledge is not a matter of propositions. We know most of what we know about Atticus's beliefs because we have known people who are like Atticus. We assume that he is like them; we don't usually think much about the resemblance. In terms of morals, we come to know about Atticus in the way we learn most of what we learn about how to behave, about goodness and good people, and that is more a matter of stories than it is a matter of moral principles. As a result of knowing Atticus in the way Harper Lee presents him I would be willing to trust him with something that is important to me, as Tom Robinson trusted Atticus with his life.

Stories

Often it is a poet or playwright or novelist who understands best how our professional morals work. She or he understands, better than we understand—or, at least she *shows* whether she understands or not—how we come to behave as we do. James Edwin Horton, the good judge of the Scottsboro cases and a contemporary of Atticus Finch at the Alabama Bar, ruined his judicial career and brought homicidal wrath on black people in Alabama when he set aside the guilty verdict and death sentence in the second Haywood Patterson case in 1933. He did all this to no effect; Patterson was put to trial a third and a fourth time and in both cases convicted. Judge Horton suffered prolonged agony in presiding at Patterson's trial. The consequences of what he did there, for himself and for others, were consequences of agony. The decision itself—the act—tells us nothing about Horton except that he was not like the other judges in those cases.

When he was asked, some thirty-five years later, why he acted as he did in those days, Judge Horton said it was because he had learned, at his mother's knee, the Latin maxim, *fiat justitia ruat coelum* (let justice be done though the heavens fall). The principle, however the judge learned it, was undoubtedly applicable, but the principle is not helpful to those of us who, in the 1980s, want to learn from Judge Horton whether a good person can be a lawyer. We want to know more about Judge Horton himself. To learn from Judge Horton about whether a good person can be a lawyer we need to hear his story.

Principles do not explain. We who teach ethics to—or with—law and medical students and those who want themselves to be teachers need to find a way to study and to teach about the ethics of character instead of about the principles we find in our codes. One can learn about the ethics of character by studying American doctor and lawyer stories, but there is serious theoretical objection to that, objection similar to the objection to the study of character in the philosophical, introspective way Aristotle and Thomas Aquinas studied character. The objection is that a morality of character is subjective and relativistic or intuitive and therefore not ethics at all. The study of virtue and of virtuous lives smacks of "situation ethics," which has come to mean a system of ponderous justification for doing what you feel like doing and, then, even when what you have done is pretty good, saying, "I behaved as I did because of the way I was brought up." Professional ethics, the objection says, cannot be a study of stories because instances from other lives do not give us objective guidance for our own lives.

If we believe that morality can be dealt with in the way we deal with law in law school, or with medicine as a science, the objection to the ethics of character will be that it is *not rational.* Those of us who claim that the interesting question in professional ethics is, "Is it possible to be a good person and a doctor or lawyer?" and who then claim that the way to answer the question is to learn from lawyer and doctor stories, have to consider whether it is accurate to charge that the ethics of character is subjective or irrational or relativistic. To put the issue positively: Can we justify a morality of character, and the study of professional stories as a way to study character, by showing those methods to be as objective and as rational as a morality of principles is? Is relativism an accurate, and, if accurate, a fatal objection?

My fourth claim, then, stated positively, is this: The truth about who we are, which explains our morality, including such things as what our communities are and what our families have been, is, as in Atticus Finch's case, more a matter of character, of life as we live it, of story, than it is of principles. This is not a matter of saying what is desirable, which is what I was doing when I extolled the ethics of character, but of saying instead that a story explains and displays such things as principles, and that one is close to the truth of one's own moral life when he studies other lives by going to the sources of morals in those lives—when he looks in that way (with the help of storytellers) at the influences that are lined up waiting for us. The life a person is living, the narrative into which his life fits, or some terms such as these, explain how that person even comes to see that a moral question exists. His seeing is there—for good or ill—in truth or in distortion—before he even thinks that what he has at hand is a moral decision.

Our stories are the sources of our moral notions and our moral notions are prior, in time and in logic, to our classifications, our categories, and our principles. Stories explain why we regard some of the things we do as moral actions and regard other things we do as reflexes or the products of routine. Our stories cause us to single out events and call them moral events. We see some events as moral because our moral notions are stirred up by them. The notions bracket the moral issues, and notions become intelligible in stories. Stories turn morals into ethics. Stories explain notions, as the presence of notions accounts for moral problems. Stories bring moral notions to light; and moral notions are prior to moral problems. To put that another way, a moral notion becomes something we see and can talk about because of a story. A moral notion is displayed and understood in a narrative context better than it is displayed and understood in a context of issues, quandaries, decisions, acts, and principles.

Consider, for example, Mark Craig's encounter with the television crew. A television producer wanted to make a documentary about Craig's dramatic abilities as a heart surgeon. Dr. Westfall, the administrator of St. Eligius's, was dubious about allowing television crews into the hospital, but Craig talked him into it—on the ground that publicity would be good for the hospital, which struggles for funding and is regarded as a second-rate, inner-city cousin to Boston's more famous hospitals. Craig deceived himself here, of course. He wanted publicity for himself; he enjoys being famous. He preened for the cameras and put up with the inconveniences of having them at his shoulder—even in the operating room—until it became clear to him (as it had become clear to everybody else, minutes earlier) that the television director subordinated people to art.

Craig practices medicine as art; he understands the importance of art. But his art is subordinate to his regard for patients. That is what makes him a good doctor, and is probably why the residents admire and learn from him. That moral notion of Craig's—medicine as art, healing art—accounts for his place in the story of St. Eligius. When he finally understood what was going on—when the television director wanted Craig to repeat a painful interview with a patient the surgeon was unable to help—Craig *saw* (then perhaps he discerned the relevance of a moral *principle*) and he ordered the television crew to leave the hospital. He acted as he did because there was something about him that was prior to his being a vain physician. That something, in him *and in ourselves,* is what we cheer. Because the director did not see what was going on he was a callous exploiter of the suffering patient—*morally* at fault in his failure to *see.* One person saw and the other did not; it was that, not the answer to the problem, which distinguished them. It happens to lawyers, too.

In professional ethics, I have had to change my view of the student or physician or lawyer who gives her answer and explains it by saying, "I can't help it. It's because I was raised in a Southern Baptist church." She is not being irrational; she is pointing out a fact that is more potent, for both of us, than any principle. This fact is prior both to moral problems and to moral principles. I have decided that I have to understand what this fact is before I can even begin to figure out how to use the problem and the answer to the problem in teaching. If we do not understand that, we run a risk even deeper than loss of a rational explanation for our morals. The risk we run is alienation from ourselves, from the people we are. And then we begin answering tough professional questions by asking not "What should I do?" but "What does a *lawyer* (physician, teacher) do?" We begin, to use a story, to live out the difference between Thomas More and Thomas Cromwell in Robert Bolt's play *A Man for All Seasons,* by choosing to be Cromwell. It was Cromwell who talked of "administrative convenience," who said that power must have its way. Cromwell's moral life is lived in alienation from his self. In such alienation, we practice our professions with disabling discontinuities between who we are and what we are doing. Too many doctors and lawyers and teachers try to do that. They end in misery, alcoholism, or repentance, and they make things worse for their clients and patients. We who ponder ethics in and for the professions should not do anything to add to their number.

This argument for the use of stories is as ordinary, I think, as the method Harper Lee used to tell us about Atticus Finch. The way we grow up morally, and in many other ways as well, is by listening to and living out stories. We recognize our morals in the moral points in stories. Some of these stories are broad, grand things, "the Jewish experience," "the story of Jesus," "the voyage of America," and so forth. Such stories have a lot to do with who we think we are, and they have everything to do with our morals. Stories need not have principles but they all have points. We often say, in this ordinary way, "The point of the story is . . ."

Stories, both the stories we live and those we hear, have plots and characters. We read or listen to or talk about a story and as we go along we ask, "What happened next?" The *point* comes out of characters creating and encountering the events of the story. It is not always a logical outcome, but it always makes sense. What was logical about Atticus insisting that the jury hear what really happened between Mayella Ewell and Tom Robinson? The point is not even necessarily a consequence of the events. That kind of story would be boring; it would be a study in causation. What comes out of a story is what comes out of our own stories, out of life itself, a sense of who people are, a sense, that is, of character.

I argue, then, that the plot of a story, which connects events and gives them a point, is a rational construct. It is an act of the mind, the act of a mind that makes sense of the story. Readers and critics make sense for themselves of stories such as Atticus's story. (Other examples of lawyers are George V. Higgins's Boston lawyer Jerry Kennedy, and Ephraim Tutt of the old *Saturday Evening Post* stories. I talk about them in chapter 5.) We make sense of our own stories, and the stories of one another, when we attempt to live purposeful lives. The two things fit together: The sense we make of the stories we hear and read is a way to make sense of the stories we live. *Ethics* can be a place where we talk about how the two meet. The ethical sense we make of either sort of story is our description of the character of the people in the story. We can be wrong in doing that, and we can argue about it. It is subject to proof and reason and, therefore, the ethics one has from stories is not only more concrete than the ethics one has from principles, it is also rational, meaning that we reason about stories.

Beyond rationality, making ethical sense of stories is an activity in which we pile one story on top of another. In telling the story of Atticus, Scout tells us her own story, and in talking about Scout's story about Atticus's story, I tell you about my story, and in arguing with me about it you will tell me about your story. We end with a diversity of people, an array of virtues and ideas, and a rich context for the study of ethics. This is not a contrivance, not merely a method; it is both how we go about living our lives in a moral way and how we go about thinking. It is also how we learn about our moral lives. We transfer the point of the story, make it our own, and keep it from being a single instance. This is the first and most ordinary way to look for—to notice—American professional ethics.

Each of us has more than one story—vertically and horizontally. I am not merely a lawyer and a teacher. I am not even most importantly either of those. I am a Christian as well and, as such, necessarily, an admirer—a child—of the Jews. A husband and a father. A mountain westerner, the only male in three generations in my family who is not a cowboy, the descendant of pioneers and frontier Christian women. Not a cowboy myself, but a Christian myself. (Eugene S. Geissler, a great moral teacher, told me once that God has no grandchildren.) Each of us changes in terms of these stories. Each of us has sequence in his life, and one of the ways—the most significant for professional ethics—is by testing one story against another, by finding that some of our stories are adequate and some are not.

Thus, Louis D. Brandeis goes along most of his life being a successful lawyer and a social activist and one day he discovers that he is a Jew. He *knew* it all along, but one day, well along in life, he *discovered* what he always knew. He noticed that he was part of Israel, of the Jewish people, an international and ancient and deeply significant story that was also *his* story. And the story Brandeis had been living, the story of a liberal lawyer, was tested against a bolder, broader, and more adequate story. The comparison changed his life. By the time Brandeis left the Supreme Court, President Franklin D. Roosevelt had learned to call him Isaiah—another story.

I have noticed an odd commonality in the many published discussions of Brandeis's professional ethics. None of them explores the significance of Brandeis's Jewishness; he is treated as morally disembodied. Of course, it is not usual for writers to relate moral theology and professional ideology in discussions of professional ethics—not even when the subject is a person who is often called America's greatest Jew. Perhaps professional ethics is also disembodied. Emergence of identity similar to Brandeis's also appears in stories of professionals and heroes who undergo Christian religious conversions. They test the story they are living against the story they hear from the Gospels. They see themselves in this new story and their lives are changed. There isn't much about them in books about professional ethics.

In *To Kill a Mockingbird,* Atticus is led right up to this comparison of stories again and again. Sometimes he changes, as he did when he tested the story of the gentleman in the old rural South against another, bolder, broader story that was also his story. Sometimes he does not change, as when he tests the story that tells him he cannot protect his battered, unconscious, teenaged son from the consequences of truth, against the story that tells him he *can* lie, however, to save Boo Radley's seclusion. What he *says* in these cases is a series of statements of principle. "I can't live one way in town and another way in my home." "Can you possibly understand?" he says to Scout, and she says, "Well, it'd be sort of like shootin' a mockingbird, wouldn't it?" But, when we think about it, we know that these moments were not primarily deductions from principle. People do, though, take direction in such comparisons, and we, when we read about such comparisons, make judgments about people and about ourselves. We can talk about those judgments. We can be rational about them, and, what is more important, rational about what caused us to make the judgments we have made.

Stories help us think about such judgments because the point of a story is something we notice in ourselves and see in our own lives. The point is found in one story and applied in another; it is transferable and *objective.* And therefore it is a way to teach, learn about, ponder, and practice in professional life.

The other initial difficulty with the approach I take to ethics is that it is bound to culture; it is (merely) intuitive; it is relativistic. I can think of two ways to cope with the charge. One is to say "so what?" That would be to deny the claim that sound ethics have to be worked out in such a way as to apply to and persuade everybody. Even people from Mars (if any). The other way is to say that my approach to ethics is *not* relativistic, to claim to meet the requirement of universality. Robert Wachbroit, a philosopher discussing the second edition of Alasdair MacIntyre's *After Virtue,* offers suggestions on both of these responses, without exactly nailing down either response. His approach appeals to me because I think it is a good idea not to try too hard to nail down a position on the question of relativism. Universality is important to many who think about ethics in the professions, and I don't want to drive them away. Not, at least, in the first chapter.

Wachbroit shows that being relativistic is not the same thing as being "emotivist," not the same as saying, "I do it because I feel like doing it." The difference is that the relativism that is in our doctor and lawyer stories depends on a tradition, where emotivism depends on will (or even on whim). If story ethics is relativistic, it is so because it insists on taking culture (Wachbroit says tradition) into account. It cannot talk about character without talking about culture (or tradition). "There is something mad in thinking that the reasons for believing that someone's friend is generous are undermined because he or she would not be considered generous in nineteenth-century Melanesia."

And we *want* to talk about character. It is attractive, appealing, helpful. "That an ancient Greek or a medieval Mogul might not judge that Gandhi had courage does not conflict with our assessment of that man, for it is not clear whether his activities would have taken courage if he had been a member of those other cultures instead." You could say the same about Mrs. Dubose. Finally, this argument is not an argument about relevance to ethical theory so much as an argument for the inclusion of selves—and particularly of the self that is poring over the ethical story at the moment. Gandhi might not have needed courage if he had been in ancient Greece, "but then he would not have been Gandhi." So there you have two thoughts on the issue of relativism: (1) the relevance of culture and (2) the relevance of self. One has to do, I think, with the plain fact that we like stories; the other has to do with the fact that each of us is interested in himself.

The Study of American Doctor and Lawyer Heroes

The procedure involved here is, in a sense, though, immediate, subjective, simple, nonrational, and even emotional. The millions of people who like *To Kill a Mockingbird* are not analytical about their liking it. An interesting fact about the novel is that there is not much reflective critical literature on it. Even those responsible for choosing its author to get a Pulitzer Prize were probably not analytical about their choice. The story of Atticus Finch appeals in an immediate way to people, and, one could say, because it appeals to them, he is a professional exemplar. He is a *hero.* To be a hero is to have this quality of appealing to other people in the hero's family or religious congregation or town. If the hero appeals to enough people, he is hero to a nation.

I don't think this immediate attraction is a sufficient way to account for heroes, but it is important. An important thing about hero stories is that they appeal from life to life. They appeal to us in the way influential people in our lives appeal to us, in a way that is for the most part unmediated by processes of analysis and comparison. One thing about an American lawyer-hero story, doctor-hero story, reporter-hero story, or police-officer-hero story is that it is attractive; it influences those who hear it in this immediate way. Trends in the popularity of such stories have a lot to do with rises and falls in the volume of applications to professional schools.

A story method in professional ethics begins with this attractiveness. American lawyer-heroes and doctor-heroes and minister- and teacher-heroes are people who have this appeal, as a matter of *fact*, at first, rather than as a matter of *analysis.* What I am proposing as a way to look for and look at professional ethics is at first a meditation on the lives of people who are already attractive in a morally influential, formative way. I am not proposing to defend the fact that they are attractive and morally influential. They just are. Those who come to professional education come in part because of this appeal. Because characters in those stories influence in a moral way I propose to call them heroes (and I don't mean for the word "hero" to carry any more weight than this point about appeal).

It is another question, a question about ourselves more than about our heroes, to ask *why* they have this appeal. This is not to explain why the hero is selected for discussion so much as it is to ask what about her or him causes me to suppose that many of my readers would join me in selecting the hero I select. The answer to that question, I think, is that the lives of others are the smallest and most immediate way in which we study experience. They are, as James William McClendon says of biography, the smallest units in which experience can be reported. McClendon dealt with stories of specific, historical people. He dealt with history in a way that is different from the way one studies fictional heroes. In some ways fiction is not as small a unit for study as biography is, since there are always two or more stories present in fiction. Jean Louise Finch (Scout) tells her own story when she tells us about Atticus, and Harper Lee tells her own story, her father's story, and the stories of both Jean Louise and Atticus. (Miss Lee is the daughter of Amasa Lee of the Monroeville, Alabama, Bar, who began practicing law in 1915.)

One way to put this special quality in fiction would be to say that the story of the community is more prominent in fiction than it is in biography. If that is so, it suggests an advantage one has in studying fiction rather than biography—or, if not an advantage, at least an opportunity. The advantage or opportunity is that it is easier to go from a fictional life to the life of the community in which that life is lived than is the case with a biographical life. It is easier to notice, as Saul Bellow did, that "I am in a crowd . . . and am part of it myself." In this way, perhaps, the moral point in a fictional story proceeds from and returns to the community more directly than a biography does. (This point is important to the argument I make about dissenters, in chapter 5.)

It is probably useful to ask at somewhat more length what is distinctive in the story of a doctor or lawyer hero. How is it that the story is, for its readers, the story of a hero rather than the story of a villain or of the common, pathetic "anti-hero" of modern fiction? Here are some possible insights into that question, insights I find in and borrow from McClendon:

Compelling Quality. Prior to explanation, and certainly prior to analysis, we find the stories of saints and heroes compelling; we are struck by them. We like them, and, more than liking them, we find in them something that keeps us from leaving them alone. That was certainly true of the stories McClendon chose for his book, particularly so of Martin Luther King, Jr., and Dag Hammarskjold. People who heard about Dr. King as he lived and worked in America were rarely indifferent to him. I had associates in those days who idolized him and I had associates who were deeply afraid of him, but I had no associates who could disregard him. He got under our skins. He bothered people in a way that was out of proportion to what people knew about him, knew as facts.

This quality is also evident in the post-death commentaries on Dag Hammarskjold. The secular humanists who hailed him as a reforming secular liberal were dismayed, after the publication of *Markings,* to find out about his Christian faith, but they were not able, even though they wanted to, to dismiss him. They tried instead to explain his faith away as a psychological aberration. A similar explanatory process occurred with regard to Dr. King, as if the liberal culture that supported Dr. King's politics could not believe that he was a Southern Baptist preacher and that it was important to him to be a Southern Baptist preacher. The white-liberal part of the civil rights movement learned that it had listened to a Southern Baptist preacher and that *it had to keep listening*.

In fiction about small-town lawyers and family doctors there is a popularity about the hero story, an immediate appeal, which cannot be dismissed, not even among those of us who tend at first to avoid a story that makes the bestseller list or sells out at the box office or is imitated in a television series. This compelling quality in the story moves around, often among popular audiences first but ultimately even among those who resist fashion. That process is a familiar one in the lives of the saints. Thomas More and Francis of Assisi come to mind. It is also familiar in the lives of contemporary religious leaders: Dr. King, for example, or Elie Wiesel, or Pope John XXIII, or Billy Graham. Leo Baeck was a leader of German Jews under the Nazis. In 1942 he went voluntarily to the death camp at Theresienstadt, to be with his fellow Jews. "When I want to conceive of the noble," Martin Buber said, "I think of Leo Baeck."

Prodigiousness. The hero goes beyond himself. There is something extraordinary about his effort. There is more in what he does than we can see ourselves doing—not in what he succeeds at, but in what he does. It is not necessary for heroes to be effective. The Hebraic hero often fails and is often a martyr. Mother Teresa of Calcutta says success is not important; what is important is faithfulness. Thomas More, a lawyer, is a better example of this distinction between prodigiousness and success than Dr. King or Gandhi or Mother Teresa, because More did not succeed at all. He did not leave behind him some ultimate triumph, as Gandhi and King did and as Mother Teresa will. Atticus Finch spoke the unspeakable in the courtroom in Maycomb and he went to the street in front of the jail in the middle of the night. His two actions are examples of this quality of prodigiousness. One act failed and the other succeeded.

In the case of the fictional lawyer-hero or doctor-hero or teacher-hero, this quality of prodigiousness seems to become clearer when seen in the context of the ordinary. Atticus is prodigious, he goes beyond himself, because Jean Louise describes his points of beginning before she describes his moments of crisis. We understand Atticus as a prodigious hero because we get to look at him on Mrs. Dubose's front walk, with his two errant children in tow, as well as on his feet in the courtroom. We see him (in the movie) calmly agreeing to be Tom Robinson's lawyer before we see him in front of the jail facing the lynch mob.

The craftsman of fiction describes a resonance between ordinary life and extraordinary life as a part of making character real; a good writer probably does this without thinking much about it. Heroes become heroic as a matter of course. The origin of the art, and the result of the art in the story of the hero, is a sense that the hero is in his community—in his family, his town, and his religious congregation. The story is about the community as well as about the hero. His prodigiousness is exercised against the backdrop of a society of people who are not prodigious but who help to explain why the hero is prodigious.

This perception of the heroic in the context of the ordinary has often been focused, in discussions of professional life, on the notion that doctors and lawyers work hard. It is not then spoken of as heroism. It is treated as ordinary, but it is not ordinary when compared with the way other people are thought to work. It is a quality of professional life—a claim for professional life that renders it distinctive—to work hard for a particular person. Eric Cassell noticed this when he reviewed Charles Bosk's book on teaching hospitals. He built on it a chain of reasoning that connects trust to competence and then connects trust and competence to work—not a claim of heroism, but, I think, an analogy. "A physician *must* learn not to make the same mistake twice . . . a patient must not be forced to pay for a doctor's temper or lack of sleep. . . . The only way to cope with the problems raised by inadequate knowledge and uncertainty is to build, in each physician, a specifically medical conscience. Such moral training is one function of internships and residencies. . . . Many of the lessons a young doctor must learn are moral lessons. . . . Moral lessons are learned best under pressure; this is one reason why interns and residents work so hard. When the training has been well done, even a fifty-year-old doctor will get out of bed at night to do what he has let lapse, because he can still hear the voice of the great chief resident in the sky."

Atticus is an example of this prodigiousness in a community. It was easy to be a Christian in Maycomb, Miss Maudie Atkinson said, because Maycomb had Atticus *to go* for it. "Attorney" means one who goes to town. Maycomb had Atticus to go to town in this symbolic sense; that is, Maycomb, more than Tom Robinson, was on trial. Miss Maudie also meant that Atticus was symbolically going to Calvary, which is what Christians (and Jews) do for one another and for the world. What Jesus did—and Leo Baeck.

The numinous. The hero is in touch with something special, something awesome and fascinating, something that attracts us and repels us at the same time. McClendon describes and relies on a moment in Dr. King's public life when he was "seized" by a physical and psychological religious experience that was extraordinary in the circumstances, but that was also the sort of religious experience that those in the black church in the South knew about and in some sense sought and could expect to have. Chaim Potok's young rabbi-chaplain in *The Book of Lights* has similar, and similarly expectable, numinous experiences. Hasidic lore is full of them—for examples, in Buber's Hasidic tales and Isaac Singer's stories.

This quality of numinousness demands judgment, in a fictional hero story, because it has a layer of interpretation (the author's) that biography, and particularly biography that is historically careful, may lack. I suppose judgment is present in all fictional stories because the author wants to make it clear that some experiences are critical to the description of the character and some are there just to move the story along. Huckleberry Finn's struggle over whether to betray Jim is more significant in this sense than his struggle with his father before Huck runs away from home. In the fictional story about a professional, the extraordinary moment, the moment of numinousness, tends to be a socially significant event—mostly, I suppose, because the story is about a leader. Atticus's courtroom performance, and his refusal to allow Sheriff Tate to lie about Jem, seem to me more numinous than his refusal to send Calpurnia away when his sister wants him to. Trollope's Dr. Thorne struggles over whether to tell his niece Mary that the wretched, drunken Sir Roger Scatcherd is her uncle. That event is more numinous than the ordinary integrity he practices among his patients.

Many of the professional hero's actions are more public than the numinous actions of other heroes. They are also more measured, more considered, and more fully explained. For these reasons, taken with the fact that the hero's actions are more public, they invite judgment. Because they are both more social and more rational (or rational*ized*), they invite judgment. This is as true of physician-hero stories as of lawyer-hero stories, but sometimes less prominent because stories about doctors often turn on private professional moments. The lives of doctors and lawyers are more alike in this regard, however, than stories of lawyers in court might lead us to suppose.

Stories about professionals who are heroes invite the reader's opinion on whether the action was good for the community. It was in those terms that Atticus was criticized for his defense of Tom Robinson. It was in those terms that he imagined himself under judgment for not lying to avoid Jem's pain and for lying to save Boo Radley's seclusion. A medical example, discussed in chapter 4, is William Carlos Williams's refusal to falsify treatment statistics when he was at Nursery and Child's Hospital in Hell's Kitchen.

Usefulness. The hero, and particularly the professional hero in fiction, becomes a hero because his story fits the moral needs of the times. It was no accident that a courageous small-town Alabama lawyer was a hero to a culture absorbed in the early turmoil of the civil rights movement, or, fifteen years later, that television made a hero story out of the experience of a brave Alabama circuit judge in a similar case. It is no accident that Judge James Edwin Horton's story was that of a hero in the Scottsboro cases *thirty years after they occurred,* when, to some extent, our country had come to its senses and the scars and tensions of the civil rights movement cried out for healing. In our pain we needed stories about heroes for both sides to admire.

Judge Horton, who acted in 1933, was a hero in Alabama in 1975, as much as he was a hero in New York. He was a hero because both places needed such a hero at that time. In 1934 Alabama turned him out of office and in 1933 New York condemned him as a bigot. In the case of a fictional lawyer-hero such as Atticus, this quality of usefulness is also a result of the fact that the author understands the times, speaks to the times, or, more accurately, speaks from the times. Harper Lee and Horton's biographer, Dan Carter, were active adults in the 1950s, writing about Alabama country lawyers of the 1930s. Both lawyers were popular heroes in the 1950s; neither was a popular hero, neither could have been, in the 1930s. The same point could be made about George Eliot's young Doctor Lydgate, who was an upstart and a disturbance when he came to Middlemarch in the 1820s with approaches to medical practice that were acceptable by the time Eliot wrote her story (1871) (see chapter 4).

Intellectual quality. The hero, and particularly the professional hero in American fiction, is a person of bravery and insight. He understands what is going on (as Thomas More did, especially the Thomas More of Robert Bolt's play, a fictional hero), and he acts in reference to what is going on in a relatively clear-sighted, skillful way. In a good hero story none of these qualities is abstracted into pure goodness. The hero stumbles and his stumbling—his sin, even—proves that it is hard to be brave and clear-sighted. But bravery and insight are more prominent in his life than in the lives of those around him.

Dr. Craig's adventures in the operating room illustrate this quality. He illustrates the fundamental value in clinical medicine of telling the truth about mistakes, but he is an arrogant man, and he sometimes has a hard time being truthful. After he nicked an artery during Mrs. Hufnagel's heart surgery, a mistake that later caused her death, he stumbled and sought to destroy the evidence of his mistake and to silence the resident who figured out what he had done. But by the time he reached the morbidity conference, he was able to explain what had happened and to take the blame for it. That was what his profession expected of him, but it was also an act of courage and of intellectual importance in professional ethics.

These qualities of bravery and insight show up when the hero is compared with others, as More, in the play, shows the same insight as Cromwell and Cardinal Wolsey, but more hope and bravery; the same bravery as the Duke of Norfolk, but more insight. The hero who is a doctor or teacher or minister or lawyer evinces courage by speaking out. This is partly because an American professional is expected to be a thinker, but also because she acts in the community, often against the community, but always in such a way as to reform the community without destroying it.

Character in Community

All of these qualities: being compelling, being prodigious, being in touch with the numinous, being useful, and being a thinker, are acts of character in community. McClendon argues that this social office, character in community, is an essential one in the use of biography as theology. Stories about American doctors and lawyers illustrate his argument. They inevitably act in the community. Fictional doctors and lawyers are what they are because their creators put them in communities. The connection between character and community is clearer in this sort of story because the connection between character and community is explained more elaborately. The lawyer is explained as a person who *talks* (witness Faulkner's Gavin Stevens). He talks about the community, about the community's story, and thus his own story is already partially interpreted by himself. He stands before a background that his own talk helps preserve. Gavin Stevens explains rural Southern custom to his nephew, and as he explains he exhibits his sorrow at the custom he explains.

The story of a good doctor or of a good lawyer is the story of character in community. This is true because, at the very least, the story of a virtuous person is a useful and fitting story. It would not be understood in categories either of sanctity or of heroism, as such stories tend to be, unless it was useful to people who live in similar situations. The fact that the story is familiar is essential to its being useful. There are also two more profound reasons why the story of the good lawyer or good doctor is the story of character in community. One of these is that she did not act alone; he was not good without spiritual support. Another reason is that the way we know what we believe is through such stories. It is the point—it may be the only point—where professional education touches the self. Not only do we learn what to do from such stories; we also learn from them what to believe. Gavin Stevens taught his nephew both what to do and what to believe. People are canonized and have tales told about them because we need their stories to live by and to learn by. There are three elements of the American community whose story is told as the story of a good doctor or good lawyer is told: family, church (religious congregation), and town.

Family. First, the doctor or lawyer comes from a family. One of the ways we know him is by knowing his family. Lawyer examples here are Fanny Holtzmann (chapter 5) and the Wall Street lawyer Henry Knox in Louis Auchincloss's novel *The Great World and Timothy Colt* (chapter 4). Another professional example is the clerical school master in his *Rector of Justin.* A medical example is Trollope's *Dr. Thorne.*

Henry Knox's Yankee Protestant clerical forebears are important to knowing him, and so are his stalwart wife, his giddy daughters, and his on-the-make son-in-law. Atticus Finch would not be who he is if it were not for his sturdy Methodist ancestors and the other "people of background" from whom he came. But for Atticus's *familial* definition of his son Jem as a gentleman-to-be, Atticus would not have come to make the distinction he did between his son's immediate welfare (and Jem's destiny, too) and the immediate welfare of the reclusive, strange, overprotected Boo Radley.

By contrast, Sinclair Lewis's doctor, Martin Arrowsmith (chapter 4), doesn't work as a story of character in community. One reason is that he is like Kafka's character in *The Trial;* we do not know who he is. His story is useful, but he is more a subject at the mercy of psychologically familiar forces than he is a person. The most ordinary way for us to learn who Arrowsmith and "K" are would be to learn about their families. Kafka's art makes "K" anonymous by hiding "K's" family. (I'm not sure what Lewis was up to.)

This works between young and old, in both directions. Dr. Carole Horn writes that her ability to go on after one of her patients dies requires faith and energy, and that she thinks she gets these from her twenty-two-month-old daughter Annie. "At three in the morning, alone and fresh out of sleep in the presence of death, it's hard not to be afraid." Part of what she finds is the moral benefit of not being rational, part of it is being compassionate by noticing—both things her child Annie knows about. Horn tells of one case where all medical attendants but one left the bed of a recently dead patient. The one remaining was a medical student, who was shattered by the experience. Maybe because of Annie, Horn noticed and came back and spent time with that student. She mentions another case in which a medical colleague came to terms with death by sitting by the bedside and talking to the corpse. Not rational, but noticing.

"I'm not sure that whatever kind of doctor I am hasn't more to do with making funny faces with Annie and singing off-key lullabies than with anything related to formal training," she says. "It's from her and my husband that most of my nurturing comes these days, although interactions with [other] people I care for contribute to it, too. The richness of the support we receive is certainly what gives us something to pass along to others, and I have been lucky in that. . . . [I wonder] if we shouldn't choose our potential doctors—and maybe our lawyers and chiefs, too—on the basis of how well they've been nurtured, with instructions that whatever else they do, they pass it along."

Church. (I mean here a sustaining and in some sense transcendent community, something that is broader culturally than a family but deeper than a town or neighborhood. For most American Christians this is the church; I use that word. There is a parallel, local Jewish religious community for which "synagogue" is hardly adequate. Lis Harris's description of the vibrant, modern, growing Lubavitcher Hasidic community in New York is an example.) The good doctor or lawyer also comes from a church. In many American stories, being part of the church is important not only in identifying, and identifying with, the doctor or lawyer; it is also important in explaining why he acts as he does. She or he could not act with courage but for a sustaining spiritual community. The church not only inspired the good lawyer or doctor to act, often beyond anything the church itself, as a human institution in a time and place, could approve of or even understand, but also gave her or him a way to nurse frustrations and failures without being destroyed by them.

This was true of Henry Knox, who probably was able to stay in his law firm and be a spiritual leader there because his work for seminary and church made up for the law firm's failure to satisfy his spirit.

This is true in an almost ethnic way for Higgins's Jerry Kennedy, a pragmatic but stubbornly Irish Catholic Boston criminal lawyer (chapter 5). It is true of Atticus, who said he could not go to church and pray unless he both helped Tom Robinson and told the truth about him. Atticus's courage went beyond what Maycomb's institutional white church could defend, but Atticus was acting as martyrs often have—for example, Leo Baeck or Thomas More, or Franz Jagerstatter. Atticus was sustained by the church even as he bore witness against it. Altruistic action depends on support from a spiritual community as much as the spiritual community depends on altruistic action.

Not all the good lawyers and doctors in American stories belong to religious congregations. Many of the modern ones resist and condemn institutional religion. But those who live outside the church have a community for spiritual support, a place to go from and a place to return to, so that they can learn how to survive their frustrations. The crusaders of adventure fiction make the point. John D. MacDonald's Travis McGee has his small cohort of dependable and honorable supporters. They sustain him even when they have no other role in the story. Ross Macdonald's Lew Archer, whose crusades against evil were lonely crusades, never went through a story without finding people of character who understood him. Camus's Dr. Rieux (in *The Plague*) had someone to talk with. Dr. Thorne had his niece Mary and his faithful friend Squire Gresham. Bolt's More has, even at the end of the play, the sustaining memory of the church which taught him about hope and martyrdom and would have continued to sustain him if it had understood what was going on. Franz Jagerstatter read the lives of the saints and declined the advice of his bishop. Gavin Stevens goes out from and returns to his relationship with his sister and with the sewing-machine salesman, V. K. Ratliff. These associations, which are typically religious in American stories, provide something the professional fraternity does not provide: Much of what is wrong with the ethics of the professions in America is the attempt to replace the church with the professional fraternity.

Town. Finally, the doctor or lawyer of American stories has a town, a society that sees his witness, that hears it as Israel heard the prophets, and that thereby fulfills its function in his life and in its own, even when it resists him and destroys him. Atticus and Gavin argued to the town, in league with the town, when they made the standard country lawyer's appeal against the social engineers of the North. Theirs was not a disingenuous appeal. If it was the product of prejudice, and it was not entirely so, it was not a prejudice they had to pretend to have. The judges and bar association officials at Henry Knox's funeral knew that he had been important to them and that he had known about their importance to him. The clarity of Dr. Thorne's character, in Trollope's story, has much to do with his stubborn and independent integrity, in and before Greshamsbury, as compared with the fashionable medicine of his rival, Dr. Fillgrave.

The importance of town as distinguished from family is that the town accounts for the doctor or lawyer as a social person, and therefore is, as we readers are, an audience for his action. It may be that a tree falling in the forest when no one is there to listen makes no noise, but the good doctor or lawyer in a good story does not fall alone; he is a hero because the town is there to see him fall. The town is distinguished from the church because it is not necessarily, or even usually, a source of spiritual sustenance to the hero. (It may, though, despite itself, be a moral teacher, as I try to show in chapter 4.) The town may be no more than the hero's foil, but it is also his necessary audience.

One Lawyer's Moral Theology

The methodological question that is consequent on this claim of the good doctor or good lawyer as displaying character in community is this: Is it legitimate, having identified the community in this way (as family, religious congregation, and town), to infer moral significance from what one finds in the community? Is it legitimate to look to the community for the professional person's point of view? Atticus Finch says little about his faith. I have been told that such a Christian lawyer-hero from Alabama would not have said much about his faith. Atticus says enough to let us know that he takes his faith seriously but the rest of what we know about his faith comes from knowing about his town, his family, and his church. The need I have had, in trying to get a professional moral theology from the story, is the need to account for the intellectual side of his courage, to explain his point of view when he himself said little about it. I do not have a diary (as McClendon had when he studied Hammarskjold). Atticus, Gavin Stevens, and Henry Knox wrote neither books nor spiritual music. (McClendon had those on Clarence Jordan and Charles Ives.)

I infer Atticus's and Knox's Christianity from their communities and I look at their faith (thus inferred) and their actions and test these against the facts and the intuitions that go into my understanding of how they were courageous. And from all of this I claim them as lessons for Americans who practice, or plan to practice, in the professions. I even claim that, with the products of this inference and intuition, I can account for ethical principles in terms of where such principles come from, as both thematic (that is, theological) and historical sources. I have claimed that lives are prior to principles. I do not appeal here to logic. The sort of story I'm talking about speaks to its reader directly, from life to life, without the mediation of concept or of explanation. Atticus and Craig speak to us modern physicians and lawyers, and speak as well to families, churches, and towns. We read and are formed by their stories in a way that is analogous to the way we are formed by the lives of people in our families, our religious congregations, and our towns.

But I do have an argument for my lesser intellectual task of inferring faith from community. The method here is not so much a matter of identifying belief, of claiming that Atticus, Dr. Thorne, and Henry Knox had belief, as it is a matter of locating a rational center that can explain their actions more plausibly than other explanations would—more plausibly, say, than relating their action to a code or a universal, verbal, professional principle. How is it that Atticus is willing to sacrifice himself as he does? Is it because he believes in the rule of law, or the Bill of Rights, or the civil rights movement? The question is not how would I explain his actions if he were Horatius at the bridge or Odysseus in Troy, but how do I explain this Atticus, of Maycomb, Alabama, United States, in 1935? What is the rational center of his actions? And I mean here to include the real moral spectrum of his actions, his regrets for his wrong actions, those he regrets and those he would regret if he were morally consistent, as well as what we readers understand to be his acts of clear heroism. His mistakes and his stumbles, his sins and his grief, are necessary to understanding his story, as his story is necessary to understanding his honesty and his courage. Without mistakes and stumbles he would be a bore and his story would be only hagiography.

My argument is that his old Methodist faith, the images and metaphors of the Cross, the Suffering Servant, and atonement, *work* better than any other explanation. And I find those images in the stories of old small towns in Alabama, of Baptist and Methodist churches in the (white and black) South, and of the Finch family as Scout describes it and as I and other American readers of her story know about such families. (Gregory Peck said he understood Maycomb, and Atticus in Maycomb, because he grew up in a small town in California.)

If this method is legitimate, it is both an *ethical* method and, within ethics, a *theological* method. My argument in this respect is like Hauerwas's and McClendon's and I will state it quickly and for present purposes. A doctrine of atonement, of the reconciliation of people with God and with one another, and, especially in stories of professional gentlemen in the South, of black people with white people, is both subjective theology and objective theology. The Hebraic tradition says that people are reconciled by and through God's action in the world, that their friendship with God is a gift that makes it possible for them to be friends with one another, to see and accept one another as gifts. For such gifts the only appropriate response is gratitude.

To this extent, Judaism and Christianity say, reconciliation is an objective fact, and the theology of atonement (at-one-ment with God and neighbor) is a theology of objective, historical, and accomplished fact. That is true, according to the Hebraic tradition, but it is not all that is true. The tradition also says that the believer shares in God's work in the world. Part of the gift he is given is a share in God's work, the invitation to be an agent in the atonement, the call to move the stone from in front of Lazarus's grave, or, in Hasidic imagery, to restore fragmented creation to the Creator. This is a theology of the subjective; atonement is both objective and subjective. Redemption has happened *and* it is an event that is going on, and will go on. It goes on in the lives of those around us and prototypically in the lives of virtuous people in our families, our towns, and our religious congregations. Such virtuous people provide to the people of God, to the congregation that hears and believes, and to the town that only hears, solid, rational information about who God is and what God is doing in the world. They provide what McClendon calls "concrete theological gain," and therefore participate in the purpose of theology, which is to inform the people of God.

The Theology of Virtue in the Professions

This method does result in what one might call second-stage concepts. It may be true, as some philosophers and theologians argue, that all concepts are removed from reality—that they freeze reality and put into words what people experience primarily without words, that concepts always "smell of the lamp," especially in academic discussions of morals. It is not necessary for an aging law professor, who is out merely to get a firmer handle on professional ethics, to get into that quarrel. It is necessary, though, to say more about the method I borrow from Hauerwas and McClendon, specifically in reference to my claim that this method is theology.

McClendon argues from the moral lives of those whose biographies he has studied that the theology of a life involves *image* and *event,* and that these are prior to principles and propositions. He defines religion as the application of the images of faith to one's own life. This application is a manifestation and a use of the grand, enduring images of faith, the great metaphors, which the person of faith (the modern, good person in Jewish or Christian life, for instance) has grown up seeing applied in prototypical ways. These images and metaphors carry for him, and for his community, the *content* of the faith. All of this is, among other things, a way to describe the force that guides our moral action. It is what a person means when he says, "I do it because that's the way I was brought up."

Possibly someone, someday, early in the life of the white community in southwestern Virginia, looked at the ungainly mountain I see from my front porch and said that the mountain was a house; he called it "House Mountain." The community accepted the name, accepted his saying that about the mountain. The Indians who were here before black and white people came would not have called the mountain a house because their houses were not like that mountain, or because they perceived two mountains where white people saw one, or, better, because a house that looked like that did not mean anything to them and could not have been the name of a mountain.

Perhaps a Spanish explorer in Colorado looked at the curious way the snow endured in the summer in a high-altitude canyon and said that the mountain and canyon made a Holy Cross. The name came from his community as much as the name "house" came from the Virginian's community. And, so, in other, more curious ways, the red-rock formations west of Colorado Springs are called the Kissing Camels and, in an example McClendon borrows from John Wisdom, a woman's new hat is called the Taj Mahal. This is the stuff of poetry. It is strong stuff and it is community stuff. The difference between such metaphors and similes ("the mountain *looks like* a house") is the difference between poetry and prose, between insight and description. McClendon's point is that such image and metaphor is also theological stuff. For example, McClendon is persuasive in saying that "*hoc est enim corpus meum*"—"this is my body"—is a similar event and image. The Cross, the nation Israel, the Suffering Servant, the atonement, are metaphors, images, and facts.

However, images as powerful as these biblical images do things mountains and hats do not do. They cut across cultures, for one thing, as the naming of mountains does not. Carl Jung showed how they tap into what he called our collective unconscious. The images Jesus used were strong among the Jews who heard him. They became strong to the Greeks and Romans who heard St. Paul and to the Africans and the Anglo-Saxons who heard one of the St. Augustines. Thus the great religious images also unify. McClendon talks about Dr. King's living out the metaphor of atonement, atonement as estrangement and as sacrifice, but also atonement as reconciliation. Dr. King sought the reconciliation of his oppressors. McClendon talks also of the power that images of reconciliation and atonement had in Hammarskjold's life—suffering servanthood as the way to understand "the meaningfulness of death and the meaninglessness of killing." Much of King's and Hammarskjold's imagery and conviction rested on the wisdom of the curious Hindu lawyer Gandhi. The images and metaphors unified.

Images are not neutral. There are true images and false images, comfortable images and stressful images. The virtuous person's living out and living under one set of images rather than another is choice (much more than choice, really, since images speak of and speak to convictions and a commitment that does not merely rise out of a decision or an act or a series of quandaries). The powerful racist images of Nazi Germany, and those that lurked in the Maycomb of Atticus Finch's generation, were false images. Reinhold Niebuhr looked at them and said the Devil was back. Believers claim that the images and metaphors of Cross, Israel, and Exodus are true images. Much of what makes Atticus, Dr. Tom Dooley, Judge James Edwin Horton, and Dr. King virtuous lies in their living one set of images rather than the other, and in their living within communities that lived both.

We celebrate in these lives a heroic quality that came from and supported the direction these doctors' and lawyers' lives took. Their stories show the difference between images of wholeness and images of dominance. That distinction (which is McClendon's) is likely, I think, to be the major issue in the professions in the remainder of this century. I think, too, that one can identify stress in the lives of these professionals, stress that evidences the enduring influence on them of images that are not images of wholeness. This stress is what I identify in Atticus as the enduring influence of the Southern Christian gentleman. I think the same thing was tugging on Judge Horton, who, asked late in his life to explain the heroism he exhibited in the Scottsboro cases, attributed his action to a Latin maxim. That maxim is in our law a motto for the wise but imperious judge, an image of dominance. What Judge Horton said he did was not the same as what he did. The image of wholeness was not what he talked about, but it helps us understand what he did.

The community looks at the lives of its virtuous professionals and understands their images and their metaphors, both as explanations for its interest in these lawyers and doctors and as an explanation for their being first interesting and then virtuous. The community asks "What sort of people are these?" and finds them familiar and challenging; it finds in them both understanding and rebuke. In religious terms, these heroes, living their images, give current, relevant, even unavoidable meaning to doctrine—and not only meaning but force as well.

These lawyers and doctors are prophets, in the Hebraic sense of the word. They show their community what its values are and how much their values cost. They *revive* the faith because they make current sense of the religious images that carry the faith. There is depth in Miss Maudie's saying that Atticus represents the Christians in Maycomb, because he and Maycomb share meaning, share, specifically, inherited, religious commitments. He represents white Maycomb as he joins Maycomb's black Christians at the courthouse, as he stands with them, white and black together, under the Cross. Professional heroes such as Atticus or Tom Dooley or Albert Schweitzer insist that the religious commitments of the church be lived as well as believed, and in this they resemble what Dr. King said, in the black church, to the black South—that "free at last" includes the liberation of white police officers.

Chapter Two

· § ·

THE BIBLE

The way, the real way, from the Creation to the Kingdom is trod not on the surface of success, but in the deep of failure. The real work, from the biblical point of view, is the late-recorded, the unrecorded, the anonymous. The real work is done in the shadow, in the quiver.

—Martin Buber

THE Bible in American professional ethics is a misty presence. It is there and not there. It is sometimes vaguely alluded to—as when Judge Sharswood speaks of the law office and the Sermon on the Mount—but more often we sense it is there only because we know that the authors of the early statements and codes were biblical people.

Rather like the Bible in American political rhetoric, the Bible was from the first there and not there in American professional ethics. Almost all professionals in America have been believing Jews or Christians. The dominant figures in nineteenth-century American legal ethics—for examples David Hoffman, George Sharswood, and Thomas Goode Jones—were all believers. Hoffman was a dogged Bible scholar, approved of even by the old-line Calvinists at Princeton Theological Seminary; Sharswood was a Presbyterian Sunday School teacher; Judge Jones was likened, in a joint session of the Alabama legislature, to "the Great Galilean, 'He who would be greatest among you, he shall be the servant of all.' " And yet none of their vast work in professional ethics—work that would fill a fat volume—gives advertent significance to biblical morality. The little they say about the Bible is a politically familiar and conventional tip of the gentleman's hat. These fathers of professional ethics were neither secular nor biblical. The Bible was carefully included in what they did, but it didn't mean anything that couldn't have been based just as well on Jeffersonian American civil religion.

The Gentleman's Ethic

Sir Thomas Percival's medical ethics (1791) are based on the "code" of the English gentleman. If this is a biblical allusion it is a vague one. The gentleman's ethic in England was in some sense a Christian cult, but Percival does not connect his code to the Bible, nor did his American disciples when they formulated the medical faculty's statement in Baltimore in the 1820s, nor did the adopters of the first American Medical Association code in 1847. The Bible contains lessons in anatomy, pathology, therapy, and nutrition, but those biblical treatments of medicine—which *must* have been familiar to these early professional ethicists—are not taken up as interesting sources of thought on the practice of medicine in a Christian society.

The development of American professional ethics took place in a culture of religious belief. Justice Douglas was right; we are a religious people. But little of the substance of professional ethics refers to or even considers religious ethics in a way that can be called thoughtful. Sharswood speaks of "the high and pure morality that breathes through the Sermon on the Mount," but goes on to decide that such a morality is of no use in a law office. Of no use to clients and therefore of no use to lawyers.

And yet Sharswood's religious culture was not merely conventional (although it was conventional). If you list two columns of events, side by side, one showing developments in the (Protestant) church in the United States, the other showing developing professionalism in law and medicine, you find Charles Grandison Finney's passionate, meaty, and successful revival sermons almost exactly parallel to Hoffman's early attempt at law-school education and the beginnings of prosperity for allopathic practitioners in medicine. (Finney, by the way, was a lawyer.) Hoffman's and Percival's mentor in ethics was William Paley, an Anglican clergyman who reasoned that scripture was compatible with the lives and habits of the dominant class in eighteenth-century Britain. He concluded, for example, that the best hope for the poor was a trickle-down theory of wealth, and that the best people to care for the poor were the "lower orders" of the Anglican clergy.

You find turmoil among Presbyterians over evangelism, parallel to the work of Sharswood as a legal educator, judge, and lecturer on ethics. Those who became members of the early nineteenth-century medical faculty at the University of Maryland were children when the Methodist church in the United States was founded; their parents were alive and alert at the time of the Great Awakening. These teachers of medicine were at the peak of their professional careers during the revivals of the 1840s and 1850s; they were able to listen to religious debate over the abolition of slavery all during their adult lives. The young men (virtually no young women) who were preparing for the professions pondered how to be good persons and doctors or lawyers or professors, or even ministers (witness Emerson's advice to the new clergy at Harvard and Hodge's review of Hoffman's *Course of Legal Study*), but there is not much evidence that they pondered in a persuasive way the significance of scripture for moral life in a profession.

It's not that they were sure of themselves. These early American professionals were likely more riddled with doubt than church history and the rhetoric of public life suggest. Philip Mason says that was true of the governing and professional classes in Britain. They were, he says, distressed at the excesses of the Enlightenment, and unhappy with early industrial materialism—but they were also bothered that they could not reconcile Genesis with science. "This combination drove some to atheism or agnosticism and tormented many others with doubts and difficulties." Perhaps the faith that survived doubt—and, mostly, faith did survive doubt then—was stolid when compared with the religion of the Wesleys and the evangelists. David Hoffman read deeply and widely in the Bible, and thought a lot about religion, but he rarely went to church.

In any case, I don't find evidence that the implications of biblical faith were disturbing to professional people who were, by and large, prosperous, erudite, and powerful. (Hoffman's generation of Baltimore lawyers had the highest professional incomes in the country.) I doubt that the biblical challenge to prosperity was faced that squarely—not any more than it is among believers now. What may have happened, with subtlety rather than apostasy, was the development of something that seemed like the traditional religion but was not—"a cult derived from Christianity," in Mason's phrase. That is an intriguing possibility because it would explain how pseudo-religion developed alongside pseudo-professionalism, and how the implications of biblical faith faded with the traditional implications of being in a calling, of being set aside for service to other people. If things happened that way, there is probably a connection between this bifurcation of religious and professional life and the nineteenth-century middle-class position on the roles of married women.

Mason (speaking of Victorian Britain) traces it this way: First, there is among those of the gentleman's class the recognition of sensitivities and etiquettes that distinguish ladies and gentlemen from everybody else. The egalitarian excesses of the French Revolution had a direct impact in Britain. Its impact in the United States was probably indirect, but it is clear that the Jeffersonian gentleman was elite and wanted to be. Hoffman's political writings are almost all devoted to ranting against Jacksonian democracy. He put aside foreign travel, law practice, and teaching to give himself full time to the Whig campaigns of 1836 and 1840. Mason shows how this whiggish elitism expressed itself in familiar Victorian prudishness about bodily functions and sex. That was true in this country as well, but the more indicative manifestation was a distaste among the prosperous lawyers and doctors of Hoffman's generation for their low-life professional colleagues and for immigrants (see chapter 5). There were two sets of professions in America then, as there have continued to be—the gentlemen in the bar association or the medical faculty, and police-court lawyers and rural practitioners who were not gentlemen and probably didn't want to be.

Stoicism is, in such a gentleman's system, taken to be courage; emotion of almost any kind (patriotism perhaps excepted) is distasteful. The gentleman doesn't talk about his love life or about his religious faith. He does talk about politics—mostly, though, to those who agree with him. In England such stoic male souls were needed to manage the Empire. In the United States they were as close as we have come to an aristocracy. This stoicism shows up in religious history as a withholding of the energy needed either to sustain faith or to support a biblical social ethic. "Austerity . . . spread over the land, and the crucifix was replaced by a plain stylized cross. Men did not care to look on the torn humiliated body that bore witness to human cruelty and divine compassion. Flesh was slightly obscene: and if the Word had been made flesh, the less said about it the better," Mason says.

"On the whole . . . it was better not to think too much about the Sermon on the Mount and the dangerously radical doctrines of the *Magnificat.* You might say in church that the poor were to be blessed and the rich sent empty away, but what was needed for everyday life was something less demanding, a sub-Christian cult, and to concentrate on a standard of behaviour altogether easier and more comfortable, something almost a religion, conduct in fact that was becoming to a gentleman." The low-church polity that Trollope describes in his Barchester novels and George Eliot in *Middlemarch* shows how that worked as theology and as a style for the country clergy in England. The priests were first among those Disraeli called "muscular Christians."

Ethics—positive ethics—lined up under this gentleman's standard. "The gentleman provided an ethical code that was a substitute for Christianity. At the same time, it derived from Christianity many of its finer points." What it did not do—and this particularly in its manifestation among the professions in the United States—was to provide a solution to the oldest problem with the ethics of gentlemen, the problem of how to regard those who were not gentlemen. William Paley seems to have baptized the English class system—and Paley influenced British and American professional ethics, through Percival, Hoffman, Sharswood, and the AMA.

You can fashion an admirable Aristotelian ethic from the Bible if you are willing to take out all the parts about the vulgar and the poor. If you leave in the parts about the vulgar and the poor, you then have also to work into your ethic something about the unrecorded and the anonymous, something about work done in the shadow and in the deep of failure. You have to take account of forgiveness and divine comfort, and the stoic professional gentleman who lurks in Paley's, Percival's, and Hoffman's ethics was not especially interested in forgiveness and divine comfort.

There is another possibility here, and if it does not explain the neglect of biblical morality in the early (and late) development of doctors' and lawyers' ethics, it might explain some of the verbal apparatus with which the neglect was excused. That is the "sexual politics" in which domestic and social life, in both countries, was divided between men and women. Nancy Woloch's study of nineteenth-century women's magazines shows how the conventional view was that the world of commerce and politics—including the professions—was the sphere of men; home and the education of children, especially the early moral education of sons, was the sphere of women. I don't argue, and I don't think Woloch argues, that this was the product of some sort of arm's-length sexual treaty; it was more likely the product of men taking the parts of life they wanted and leaving the rest to women. However, the result was feminine control of what psychology later identified as the critical years of moral formation for those (boys) who were to become doctors and lawyers. The Bible was undoubtedly a large part of that moral education. One consequence of the woman's sphere was that women had influence in the church (although not much in the clergy) and were prominent if not dominant in such things as the beginnings of the enormously successful Sunday school movement in the United States.

On the other hand, men were in control of professional education, once the doctors and lawyers of the future were pointed in a professional direction. Such university education as there was for the professions (not much in the United States before the Civil War) was entirely male, and the law and medical schools that became increasingly significant as the nineteenth century wore on were entirely male. Most of the medical schools excluded women or severely limited the enrollment of women. Law schools excluded women entirely. In 1910 there were only fifteen hundred women lawyers in the United States, and they were educated in apprenticeships. The informal associations of doctors that antedated medical societies as significant professional guilds (e.g., the medical world described by George Eliot in *Middlemarch*) were male, and the formation of later, more formal and influential societies was male. The same was true of the legal fraternity in David Hoffman's Baltimore and George Sharswood's Philadelphia; and, when the first modern American bar associations were formed in the 1870s, and began to promulgate codes of legal ethics, membership, formulation, and such enforcement as there was were all male. When Fanny Holtzmann, who is discussed in chapter 5 of this book, joined the Bar in 1923 in New York City, she was, because a woman, ineligible for membership in the bar association.

The *professional* world was (depending on how you look at it) left to or retained by men. The biblical *moral* world, as even these professional men thought of it, was, though, left to women. Home, the woman's sphere, was a moral island, a place of relative purity, and the principal source of moral education. That meant that the male sphere could become a place of relative callousness. Since morals—and particularly biblical morals—had been taken care of by handing the subject over to women, men in professional societies could turn their attention to exploiting natural resources, empowering the robber barons, and making a profit. They were free to claim that the path to soundness in medicine was science rather than healing, and to look the other way when someone suggested that the popular therapies were more exploitation of the sick than care of the sick. Examples here are the fraternity of physicians George Bernard Shaw described in *The Doctor's Dilemma,* or the professional world in which Martin Arrowsmith, as a medical student, would be understood and accepted when he said, "I don't want to influence anybody. I want to learn the doctor trade and make six thousand dollars a year." It was also, perhaps, the sort of moral world—this male, professional world—in which Arrowsmith would later be supported and encouraged in his decision to pursue science rather than healing, and in doing that decide to abandon (as he did) civility and ordinary responsibility to other people, including his wife and son.

When Arrowsmith and his second wife, Joyce, were about to split up—and that because he would neither join in her world, not even for dinners among friends, nor share his world with her—she argued that it was immoral for him to leave her and their son and go off into the woods of Vermont to do his experiments. Martin said to her, "It's just that argument that's kept almost everybody, all these centuries, from being anything but a machine for digestion and propagation and obedience. . . . We could prove that I'm a hero or a fool or a deserter or anything you like, but the fact is I've suddenly seen I must go! I want my freedom to work." He thought he was a hero. His complaint about Joyce was that she did not *belong* to him, as his first wife, Leora, did. "You've been generous to me. I'm grateful. But you've never been mine. Good-by." It is significant for my present argument, I think, that *Arrowsmith* was regarded, and regarded by Lewis himself, as Sinclair Lewis's most idealistic novel.

It may be indicative on this argument that nursing in England and America began among the poor (those whom Paley left to the "lower orders" of the male Anglican clergy)—in hospitals, which were, then, not places of medical treatment of the sick but were rather well within the woman's sphere. They were places where the poor were put to die, where their suffering and death would be invisible and therefore safely in the hands of women. Nursing was, then, from its beginnings in the cultures that give us modern American professional ethics, a radically separate profession from medicine. When nurses first went into military hospitals in this culture's wars, they came for the first time into significant struggles with professional men—with the military surgeons who sawed off the limbs of wounded soldiers. The struggles between surgeons and nurses were struggles over the nonmedical care the soldiers were given (and over such things as sanitation in the hospitals). In that struggle, the arguments the nurses made for control were religious and often biblical arguments. Mary Ann Bickerdyke, one of the early combatants in this struggle, said to a military surgeon: "I have received my authority from God Almighty. Have you anything that ranks higher than that?"

· § ·

All of this may explain the neglect of biblical morality among the professional gentry in Britain and North America. It does not describe the significance the Bible had for a thoughtful professional in a culture of Jews and Christians—and the Bible must have had *some* significance. Nor does it explain what a late twentieth-century consideration of biblical morality in professional ethics might turn up. For the first of those questions, I propose now to take more careful looks at David Hoffman as a Bible scholar and at biblical medical ethics. For the second, I propose to consider the Bible as a source of professional ethics, and, particularly, the prophet Isaiah's enigmatic "Servant of the Lord" as a biblical model for professional life.

David Hoffman

Hoffman was, I think, the father of American legal ethics. He was one of the second generation of American legal educators (along with Joseph Story and Judge Tapping Reeve, a generation after Virginia's George Wythe). He held the country's first appointment as a university law professor (at the University of Maryland, 1814–1843). He was the author of the first systematic American outline for the study of law. Story called Hoffman's outline "an honour to our country . . . by far the most perfect system for the study of law that has ever been offered to the public." Chancellor James Kent of New York said, "Whoever follows its directions will be a well read and accomplished lawyer."

Hoffman's work on legal education has not been republished since he asked a printer in Baltimore to bind the remaining copies of his second (1836) edition into one volume. His work on the law lingers, if at all, as a vague influence among a host of nineteenth-century American scholars who proposed to make law a science. His theories of legal education—some of which are still followed—were swallowed up in the beginnings of other law schools. The law chair he occupied at Maryland was left vacant from 1843 to 1869. He wrote several books of social observation in the 1840s and six volumes of religious history (he published three of them) in the 1850s. None of these has been reprinted. His popular literature was never popular. None of his work on substantive law or legal education has been reprinted either. But his 1836 "Resolutions on Professional Deportment" are revived in every generation. His professional ethics were and are influential.

Hoffman's professional ethics rests on a Jeffersonian sense of responsibility. Since, as he saw it, a lawyer was a specialist in justice, professional responsibility meant responsibility for justice. Thus, he said, a lawyer should not advocate a legal interpretation that will benefit his client unless the lawyer believes the interpretation is good for the country. A lawyer should not plead technical defenses to civil lawsuits (defenses such as statutes of limitation or the rule that a child cannot make a binding contract) unless the claim against the client is morally invalid aside from the technical defense. "He shall never make me a partner in his knavery," Hoffman said of his client.

When it came to people accused of crime, Hoffman taught (as Sharswood did in the next generation) that legal representation should be diminished when the client appeared to be guilty as charged. He said it was wrong for a lawyer to urge in such a case all the defenses the law allowed. Hoffman believed in justice, and by justice he meant what was dispensed by people of his class, acting as the government. Hoffman was a Jeffersonian gentleman; he saw himself as responsible for what the government did. His ethical propositions do not rest on scripture, neither in the 1817 essay and bibliography nor in the longer, more durable, and more precise 1836 Resolutions. His and William Paley's bias against the poor and the vulgar is gentlemanly rather than unbiblical.

Hoffman believed in broad, lasting learning for law students, as he believed in lawyers as the natural cultural and political leaders of American society. He fought incessantly with the medical faculty at Maryland, mostly over turf but more interestingly over scientific assumptions in law and medicine. His recommended reading in the *Course* is studded with references to Roman and continental legal sources as well as British and American law books. He insisted that his law students come to him with a solid liberal education. He emphasized public responsibility as the essence of a lawyer's moral life.

Much of Hoffman's writing contains references to scripture and to biblical characters, but these were common literary devices in his day, as common as references to figures in Greek and Roman mythology. Even a freethinker (Benjamin Franklin for example) could, when he wanted, sound like a Sunday school teacher. The Bible was then, in every sense, a common book in America. But there was more than convention in Hoffman's biblical interest. He was not only a careful student of religion (his last major writing project was a six-volume history of Christianity) but also a law teacher who claimed that the Bible was essential to his craft. An interesting piece of evidence that he found the Bible important in law teaching and legal scholarship, and that he kept up with what was written and said about the Bible, is the array of references he gives to contemporary secondary literature on the Bible. Most of his 1836 references were to books published, several of them in the United States, after the 1817 edition of his *Course* was published. Many of the works he cites (e.g., Jahn's *History of the Hebrew Commonwealth,* which was published at Andover in 1828) are narrow, technical works by biblical scholars.

Hoffman's 1836 edition was reviewed, at length and with elaborate praise, in *The Biblical Repertory and Princeton Review.* The author of the review recommended Hoffman's work to divinity students, and its outline of legal process to those who conducted ecclesiastical trials. Hoffman's biblical title, he said, "shows the author's high estimate of [the Bible's] importance . . . and . . . is well worthy of an attentive perusal . . . [it] contains much information . . . relative to the sacred volume, calculated to be highly useful to the theological, as well as the law student. . . . The author then states the difficulties which must be encountered in perusing the sacred volume with profit, and under each head refers the reader to such works as will tend to obviate these difficulties." This evaluation from the seminary is evidence that Hoffman's biblical learning was sound as well as up to date. The editor of the Princeton *Review* at that time, and the probable author of the unsigned essay on Hoffman's *Course,* was Professor Charles Hodge, a Bible scholar and a teacher not given to the praise of novelty or to underestimating lapses from orthodoxy. When Professor Hodge was feted for fifty years of teaching, in 1870, he said he was proud to report that "a new idea never originated in this seminary."

Hoffman began his consideration of *the law*—not ethics, but law—with the Bible. But this was not—as might have been expected in his generation—because the Bible was useful background. Hoffman promoted the Bible as a law book, as a source of law. Almost all law students were then Christians. The United States, according to foreign visitors of the 1820s and 1830s, had a Protestant state religion. It might have been expected that a professional book would give a conventional nod, at its beginning, to the scriptures. But Hoffman was serious; he put the Bible at the beginning because he regarded it as the most important *law book.* His advice on background reading (classics, philosophy, poetry, works on art, etc.) was that law students should study them as recreation, or, better, study them before they began to study law. His recommendations on using the Bible were recommendations for office hours. He recommended it as a primary source for learning law, for learning professional skill, for being introduced to professional culture, and for personal advancement in the profession.

For example, he says, the Bible explicates the origin of all law and of civil government itself; it gives an account of how law came about—and this in two senses. First, it reflects "a form of government and law originating in the great Legislator of the universe," which is to say that the Bible shows the source of government in the sense in which Sir William Blackstone taught about legal origins. It is a way to learn about natural law. Second, the fact that the Bible contains guidance on the origin of the specific government in a more narrow, more historical sense, is important because it is "in many instances, the foundation of the law" (and also because it gives "the clue to the controversies of the Canonists").

The Bible also gives the law student a political philosophy, a coherent and dependable theory of "the social compact." When that point is pondered, it seems to mean that the Bible, to Hoffman, provided a theory of government that is to be contrasted with "the social compact" of the Enlightenment philosophers. What Hoffman meant to do, in referring the law student to the Bible as a source on this point, was to suggest that the biblical covenant that originates government in Hebrew scripture, and that was important in the political philosophies of the American Puritans, was a more dependable theory of the state than, say, Hobbes's and Rousseau's theories of a social contract among noble savages. The Bible, Hoffman says, exhibits "the actual manner in which society was generated . . . and . . . offers the best theory of the social compact; a point on which there has been no small misconception."

The Bible demonstrates how moral principles governing primitive people—"the rudest and most unlettered nations"— were more likely the product of revelation from God than of natural law. Hoffman does not trust the more naive end of the eighteenth-century English natural-law jurisprudence. He has a wary Calvinist's suspicion of fanciful suggestions about noble savages, and—more to the point—he believes the Bible demonstrates how a revealed system of morals is superior to a natural-law system of morals.

America is, he says, a Christian nation. The Christian religion is a part of the law of the land. For this reason alone the Bible is an important legal document; it is, in any case—and here he views legal sources as both English and American—the foundation of the common law. That is Blackstone's view, too, and was conventional wisdom in the popular American jurisprudence of Hoffman's day. Aside from religion, and aside from a view that biblical morality is revealed, the moral teachings of the New Testament are superior to all other moral teachings. Here Hoffman's argument relies on Enlightenment thinkers. He cites John Locke (and might as well have cited Jefferson) to that effect. Locke says he would send a student to the New Testament alone for "a complete knowledge of genuine morals"—and this aside from belief in the divine origin of New Testament morals. "Legal education," Hoffman says, "should be raised on the broad and solid foundation of ethics." The ethics of the Bible are culturally relevant for Americans and are analytically superior to the ethics of Aristotle, Plato, or Cicero. He is not talking here about professional ethics but the ethics that are first cousins to the law. He is talking about politics and jurisprudence, not about how a good person can be a lawyer.

Hoffman also argues that there is law—that is, explicit legal norms—to be found in the Bible. He speaks in this connection of the law of marriage and inheritance. Part of his point is that the Bible provides comparative law, in the sense in which a modern law student studies comparative law to better understand municipal law, as the student of English learns more grammar from studying Latin than he does from studying the grammar of his own language. He mentions the biblical law of property ownership, of conveyancing, and of master-servant relationships.

The Bible teaches professional skill as well as legal information. Hoffman finds biblical literature valuable for lawyers because (among other reasons) it teaches eloquence and provides useful allusions for public speaking. He quotes several eloquent passages to show what he means. In this way, too, a knowledge of scripture is a way for a young lawyer to get ahead; it is a way for him to find his way into the culture of lawyers. "All the distinguished lawyers with whom we have been personally, or through the medium of books, or otherwise acquainted, have not only professed a high veneration for biblical learning, but were themselves considerably versed in it."

He ends his essay on the Bible in what seems to me a defensive mood. "We make no apology for the length of this note" (some twenty pages), Hoffman says at the end of this, the first title of his *Course of Law Study*, "nor for any matter in it which may be conceived, by some, not strictly within the design of this volume. We think differently; at all events, the Bible may be allowed to form an exception; for upon no occasion, where it is recommended, can any matter be irrelevant which in any degree unfolds its excellencies, or facilitates its study."

Hoffman did not neglect, as a separate inquiry, the question of how a good person goes about being a lawyer. His professional ethics are, in both editions, in appended essays on "professional deportment." These rely repeatedly on collections of moral (and in some cases legal) maxims. For example, he devotes most of a page of the essay on deportment to La Rochefoucauld's *Maxims.* Because he liked a neat phrase, and was willing on occasion to celebrate authority more than reason, he found comfort and educational value (as many law teachers do—still do) in short, unelaborated moral rules. There is a curious, pervasive distinction between his affinity for this moral teaching and his use of the Bible in legal education. The Bible appears in his *Course* as the first title, as the point of beginning for the process we still call "learning to think like a lawyer." The maxims appear at the end of his work, in the appendix on professional ethics, as part of a less reasoned approach to what he called "professional deportment."

Hoffman talked of morals in two places, and in two senses, and he separated the two as widely as he could. His article on the Bible as law (as politics and jurisprudence) appears first in the first volume of the 1836 *Course.* The essays and Resolutions (his legal ethics) appear last in the second volume. The Bible is prominent, or at least primary, in the way he outlines what the law is, and what philosophy Anglo-American law rests on. But the Bible is noticeable by its absence as a basis for reasoning on the day-to-day moral behavior of lawyers. (He discusses the Book of Proverbs in an appendix to his ethics, but only as a set of maxims, not as a doctrinal or even cultural basis for ethical thought.) It is almost as if by raising the Bible to the altar in his temple of justice, Hoffman was able to keep it from having much to do with ethics. By making it the foundation of all law, as he did, he need not have bothered to make it the foundation of a lawyer's behavior on an ordinary Wednesday afternoon. This division probably had a lot to do with his ability to overlook—at least in ethical theory—the biblical bias for the vulgar and the poor.

The Bible as a Source of Medical Ethics

It may be important to many doctors and lawyers to read what the Bible says about what they should do in their professional lives. While that sounds plausible to a believer, particularly in view of the paternal image of God that most believers have inherited, it may not be as simple as it sounds. I think here of a useful analytical essay on biblical medical ethics by Richard J. Mouw.

Mouw says it is sometimes possible to take the imperative biblical language as a direct and firm (as the philosophers say it, "deontological") command. "Thou shalt not kill," for medical ethics, then is no more nor less authoritative than the usual tradition, conventionally traced to Hippocrates, that has so far kept physicians in America from administering capital punishment. But nobody in the medical profession is prepared, I think, to follow all the relevant imperatives in the Bible on medical practice; I do not know of anyone (nor, apparently, does Mouw) who follows the prescriptions of Leviticus 13 in treating skin disease. The rabbis early decided that those prescriptions dealt more with ritual purity than with medicine. A modern Torah commentary, directed to Leviticus 13, even says "The Bible says almost nothing about medical practice." That is, at best, a rigorous bit of interpretation; it might not be the explanation that would have been chosen by the Talmudists who consigned "the best of physicians to hell" and said that one who cures the sick without pay is worth as much as he gets.

At the other end of a scriptural view of medical ethics are those in "situation ethics" who say that the only biblical command that must be followed is the command to love. At its most literal, that school of thought leaves it up to the obedient follower of the law of love to decide when his feelings are love and when they have other explanations.

In between, and, I think, more consistent with what the rabbis (including Jesus) announced as the law of love, is the view that other biblical commands show what love is. An even more comprehensive view might be that the entire Bible shows what love is—in its songs and stories, as well as its commandments. Love is a way of life; the Bible shows what that way of life is like. From that point of view, the Bible is a source of tests for moral commands, both those that come from the Bible and those that come from other sources. This last is the way most believers have come to live with the Bible, and is probably the only way it can be useful for professional practice.

But not without some discomfort. Lawyers, for example, from any of these points of view, should probably wonder about the Bible and litigation. The New Testament tells Christians to stay out of the courts. It provides a specific procedure (at least as specific as the procedure for treating skin disease in Leviticus 13) for resolving disputes within the community of believers, and, as to disputes between members of the community and others, says it is better to give in than to litigate. It is possible, no doubt, to do some interpreting there, as the rabbis interpreted Leviticus 13 in medical practice, but anyone who is serious should be uncomfortable about it (as the rabbis, including Jesus, no doubt were; see Mark 1:40ff). The risk in interpreting the issue away is that one will thereby interpret the Bible away. I think that is exactly what the Anglican priest William Paley did, in his decision that the injunctions against litigation did not apply to English law—which, in Paley's day, denied property ownership to married women, permitted commercial traffic in African slaves, and imposed capital punishment on children. Paley's view, and analogous views on medical issues, taken with his popularity as a source of seminal professional ethics in Britain and the United States, may explain why professional ethics say nothing about the Bible. The Bible is left out because it doesn't make a difference.

Mouw suggests that the analysis might go another way. Any moral command, including an article of professional ethics, has some explicit or implicit justification—so that David Hoffman counsels against advancing the defense of the statute of limitations or of infancy because to do so might defeat a just claim. Or Sir Thomas Percival suggests that surgeons put on a clean apron between operations, so that the new patient will not be unduly upset by the sight of somebody else's blood. He also advises that hospital schedules be set up in such a way as to allow physicians to go to church on Sundays—because, I take it, gentlemen go to church.

There are different ways to invoke the Bible as a justification for a moral rule in professional life. One might say: I obey God because God is the Supreme Power. Mouw says that view is from Thomas Hobbes—"The appeal is not so much to a sense of the moral fittingness of . . . submission as it is to a prudential awareness of what is in our self-interest." George V. Higgins's lawyer, Jerry Kennedy, says he will never complain to God about anything, because God led him to a wonderful wife and complaint about anything else might be taken as ingratitude. One might say, as my Roman Catholic tradition usually has said, that she or he obeys God because God made him to be happy when he is obedient—or (the Catholic moralists have said it's the same thing) because what God commands is consistent with human nature. Either way God knows what's best. The Protestant tradition has tended more to say that we obey God's commands out of gratitude to God, Who, in love, has offered us salvation (meaning eternal life, or well-being, or both).

In the spirit of the way-of-life view of the Bible as a source of ethics for the professions, Mouw, who writes for doctors, suggests a consideration of a biblical view of medicine. What might that look like? These answers are products of my own liberal interpretation of what Mouw says.

First, God did not make us to be sick—and (usually anyway) God is not the one who makes us sick. God is our healer. "Remember us to life, O King who delights in life," says the prayer-book service for Rosh Hashanah. "You revive the dead; you are powerful to save. You sustain the living with kindness . . . support all who fall, and heal the sick. . . . You bring death and restore life and cause salvation to flourish." The promise of the messianic age and of the Second Coming speak of a God who "will wipe every tear from their eyes" (Revelation 21:4).

Second, illness is appropriately a concern for the community, not only for the person who is ill and the persons who treat him. St. James called for the early Christians to "call for the elders . . . and let them pray over him, anointing him with oil . . . and the prayer of faith will save the sick man" (James 5:14–15). Whatever else Leviticus 13 meant in Israel, it was followed as a piece of community regulation, one that Rabbi Jesus, in healing, respected (Mark 1:40ff).

Third, the emphasis on the community as healer seems to imply a canon of professional ethics for the healer—that the healer represent the concern of the community for the sick, and that the healer be open to learning about sickness from those who are not professionals—including the sick person himself. "I whisper silent thanks to the old man at St. Elizabeth's who convinced me of the importance of asking people what *they* think is causing their symptoms," says Carole Horn. The old man had been diagnosed by another doctor as a paranoid schizophrenic because he wore three pairs of eyeglasses. When she asked him what he thought, he said, "Oh, these. . . . You know my eyesight ain't what it used to be, and I don't have no good glasses. I found all these and put 'em together, and now I see just fine."

For the community itself (and that includes the medical professionals in it), this biblical perspective would, consistent with the part of the biblical tradition that speaks of a variety of gifts, look for different things from different people. Mouw suggests that one perspective might be, in effect, priestly—might ask how the practitioner can go about what he does with love for the patient, openness to those who might give him information, respect and deference for other experts. This is a *priestly* perspective, Mouw says, because it assumes "the legitimacy of current standards and norms for medical practice, asking how we can be more loving or just within those patterns."

Another perspective might be *prophetic.* (Martin Buber says that the priest and the prophet are eternal types in Judaism; the priest wants power, the prophet truth.) Here a biblical view of medicine would be open to the possibility that religious and professional renegades might have something useful to say—the Jehovah's Witnesses refusing blood transfusions; the Christian Scientists refusing most medical care; some other groups refusing polio vaccine; the disciples of Ivan Illich saying that medicine has become an illegitimate metaphor for all of life; the school of Thomas Szasz, which says that medicine is the new American state religion.

Those three biblical perspectives, elaborated in this way, might, then, Mouw says, make a difference. It might make a difference, for example, to insist that the practice of a profession be subordinate to what one can figure out from a biblical moral perspective. Christian lawyers have worried, openly sometimes, about what seems to be the clear language of chapter 18 of St. Matthew's Gospel. Many of them have given up litigation practice and some have given up ordinary law practice altogether and now work in forums and processes set up to follow Matthew 18. Traditional Jewish rabbinical courts have always been forums for reconciliation. American Jewish communities, particularly in New York, began some time ago to establish special, more public reconciliation courts that would keep Jews out of civil litigation. The point is that it is possible that the Bible might make a difference.

Any of these biblical perspectives, when directed at the patient or client, would part company with the dominant ideal of professional ethics in America, which is that the goal of professional service is that the client or patient be free, that he be autonomous. A biblical perspective would take into account the relationship between the patient or client and God, and it would work out professional service in light of that other relationship. An example Mouw uses, for medicine, involves disclosure to the patient of what her condition is. The patient, who is in pain, cannot suffer, in the biblical sense, unless she knows what she is suffering from. "The spiritual significance of suffering corresponds . . . to a right to know the facts about one's physical condition." In my view, this giving of information is not an issue about paternalism (which might or might not be appropriate, on other grounds, some of them biblical); nor is it, as Mouw suggests, an issue about a "plurality of perspectives on the issues of life and death, health and suffering." The reason for giving the other person information about her situation (and this applies to legal matters as well as medical matters) is that she is a child of God. Her relationship with God is, from a biblical perspective, a fundamental fact in professional service—a goal in many cases, I think; a condition in all cases.

Beyond these biblical perspectives, which bear on the professional-client relationship, Mouw suggests that a biblical perspective carries a bias for the poor, a concern for the context in which professional services are rendered, and a responsibility for the political consequences of professional service. "No moral perspective that takes divine commands seriously can ignore the overwhelming number of occasions on which God has commanded . . . people to defend the cause of those who are helpless before the structures of society." It is, from that point of view, consistent for doctors and lawyers, as doctors and lawyers, to associate for opposition to nuclear weapons. They don't really have to say (although I suppose it doesn't hurt) that atomic annihilation is a matter of health or of justice.

The Servant of the Lord

A lawyer or doctor or teacher has to give some reason for her or his privileges—licensed access to mysteries, social power, status, and, usually, high income. He and his fraternities (she and her sororities) feel the need anyone does, and particularly anyone in the modern world, to fit his or her situation into some universal and objective morality. The usual way this is done in the professions is through the claim that professionals are set aside for service. It is not the *noblesse oblige* that advertently class-oriented societies—Percival's and Hoffman's, for examples—have seen (the notion that the price of status is care for those who don't have status), but an argument that admits that the only purpose of being set apart is to be of service to those who are not set apart. This is the modern way to take account of the vulgar and the poor.

This claim of service, mixed into the reality of professional practice, leads to a fundamental fact and the distinctive moral situation of professionalism. The professional person is involved in the conscience of his client. Professional morality is vicarious morality. We professionals, by definition, act for other persons. Their ends become our ends as we act for them. A pastor's concern, as professional, is the spiritual health of her or his parishioner. The physician practices the medical art so that the patient may realize a wish to be healthy, as the mechanic repairs the machine so that the machine will do what the mechanic's client wants it to do. The word "attorney" means one who goes to town for another. The American legal profession has exalted the fact of vicarious morality into the ethics of the professional adversary. A lawyer will sometimes refer to himself as a "hired gun," that is, a mercenary—one whose morals are so entirely vicarious that (in metaphor) she or he kills those his client wants to be dead.

On the most conventional reasoning, then, the professional is involved in his client's moral choices. The most conventional difficulty here is that the professional person also has a conscience of his own. Judge Jones's 1887 Alabama code for lawyers implied a consequent misgiving and met it with a vehemence that lawyers in America have always found discomforting. "The attorney's office does not destroy the man's accountability to the Creator . . . and the obligation to his neighbor; and it does not permit, much less demand . . . any manner of fraud or chicanery, for the client's sake."

Arrayed against that Jeffersonian vestige is most of modern professional ethics. The physician and the mechanic argue that the client's use of health or of an automobile is no part of the professional's concern. The pastor and the counselor speak of the client's liberty, and the professional's involvement in the client's life as a concern for liberty. How the client uses liberty is his business. Part of being set apart for professional service is setting one's conscience apart from the consequences of professional service, Judge Jones to the contrary notwithstanding.

The moral question being asked is, "What is the client up to?" The modern, professional moral answer is, "That's none of my business. I'm just doing my job." But the moral question can be answered in another way, a way (to use the rhetoric of H. Richard Niebuhr's school of ethics) that would interpret the question, "What is the client up to?" as a different and more troubling question. "How is the client, in his association with me, changing? What is she or he becoming *because* of me?" Not only does my professional assistance enable him to *do* something; it also enables him to *become* something. When I understand that this is so, I may say to myself, my hope is that the new person will be a better person than the old person was. Pastors do not point their parishioners toward evil; physicians consider it immoral to administer lethal drugs, even at the behest of the state (that is, they do not seek to change their patients from life to death); lawyers consider it immoral to advise clients on how to become criminals. We professionals try not to make things worse. My client will be a different person because of his association with me, as he will be a different person after any intense association. And to notice that is to ask, "What do I want him to be?" or, to put that another way, "What am *I* up to?" Professional morals, because they are vicarious, tend to obscure the moral question, "What am *I* up to?"

Consequently, professionals find it necessary to protect themselves from their clients. Otherwise we end up asking whether it is moral for us to lie, to kill, or to destroy—questions that would be readily answered if one of us professionals was acting only for himself.

The professions in America have not talked about these vicarious ethical questions in reference to the Bible. That could be because they are questions of such elementary and universal moral significance that the Bible is not needed for them. David Hoffman perhaps thought so. But it is an odd result in a culture where the professions have been dominated by believers. I wonder if the reason biblical morality has been peripheral, in this interpersonal view of what American professional ethics is, is that the Bible speaks too clearly and too plainly. Maybe the reason biblical morality has been left out is that it is both insistent and unpleasant; it demands too much.

· § ·

Biblical notions of service to others are rooted in a culture that understood and accepted the morality of service, of doing unto others as one would be done to. Jesus quoted that ancient Jewish moral principle, as his contemporary Rabbi Hillel did. "Deal lovingly with your fellow man, who is like you" (Leviticus 19:18, Buber's translation). That moral principle supports offering service and then carrying out the service for the well-being of the person served. Service to the other was and is consequent on serving the God of Israel, a loving God, a God who is addressed as parent. It is a relentlessly difficult and demanding ethic, but it is not a naked do-or-die moral absolute. It is the commandment of a forgiving God, a God who says, "I will make allowances for them as a man who makes allowances for the son who obeys him. Then once again you will see the difference between an upright man and a wicked one, between the one who serves God and the one who does not serve him" (Malachi 3:17–18, Jerusalem Bible).

Jesus announced the Jewish moral principle of obedient service in three ways, ways that are characteristic of Hebrew prophets:

1. The service Jesus enjoins is pursued to the point of suffering.
2. The service Jesus enjoins is powerless.
3. The service Jesus enjoins is given a justification in terms of its social consequences; that justification is the reconciliation of one person to another.

Taken as a whole, this Hebraic emphasis points to a professional morality of servanthood—of being *a servant* and not merely being *of service.* The refinements turn service into servanthood. A biblical professional ethic is an ethic, not of service, but of servanthood.

Suffering. Jesus said, "Among pagans it is the kings who lord it over them, and those who have authority over them are given the title Benefactor. This must not happen with you. No; the greatest among you must behave as if he were the youngest, the leader as if he were the one who serves. For who is the greater: the one at table or the one who serves? The one at table, surely? Yet here am I among you as one who serves" (Luke 22:25–27, Jerusalem Bible). Jesus drew on the moral theology of Israel, the morals of obedient service to God. He also drew specifically on four mysterious songs from the book of the prophet Isaiah. His followers laid claim, for the Christian church, to the image in Judaism of the Servant of the Lord, the servant who suffers. One of those songs said that the Servant of the Lord brings justice (Isaiah 42:1–4). One said that this servant brings "light to the nations . . . salvation . . . to the ends of the earth" (Isaiah 49:1–6, Jerusalem Bible). One spoke of the Servant of the Lord as humiliated in his own generation but finally vindicated by God (Isaiah 50:4–9). And one of them spoke of the servant as a deviant, one who is made ugly by the touch of God and who suffers for his deviance:

> a thing despised and rejected by men,
> a man of sorrows and familiar with suffering,
> a man to make people screen their faces;
> he was despised and we took no account of him. . . .
> Harshly dealt with, he bore it humbly,
> he never opened his mouth,
> like a lamb that is led to the slaughterhouse,
> like a sheep that is dumb before its shearers
> never opening its mouth. . . .
> They gave him a grave with the wicked,
> a tomb with the rich,
> though he had done no wrong
> and there was no perjury in his mouth.
> [The Lord] has been pleased to crush him with suffering.
> If he offers his life in atonement,

he shall see his heirs, he shall have a long life
and through him what [the Lord] wishes will be done.
(Isaiah 53:3, 7, 9–10, Jerusalem Bible)

The Servant of the Lord brings justice to Israel, and salvation to the other nations. He is, like the prophets, vindicated by God, but before vindication, he is, like the prophets, despised and rejected of men—a deviant, a leper. The first Christians made dogmatic claims from these songs—most notably the claim that Jesus' death by torture was resolved, as Isaiah said, in glorification, in the Resurrection. The Jewish tradition sees the image in Isaiah as the personification of Israel, which is chosen by God—chosen for suffering—for the good of all nations. The moral point is not either dogmatic claim, but the claim that Jesus and Israel recognize this image of the suffering servant as a divine command, a divine command that speaks to the question of how to be a doctor or a lawyer and a good person as well.

That is the way the followers of the prophets are to be—the way Jews and Christians are to live with their clients—not merely to *serve* them but to be their servants, and to expect to suffer for it. This is a clear and radical command. It brings to mind Kierkegaard's melancholy observation: "Remove from Christianity its ability to shock . . . and it is altogether destroyed. It then becomes a tiny, superficial thing, capable neither of inflicting deep wounds nor of healing them."

Martin Buber, facing with his fellow German Jews the horrors of the 1930s and 1940s, made such a claim for modern Israel: " 'Israel' means to practice community for the sake of a common covenant in which our existence is founded; to practice in actual living the community between . . . person and person. . . . And today this means to preserve directness in a world which is becoming more and more indirect, in the face of the self-righteousness of collectivities to preserve the mystery of relationship."

Powerlessness. Jesus announced that a kingdom had come. The way one belonged to the kingdom that had come was to be powerless. "Let the children come to me," he said, "and do not stop them; for it is to such as these that the kingdom of God belongs. I tell you solemnly, anyone who does not welcome the kingdom of God like a little child will never enter it" (Luke 18:16–17, Jerusalem Bible. St. Mark's account ties these two teachings—the little-children lesson and the lesson on servanthood—together; Mark 9:35–37). One could ponder what it means to welcome anything as a child welcomes what happens to him. It does not mean innocence; children are not innocent. It does not mean simplicity; children are as complicated as adults are. Being a child means being without power. The kingdom Jesus speaks about is a kingdom one enters when he is able to welcome it as one who does not share in worldly power. The way to the kingdom is, in Buber's phrase, not trod on the surface of success. Or, as Mother Teresa of Calcutta puts it, our concern is not to be successful; it is to be faithful.

But this absence of power—renunciation of power—is not a circumstance; it is a choice. And it has a purpose. "The self-abasement of Christ to powerlessness, to the renunciation of all obvious marks of distinction, is . . . *intended to render a service,*" Helmut Thielicke says (emphasis added). For example, Jesus' refusal to use power at the behest of Satan (Luke 4:1–13) serves the dignity and freedom of those Jesus serves; it shows that the divine parent Jesus speaks of makes women and men subjects through their own free decision rather than as objects of the power of others. When Jesus performs miracles he uses them to teach with rather than to compel with or to threaten. He seeks powerlessness even when he *uses* power, as in the curing of the leper. By touching the leper he cures the man's disease; but in the process Jesus makes a leper of himself (Mark 1:40–45).

Reconciliation. In the Letter to the Hebrews a Jewish-Christian moral theologian says, "Let us keep firm in the hope we profess, because the one who made the promise is faithful. Let us be concerned for each other, to stir up a response in love and good works" (Hebrews 10:23–24, Jerusalem Bible). The Jewish follower of Jesus here claims his Jewish heritage. Rabbi Hanina bar Hama, commenting on Proverbs (25:21–22), said, "even if the enemy come to your house to slay you, and he is hungry or thirsty, give him food and drink; for thereby God will reconcile him to you" (cf. 2 Kings 6:21–23). Jesus, when giving directions to his followers on how they were to resolve their disputes, said, "If your brother does something wrong, go and have it out with him alone, between your two selves. If he listens to you, you have won back your brother" (Matthew 18:15, Jerusalem Bible).

The aim of moral life with patients, students, or clients, according to these texts, is to serve in such a way that the person served will himself become a servant—that he will himself be moved to love, to good works, to the company of those who serve. This is a *social* ethic; it makes an argument, a consequential, ethical argument, for these otherwise curious demands for suffering and for powerlessness. It gives suffering and powerlessness a social consequence and uses that consequence as a reason for being a servant. These teachings do not show how reconciliation will occur; what they say is that it occurs as a consequence of suffering, powerless servanthood. The teachings rest on stories—the stories of Israel and of the Cross, and on the understanding of these stories that is preserved in Israel, among the rabbis, and in the church. The teachings do suggest, though, that one result is the conversion of the person served. Conversion to what? *To suffering and powerlessness.* This social ethic is curious. St. Paul says, "If my blood has to be shed as part of your own sacrifice and offering—which is your faith—I shall still be happy and rejoice with all of you and you must be just as happy and rejoice with me." The Talmud speaks in a similar way of the martyr Rabbi Aquiba, who smiled as his death by torture neared, because he understood at the end of his life what it means to love God with soul as well as with heart and might (Deuteronomy 6:5).

St. Paul speaks of a fellow believer Epaphroditus, who has been persecuted, and says, "It was for Christ's work that he came so near to dying." And of Jesus himself, the early church said in one of its songs:

> His state was divine,
> Yet he did not cling
> to his equality with God
> but emptied himself
> to assume the condition of a slave. . . .
>
> (Philippians 2:6–7, 30; Jerusalem Bible)

A curious teaching. Karl Barth says of it, "No one is . . . to be pitied if he cannot at first belong to this minority, nor to be envied if he really must." And yet:

The biblical command and example for professionals is to take on the servant's task, a task that summons the professional out of what Karl Barth called an "impossible isolation and concentration on [self]," that one do that, not in order to be satisfied in his altruism, but in order to make his professional action correspond to the biblical model, the suffering servant, who works in the shadow and whose achievement may be in the deep of failure. In this response one serves God by being servant to his clients, by being a servant in suffering, in powerlessness, and in reconciliation. That is the professional ethics of servanthood. It is apparently the biblical way to be a professional person. The theology behind the ethic is specific for believers, in any case, and it is that the follower contributes in his obedience to God's action as Creator and Redeemer. For Christians the focus of obedience is Jesus as Lord and Savior; for Jews the focus is a personal identification with and within Israel as Servant of the Lord. There is nothing obscure about it, but it *is* hard to take. It would have caused problems for Hoffman's and Percival's professional ethics. It was simpler for them to confine the Bible to jurisprudence, to use maxims for ethics, and to depend on the decent instincts of gentlemen.

Even so, I think the American professions have been affected by this radical, biblical ethic of servanthood. It is *so* radical that one might guess that it would be made trivial among the faithful and ignored by everybody else, and from those guesses might suppose that nothing would come of it. But you will find in our professional histories and in our lawyer and doctor stories more than a trace of the notion that we overcome evil by suffering the outrage of evil.

Take, for example, stories of nurses and doctors among the poor such as Tom Dooley, or of models held up to law students—of Andrew Hamilton, the champion of free speech, who represented the journalist Peter Zenger before the colonial tyrants of New York; or of John Adams defending the British soldiers after the Boston Massacre; or of the brave Army lawyers who defended Generals Homma and Yamashita and in the process defied Douglas Mac-

Arthur. It is possible to claim for such American hero stories, and to claim seriously, the powerlessness and suffering and reconciliation of the biblical ideal.

But the point is in our hero stories, not in our codes of ethics. James McClendon argues, of some of these stories, that they are themselves a theology of suffering servanthood—Dr. King as the hero and exemplar of the civil rights movement; Hammarskjold as the model peacemaker. King was also a Baptist preacher; he came from, returned to—never left—the Southern black church. His life was a theology of exodus and atonement. The images of his leadership (those he followed and those he left to us) are the images of the servant who overcomes evil by suffering it, who is powerless, who kneels in the street and prays for his persecutors. Hammarskjold, the man of peace, is seen in his diary as a follower of the Cross and not as the practitioner of peaceful coexistence that he seemed to be at the United Nations—another powerless sufferer whose life was a theology of reconciliation.

So, too, of lawyer heroes—Thomas More, for example, or Atticus Finch. Miss Maudie says, about Atticus's defense of Tom Robinson, that the Christians of Maycomb had Atticus *go for* them. Go where? To the Cross. There Atticus and, even more, his innocent client suffer. There Atticus is the white church, gathered with Reverend Sykes and the black church, gathered in reconciliation at the Cross. The courtroom is the Cross, the Cross showing what men do to one another in the name of the law. Tom Robinson is on the cross. The agony of Southern Christianity is in that story, and it is a recent story about an American lawyer.

· § ·

Professional morals are vicarious. That is implicit in any professional's undertaking to be of service. Biblical professional morals are, as well, the morals of those who serve the Lord. The Lord of Jews and Christians is the loving parent Who serves people and Whose command is that His servants serve people, too, and serve them in a specific and radical way—in suffering, in powerlessness, toward reconciliation. This command has continuing influence in professional ethics in America, which may prove that we are more biblical than we thought we were.

What I have to try to do, then, is to connect this moral theology with the basic question in the professional ethics of responsibility: What do I wish for my client? That is the professional version of the basic moral question for anybody: What am I up to? I have often thought that I could talk about the question of what I am up to as the professional in professional relationships, which is also the question of what I hope for my client, in terms of three alternatives.

1. Autonomy. I hope that my client will be *free;* what I seek for him will be realized when he can choose for himself; or
2. Rectitude. I hope that my client will be *right;* what I seek for him will be realized when, looking at his act, I can see that he chose to do the right thing; or
3. Virtue. I hope that my client will be *good;* what I seek for him will be realized when he develops and rejoices in his own moral qualities, when he becomes virtuous.

These answers now seem to me to be too much like moral rules and too little like the rabbis (Jesus and Moses Maimonides among them) who said that the Sabbath is made for man, not man for the Sabbath. Perhaps we could say that the moral ideal that is most prominent in the Bible is not so much a matter of rules as a matter of how to live with rules. Whether that is right or not, the Sabbath is made for man, not man for the Sabbath. Rules and moral dilemmas are subordinated to the law of love. Servanthood, in suffering and powerlessness and toward reconciliation, approaches the other not as the occasion of professional moral choice but as one who is cherished. First he is cherished and then he is a moral dilemma. He is cherished whether he is a moral dilemma or not.

It is even starker than that. The other—patient or client—is cherished, but not as an equal. He is cherished as a superior, as my master, as the boss. First he is cherished and then, if he becomes a moral dilemma for me, he is given the benefit of the doubt. If we disagree, *he* is probably right. Bosses are entitled to the benefit of the doubt. Servanthood is, in scripture, a literal notion. The Greek word St. Luke uses to render Jesus' meaning is the word for a table servant—"waitress" might be a modern English equivalent. St. Paul uses "slave" to express the idea to the Greeks. The New Testament writers thought that Jesus meant for his teaching on servanthood to be taken literally. Notice, for example, that St. John's Gospel focuses the events leading to the Cross and Resurrection on Jesus washing the feet of his companions.

Autonomy. The legal ethics of servanthood will therefore balance my hope that my client will be free against the command that my serving him will reconcile, that she or he will be restored to his brothers and sisters and be stirred up to love and good works. His destiny is, certainly, to be free, but that is so that he can choose to be reconciled to others and so that he can be liberated, in suffering and without power. My hope for him in his freedom is like my hope for myself in my freedom. Mouw puts this in terms of the Hebraic notions of covenant and idolatry, which are, I think, another way to look at reconciliation and atonement. Medical intervention, he says, is not so much a threat to patient autonomy as it is a threat "to one's fidelity to the primary covenantal relationship with God. The danger is not so much a loss of freedom as it is a temptation to put idolatrous trust in medical technology." And the medical professional is more vulnerable to that risk than the patient is.

Rectitude. In this way of looking at things, I hope, too, that my client will choose what is right. In his freedom, I hope, he will see clearly and choose bravely and end up doing the right thing. But my servanthood is the renunciation of power—and this means, in professional relations, the renunciation of the clout that professionals in our culture have—the power of special knowledge, the status, the paternalism I am seduced into because my client seems to be dependent on me. I am not his master; he is mine. I am not his mother or father; we are together sisters and brothers of a Lord Who wants us both to be waitresses. If I have power—and heaven knows doctors and teachers and lawyers have power in America—it is as a means of servanthood, a means inferior to love. Otherwise I should renounce it, as Jesus renounced the power to work miracles, lest my power coerce those whom God wants to be free.

Virtue. And, finally, I hope that my client will grow in virtue. I hope she or he will not only make right choices, but will become the sort of person who makes right choices. I want him to be better than he would have been if I had not stumbled into his life. But the price of that growth may be suffering—my own, by definition; that is what "compassion" means—but also *his* suffering; his identification (as well as mine) with the vulgar and the poor; his concern for justice as a gift we give one another; his rejection of the idolatry of institutions.

That suffering part of servanthood is hard for doctors and lawyers, so radical that it is all but unacceptable. Our training and self-selection is competitive. Our professional metaphors speak of rescue and rivalry; we speak of ourselves as warlike. We lawyers aim to win for our clients in court and, in the office, to prevent their losing. Death and pain are the enemies of medicine. Our best moves are assaults, bombshells, forays, frontal attacks, and rear-guard actions. Everything turns on victory. And so when Anthony Lewis wants to write a book about poor old Clarence Earl Gideon's finding a friend in court, he uses a biblical battlefield for his symbol. *Gideon's Trumpet* tells of a lawyer who no doubt served his client but was not his client's servant. I suspect that servanthood would have involved more contact, and, maybe, less victory. Jesus cures the leper, and becomes a leper in the process. Jesus saves the good thief, but he does not rescue him from suffering; the good thief does not come down from his cross until he, too, is dead. Leo Baeck expresses his leadership of Hitler's Jewish victims by going to the death camp to join them. It is always possible that the real biblical work that my patient or client has to do is, like my own, trodden not on the surface of success, but in the deep of failure.

Chapter Three

· § ·

THEOLOGY

Man, fearfully and wonderfully made, is the workmanship of his all perfect Creator: A State, useful and valuable as the contrivance is, is the inferior contrivance of man; and from his native dignity derives all its acquired importance. . . . A state, I cheerfully admit, is the noblest work of Man. But Man himself . . . is . . . the noblest work of God.

—Justice James Wilson

In Hebraic theology, God is one and there is no other god. Ethics based on that theology begin with a negative injunction against idolatry: You shall have no other god—not, for example, the profession, or what Ivan Illich calls the medicalization of life. Not the work of a lifetime. Not even clients. No other God. All of Hebraic theology tends from this oneness of God to a consequent striving for unity—oneness—in creation; to the deed that manifests obedience; and to the hope that follows from oneness and from obedience. If the question in the narrower focus of professional ethics asks whether one can be a doctor or lawyer or teacher and a good person, the Jewish and Christian theological answer to the question will begin with this unity, obedience, and hope. Curiously, though, a theological orientation may not involve a single morality. Theological ethics has often taught a separate morality for professional life. In the light of this theological experience, if not in the light of logic, the question for professional ethics becomes: Is there a separate morality for professional life? In terms of experience, convention, and argot, the answer to that question would appear to be: Yes, there is a separate morality for professional life. Our forebears have not followed, and we do not follow, the same morals in public and professional life that we follow in personal life:

1. The earliest statements of rules of behavior for American lawyers made no distinction between personal and professional life. These were admonitions by law teachers (Hoffman, Sharswood), though; they were not the work of bar associations or committees of practicing lawyers. When, in the age of the industrial robber barons and their lawyers, the profession began to put its ethics into codes (such as Jones's Alabama Code of 1887), there appeared a distinction between etiquette and regulation on the one hand and morals on the other. The same distinction is implicit in codified American medical ethics as that subject has developed from Sir Thomas Percival's code of 1791. Each generation of American lawyers since Judge Jones's has revised its code of ethics; and each revision says less about morals, and says what it does say about morals less precisely.

The American Bar Association's proposed Rules of Professional Conduct for American lawyers (1983) bring this development to new fullness by avoiding the traditional words of ethical argument—words such as conscience, morality, right, good, and propriety—in favor of the words of mandate and permission that are the stuff of statutes and court orders. The position implicit in the Rules is that the nationally organized bar is not interested in providing, or is interested in but not able to provide, moral admonition to American lawyers. Moral admonition has become either private and non-professional or it has become a concern appropriate in more local or more specialized organizations of lawyers. Other contemporary comment on the morals of professionals suggests that lawyers should keep their personal morals out of their law practices, and that doctors who offer their moral opinions on what patients decide to do are paternalistic (bad word). Our lives are described by the cartoon in *The New Yorker* that shows two judges robing for their day's work. One says to the other, "This daily metamorphosis never fails to amaze me. Around the house, I'm a perfect idiot. I come to court, put on a black robe, and . . . I'm it."

2. A common professional and political view is that a lawyer may do for his client, or an official for his country, or a physician for his patient, what would be immoral if either acted in the same way for himself. John T. Noonan, Jr., gives as an example the Wall Street lawyer who bribed a federal judge, escaped prosecution, and gained or retained the esteem of his law firm and of the Bar. The published history of that lawyer's law firm says of him, "No lawyer ever unreservedly gave more of himself for a client."

Noonan mentions Sir Winston Churchill's order to bomb Dresden in World War II, an act that incinerated thousands of civilian refugees in revenge for the bombing of Britain. Sir Winston acted for his countrymen, not for himself. If his conscience gave him pause, he kept his conscience to himself. Even the comics provide an example. Mark Trail, outdoorsman and righter of wrongs, went mountain climbing with a government agent. They were searching in the high timber for a hijacker who had bailed out of an airplane with a million dollars. They split up. Mark found the body of the hijacker but no money. Mark called to the agent, who joined him and the body and suggested that Mark had found the money and hidden it. Mark, who is a person of formidable integrity, objected to this; the agent said, "I'm just doing my job, Mark."

"Forgive me for lying to you," says one of John D. MacDonald's characters, and forgiveness is given as it was asked for: "Oh yes! You've got a job to do." Medical ethics has come to this position—as has the ethics of journalism—more slowly than law and government service have, but medicine and journalism now proclaim separate vocational ethics as relentlessly as the law does. Witness positions taken on abortion, or the withholding of medical treatment from newborn children who have Down's Syndrome or some other serious disability. What the doctor is to do in such cases is said to be a private matter, not up to the doctor but up to the patient or patient's family. Witness the defense of intrusive investigative journalism, a defense that says, "I've got a job to do."

3. When political questions in our country are tense, we make continued deliberation of them possible by making morals private. Abortion is a prominent and recent example, one that imposes a vocational ethic on government service, journalism, medicine, and

law. A similar protocol was followed in the 1840s and 1850s when slavery was a tense issue; partisans on both sides of the abortion issue have noticed a resemblance between today's pro-life groups and yesterday's abolitionists. In more civil political discourse, it is impolite to claim moral reasons for opposing abortion or moral reasons for approving of abortion. And it is improper to consult one's morals in deciding how to act politically or legally or medically on the question. When one is responsible for law or public policy or health care, and the issue is abortion, he is to keep his morals to himself. One may, for the benefit of the voters, announce his personal moral views, but he is expected to add that he won't consult personal moral views when he acts officially.

A public debate, in the 1870s, between the illustrious Wall Street lawyer David Dudley Field and the Yankee editor, Samuel Bowles, over Field's representation of the villains in the railroad scandals and Bowles's editorial condemnation of Field and other such lawyers, is a benchmark in this development of a separate professional morality in the United States. Field did not claim that his relationship with his clients, and his focus on what lawyers were coming to call interests, was beyond moral analysis; he claimed the subject was private, not the business of an editor. Bowles did not claim that Field had no right to privacy, or that Bowles violated the civility one gentleman owes another; he claimed that the morals of a newspaper editor require the editor to intrude and criticize professionally where it would be immoral to intrude and criticize interpersonally. Neither understood the other's notions of responsibility and of privacy; neither was willing to accept the identification of public and private morals that was the substance of David Hoffman's legal ethics, of Thomas Jefferson's politics, and of Sir Thomas Percival's medical ethics.

"What gives you, sitting in private and writing anonymously, the authority to render 'judgment' upon me?" Field asked Bowles. "You must know that you would not have ventured to say what is contained [in an editorial in the *Springfield Republican*] to my face, in any company whatever." Bowles, whose editorials accused Field of avarice, meanness, and pettifoggery, admitted he would not have said such things to Field personally, but he claimed for journalism a license to make sweeping moral judgments on "the conduct of private men, before the public." A lawyer, he said, "first, in accepting this position, and next, in discharging it . . . takes a responsibility to the public, on which it [meaning editorial writers] may arraign, dispute and judge him."

Field claimed a dispensation from having to answer for what his clients did. "I shall, whenever I speak for them in the courts of the country, stand between them and popular clamor, just as I would stand between them and power, if they were menaced by power of any kind, monarchical or republican." He identified himself with the revolutionary lawyers who had represented Thomas Paine. "A lawyer," he said, "is responsible, not for his client's causes, but for the manner in which he conducts their causes." Bowles answered that Field had "offended the moral sense of the public,—that is what I insist upon; that is what, in my duty as a journalist, I have proclaimed to the public." They could not agree on what their moral words meant—private, public, responsible—but both implied that their professional morals were separate from their private morals; both implied professional reliance on a teleology of professional success, on what Emile Durkheim called a market morality.

Sometimes the argument in such examples is that public and professional life has no morality. If that is the argument it is not interesting ethically, since ethical discussion begins with a first principle: Do good and avoid evil. One who won't agree on that beginning point is not interested in ethics. It may be possible to talk with him about football, but not about morals. I'm not sure I would want to play poker with him, particularly if he viewed poker as a professional activity, or his professional activity as a poker game. The examples I have given are not arguments that professional life has no morality. In them the argument is that public and professional life has a morality, but that it is a separate morality. The argument behind the agent's saying "It's my job" is that it is a good thing to do the job and that there is a good way to do the job. That argument, like both Field's argument and Bowles's, is a moral argument. All three also imply that their jobs dispense them from the personal morals they would otherwise follow in their work—and that, too, is a moral argument. A distressing example of this moral argument, for me, came up in the country's agony over Vietnam. The Doves said, "That war is immoral." Some of the Hawks said "All war is immoral," which seemed to mean, in that instance, that it was moral to be immoral. However, I don't think the Hawks were deciding to be evil; they were deciding, instead, that the circumstances carried a dispensation from ordinary morality. Sometimes the argument went beyond that and said that American intervention in Vietnam with violence and death was the moral thing to do, an argument that is implicit in some of the talk in the 1980s about being just to American veterans of that war. For some of the Hawks, that argument implies that international statecraft has a different morality than personal life does; it is only in that sense that all war is immoral. It seems unlikely, in any case, that a professional soldier would say, "All war is immoral."

Atticus Finch, who was, I think, the most popular American lawyer of the 1950s and 1960s, would probably, and even in the face of these examples, answer my question the other way. He would probably say, "No. There is not a separate morality for professional life." It was Atticus who said, "I can't live one way in town and another way in my home." Atticus's moral system was the "code" of the Southern Christian gentleman. When young Jem began to understand how Atticus lived, and how he too would live, he said, "Atticus is a gentleman, and so am I." A dual system of morals for a gentleman was unacceptable; it was necessary for Scout and Jem, who were in training to be gentlemen, to know that. It was necessary even that they suffer—as they did—in their learning of it. A gentleman may not be able to change evil, or to overcome it, but he must learn to endure it and not to be duped by it. The most fundamental canon of the gentleman's ethic is integrity, or constancy, being all of a piece, consistent with himself, the same person yesterday, today, and tomorrow, whether in town or at home, in peace and in war. Faulkner's Gavin Stevens's final advice to his nephew, on resistance to racism, was, "Don't stop." (It says something about popular discussion of morals, by the way, that the movie version of Atticus's story leaves this point out and that Faulkner was regarded in the North as a defender of racial segregation.)

This is an ethic almost any American lawyer of the period before

1850 would have understood. The gentleman's point of view was taught to law students by David Hoffman, who said that a lawyer ordinarily should not plead the statute of limitations: "If my client is conscious he owes the debt, and has no other defense than the legal bar, he shall never make me a partner in his knavery." From the point of view of these gentlemen-lawyers, professional and public life are governed by the same morality. By and large, Hoffman would say, a gentleman-lawyer is as responsible for justice in the community or in his client's life as he is for justice in his own life. The gentleman's ethic would warn that a different point of view leads to evil, corrupting results.

Another hero to modern American professionals is Thomas More—not so much the Saint Thomas More who has been the popular patron of Roman Catholic lawyers, but the existentialist Thomas More of Robert Bolt's play, *A Man for All Seasons.* In Bolt's rendering, More is the hero who has "an adamantine sense of his own self," who cannot claim a special morality for professional and public life because he cannot cut himself in two. Consider the first encounter in the play between Richard Rich and Thomas Cromwell. Rich was a friend of Sir Thomas More. Cromwell, then secretary to King Henry VIII, was out to stifle opposition to a papal annulment of King Henry's marriage. More did not—dared not—oppose the annulment in public, but Cromwell suspected that More opposed it in private. He turned to Rich to discover More's private conversations because Rich was corruptible. It turned out that Cromwell was wrong about More's private conversations, but right about Rich. More said nothing to anybody about his views on the king's marriage, but, late in the play, Rich gave false testimony against More, and was rewarded by being made attorney general for Wales. You may remember the point in the play where More heard the false testimony in court. He said to Rich, "It profits a man nothing to give his soul for the whole world. . . . But for Wales!"

Earlier in the story, when Cromwell was testing Rich, he asked Rich whether he was capable of providing what the state needed, if the state needed faithlessness toward his friend and even falsehood. Rich replied that the answer depended on what he was offered. Cromwell said that he admired that answer. Many people, he said, believe faithlessness is a matter of price, but few will say it. Rich objected a little. "There are some things one wouldn't do for anything. Surely." And Cromwell said it was all a matter of "administrative convenience. . . . Our job as administrators," he told Rich, is to make convenient what power wants. "There are these men—you know—'upright,' 'steadfast,' men who want themselves to be the constant factor in the situation; which, of course, they can't be. The situation rolls forward in any case. . . . If they've any sense they get out of its way. . . . [If not,] well, they're fit only for Heaven." Heaven has one morality; the "constant factor," power in the court of a king, has another.

More's moral argument against a separate morality was interpersonal, but also, like Cromwell's, professional and political. "I believe, when statesmen forsake their private conscience for the sake of their public duties . . . they lead their country by a short route to chaos."

The Theology of the Two Kingdoms

So far this comparison of those who believe that public and professional life has morals of its own, with those who believe that life in town and life at home are governed by the same morality, looks like a comparison of good guys with bad guys. In reference to Thomas More, I might instead have done with him and Cromwell not what Robert Bolt did but what the curator at the Frick Museum in New York City did with Hans Holbein's portraits of them. The curator put More's portrait on one side of a fireplace, Cromwell's on the other, and El Greco's St. Jerome, like the Father in a Renaissance Fresco, over the fireplace and high above them both. More and Cromwell in the museum are opposites, as the men themselves were. They are, though, opposites under God. The curator used the wall around the fireplace to make a theological statement. Cromwell talks about administrative convenience in a useful institution; More says he is the king's good servant but God's first. The argument looks more modest with St. Jerome looking down on it. Cromwell might have enjoyed the arrangement; I'm sure More would have. The position of the three portraits suggests the possibility of a respectable moral theory to support Cromwell's point of view, a theory that might interest St. Jerome.

The separate-morality argument qualifies for ethics—because it is interesting. The view that public and professional life has rules of its own is an ancient, religious, biblical point of view. It has to be taken more seriously than it was in Bolt's play and in the flippant manner in which Hollywood bowdlerized Harper Lee's novel. There is something to be said for Cromwell. At the very least, we might notice that Cromwell understood, better than More did, what was going on in England and in the world, that he was at least willing to remain in public life (to remain an active professional), unlike More, who resigned and tried to survive in seclusion. Cromwell has going for him the argument that he was competent in an institution that kept civil war from returning to England. Finally, Cromwell gave his life, as More had; and Cromwell gave his life, in a sense, for his theory—or at least as a consequence of remaining, true to his theory, an active force in public life.

Cromwell was an able public official, although he also went to the block when he was not administratively convenient to the king. His nationalistic politics was more appropriate to the times than More's attempt to preserve a medieval, theocratic public order. (It is convenient for fans of Bolt's play to forget that More was in favor of burning heretics and that he was, in terms of realistic, sixteenth-century European politics, a crank.) Which is to say that the struggle between More and Cromwell was more political and less theological than Bolt's play suggests, or, better, to say that Cromwell might have had a theological argument to make, and that much of the cultural self-deception at work in England then was on More's side, the side of those who were disposed to resist the king and support the pope.

In this climate, Cromwell's political skills—and political skills are always moral skills, too—were considerable, whatever his theology. Hackett's biography of Henry VIII makes this point. Cromwell "was not a fanatic . . . not a mere Philistine. . . . He was a cold-blooded man of action, with the prime quality for success: singleness of purpose joined to a wide practical vision. . . . He was not a man of unsteady nerves. Nature had given him the useful cortex of a plebian—of the turnkey, the lunatic attendant, the best of thick-set public guardians." "Wide public vision" and "public guardian" are or can be words of approval; they are words of moral and theological argument.

In defense of Cromwell and of the ethics of administrative convenience, consider how deep are the origins of the view that the larger affairs of a culture require a separate morality. The God of Abraham, Isaac, and Jacob does not, for example, appear to follow the morals of righteousness imposed on Israel. God chooses Abel, rejects Cain; chooses Jacob, rejects Esau; chooses Isaac, rejects Ishmael; chooses Israel, rejects the other nations—and even requires Israel to destroy the other nations. God deprives King Saul of the throne because Saul, in the midst of slaughter, spares a single life. This sometimes seems to be a God Who is not governed by morals at all, to be a God Who—to use Browning's irreverent phrase—"Doth as he likes, or wherefore Lord?" Notice the rhetoric of the description of God in Psalm 111 (New English Bible):

> He showed his people what his strength could do,
> bestowing on them the lands of other nations.
> His works are truth and justice;
> his precepts all stand on firm foundations,
> strongly based to endure for ever,
> their fabric goodness and truth.

These are moral words—truth, justice, goodness—but they are also the words, in the context, of a separate morality. It is hardly a wonder, given these stories and this description, that the great problem for Jewish and Christian theology has been to show how the God of Abraham, Isaac, Jacob—and of Job—is a God Who demonstrates in the world both justice and mercy.

In the Jewish tradition this God is argued with, is told to see to His own morals, is even told to be consistent for a change. "What is Jewish history," Elie Wiesel asks, "if not an endless quarrel with God?" Abraham Kaplan of the University of Haifa tells of the Jew in the Warsaw Ghetto, in the early days of the Holocaust, who prayed, "I believe in You, God of Israel, even though You have done everything to stop me from believing in You." He tells the Hasidic anecdote in which a pious Jew says to God on Yom Kippur, "Sure, I have sinned; but what about you, O God? What about the suffering of innocents, unjust persecutions, the triumph of evil? Let's call it quits—You forgive me, O God, and I will forgive You!"

In trying to say something for Thomas Cromwell, consider the first and the greatest of Christian theologians, St. Paul, the Pharisaic rabbi from Tarsus, who told his Christian followers in Rome that "[A]ll government comes from God, the civil authorities were appointed by God, and so anyone who resists authority is rebelling against God's decision. . . . The state is there to serve God for your benefit. . . . The authorities . . . carry out God's revenge by punishing wrongdoers. . . . [A]ll government officials are God's officers" (Romans 13:1–6, Jerusalem Bible). St. Paul was not talking about the Environmental Protection Agency or Marshal Dillon. He was talking about Nero and Caligula—about governmental officials who fed Jews and Christians to lions in order to preserve imperial institutions, that is, in the interests of law and order.

I can imagine a puzzled believer in the Catacombs reading that letter from Corinth and saying, Okay, but if Nero and Caligula are God's officers, God must have a special set of rules for officers. He may or may not have been comforted in his puzzlement by recalling that Cyrus the Conqueror was God's anointed, even though Cyrus didn't know it (Isaiah 45:4–7). Martin Luther said, "Even Satan is ultimately drawn into [God's] service." With such minions, and such methods, it would have been logical to reason that God's public purposes were different from God's interpersonal purposes—one teleology for the world, another for each child of God.

Faithful Jewish and Christian theologians have had a hard time understanding the God of Israel and of Job, and making sense of St. Paul's political theology. This difficulty is no doubt one of the principal streams in the long and faithful tradition of faith seeking understanding. For the public official—and sometimes for us doctors and lawyers, too—it is an enigma. Luther said, "We are taught nothing of how this rule is to be exercised and carried out, but are only commanded that it should be honored and not resisted." We are like Mr. Rumpole of the Old Bailey. We are given morals for those who must obey, but she-who-must-be-obeyed has morals of her own. St. Augustine noticed with some small sympathy how the faithful "remain scandalized at [these] differences shown in Scripture." Augustine's solution involved a distinction between the City of God and the earthly city; in the City of God the faithful live and work and follow the law of love. In the earthly city, earthly rulers live and work and follow other rules. And, still, God is Lord of all, Lord of both. All the rules are moral rules; and the rules come from the One God, the only God.

Medieval Christian theologians, who had to deal more than Augustine with the fact that Christians had become princes, that the Roman emperor had become the Holy Roman Emperor, read the Sermon on the Mount and decided that, when it comes to public and professional life, the radical mandates of Jesus are, as they put it, "counsels of perfection." The Beatitudes are for nuns and monks, not for busy, professional wielders of power. It was Martin Luther who, more than any other in the Christian tradition, gave this dilemma a name and a structure for ethical thought. Luther was offended by the Scholastic category "counsels of perfection." He was unable to accept the view that the Sermon on the Mount was only for nuns and monks, and St. Paul's teaching on civil authority only for subjects. His solution has come to be called—not so much by Luther as by others—the moral theology of the two kingdoms. In one, the Kingdom of Law, God has, as St. Paul said, instituted civil authority to keep the peace and to punish evildoers. In the other, the Kingdom of Love, God has established love of neighbor as a mandate—not as a counsel of perfection, but as a command. And each kingdom, under God, has its own morality.

In the first kingdom, the kingdom of tribute, custom, honor, and fear, one obeys with his life, his goods, and his honor. One follows, there, not the morals of faith but the morals of reason. In the other, the Kingdom of Love, one obeys with his faith and his books. One is the kingdom of shepherds, one the kingdom of hangmen, and the faithful live in both, in obedience to both. Called to be a shepherd, a Christian may be a hangman too if her or his neighbor requires it, because, in one of Luther's colorful and vehement phrases, "Frogs need storks." As the Lutheran theologian Richard P. Baepler puts it, "The absolute imperatives of the law do their work of terrifying the conscience and breaking through all pretension and hypocrisy." God acts in the civil order, but acts there with a mask. The mask is the face of Caligula; those who serve Caligula serve God when they obey Caligula, even—as in the case of the hangman—when they are Caligula.

In twentieth-century American Christian theology, some thinkers have been chastened by what they saw as the naive simplicity—if not hypocrisy—of David Hoffman's generation of Americans. They decided that we Americans have not realized that it is impossible to act in the world without doing wrong. Theologians such as Reinhold Niebuhr, Paul Tillich, and Harvey Cox said that those in public life who try to follow the Sermon on the Mount kid themselves and do great harm because they do not understand that justice is one thing and love is something else. The best you can hope for in exercising power in the world, as doctors, journalists, and lawyers do, is what Reinhold Niebuhr called "the relative good." You can't follow the law of love in public and professional life; you do the best you can and that is always to some extent evil. If the morality of public and professional life is not exactly a separate morality, it is inevitably a compromised morality. (I do not risk claiming a causal connection between these thinkers and Luther. I notice only that both schools of thought are on the "yes" side of the separate-morality question.) So there is something to be said for the view that public and professional life has morals of its own. There is something to be said for a morality of administrative convenience in town—it can, maybe, be worked out theologically—even if we follow biblical morality when we are at home. Even Atticus Finch demonstrates this point of view. He believed that the ethics of the Christian gentleman provides one morality for public and private life. He did not believe in a separate set of morals for his life as lawyer and legislator. But the need he felt to protect Boo Radley, by lying to cover up the fact that Radley killed Bob Ewell, brought him to the place where his behavior, if not his point of view, was on Cromwell's side of the fireplace and not on More's. He came to behave as if life in town had to have rules of its own. The Boo Radley episode gives the novel its theme and its title; the theme and the title seem to say that a gentleman who is uncommonly devoted to the truth need not or cannot live as truthfully in town as he does at home.

I suspect that this story, and stories like it, do more to make us believers in separate morals than the theologians do. It is hard to sustain a principled disapproval of Atticus Finch. (I have tried, and it is hard.) We tend—all of us—to sympathize with Atticus, as his daughter Scout did, and we do this regardless of our theories. We sympathize even as we are tempted to say that Atticus followed different morals in one situation than in the other. In one case he was not willing to lie—not even to protect his injured son, whom he loved; in the other case he was willing to lie, even though he was a man uncommonly devoted to the truth. Somehow, we say, it is too simple to put Atticus on Cromwell's side of the fireplace. Or maybe we do have to put Atticus there and then see to our theories, to say something positive about Thomas Cromwell. It is important for us to see that righteousness is more complicated than we thought it was. In fact, to return to the Bible and to the theologians, it is important for us to see that both ways of thinking—telling the truth, and not killing the mockingbird—are consistent with faith, and maybe even with sound morals.

(Atticus's story is too tempting not to use in this context, but a better theory for his deciding not to kill the mockingbird is that he acted against his own moral grain. I don't think he believed in the morality of the two kingdoms; he did not justify his behavior by appeal to that morality. What he did was to agree to share in Sheriff Tate's lie, a lie that said Bob Ewell, persecutor and would-be murderer of Atticus's children, had killed himself when he fell on his own knife. In fact, Ewell was killed by the reclusive Boo Radley. Atticus and the Sheriff lied in order that Boo Radley not become a celebrity. Atticus did not believe that telling a lie was the moral thing to do—in town or at home—but, still, he lied to protect his friend. His was the single-kingdom morality of the Christian gentleman. Shirley Letwin, referring to such gentlemen in Trollope's novels, and to Kant's famous "which way did he go" example, says that the gentleman will lie to protect his friend, but he will not pretend that he has not lied.)

The Two Kingdoms in American Professional Ethics

The doctrine that professional life has a separate morality has been the central theory in American professional ethics for about a century. Although it shows wear and tear, it has been the most prevalent moral justification American lawyers give for what their profession does. It is becoming the dominant answer medical ethics gives for doctors' carrying out the decisions of patients and their families. (Doctors have, so far, though, refused to become hangmen.) We lawyers don't call this theory the doctrine of the two kingdoms or the moral theology of Reinhold Niebuhr. We call it the adversary ethic. It is not argued theologically; theology had disappeared without a trace from both professions' official thinking before the adversary ethic was invented. But the adversary ethic in the law, and theories of patient privacy in medicine, look like secular, post-Christian, God-is-dead versions of what might elsewhere be called the theology of the two kingdoms.

The adversary ethic appeared in the legal profession's collective morality at about the time lawyers such as David Dudley Field began acting for the robber barons of the American industrial revolution. Or, more accurately, it appeared when lawyers began to defend themselves for acting for the robber barons, and at the same time began to design limits on what a lawyer could do when acting for such clients. The ethics of privacy in medicine appeared when the culture seemed to turn aside from any persuasive way to say that the community has a stake in the life and health of each of its members.

The adversary ethic was stated in many sentences, most of them querulous and tentative, by Judge George Sharswood, in his lectures of 1854 on legal ethics. Sharswood's twentieth-century counterparts are usually more forthright, not to say bombastic:

1. The late Justice Abe Fortas, defending his former law partner, Thurman Arnold, said, "Lawyers are agents, not principals; and they should neither criticize nor tolerate criticism based upon the character of the client whom they represent or the cause that they prosecute or defend. They cannot and should not accept responsibility for the client's practices. Rapists, murderers, child-abusers, General Motors, Dow Chemical—and even cigarette manufacturers and

stream-polluters—are entitled to a lawyer; and any lawyer who undertakes their representation must be immune from criticism for doing so."

2. Monroe Freedman says, "Once a lawyer has assumed responsibility to represent a client, the zealousness of that representation cannot be tempered by the lawyer's moral judgments of the client or of the client's cause." He argues that if the client wants to lie in court, the lawyer-as-advocate should help the client lie; if the client appears to be the sort who will use legal information to do evil, the lawyer-as-advisor should nonetheless give the information. He argues that the lawyer's stake in his client's life is that the client be free, and that faithfulness to this investment focuses the lawyer's concern on the law that assures the client's freedom—the adversary (judicial) system, the Constitution, and, I suppose, free-market capitalism. The lawyer's specific moral duty is to see that his client is free, under the law. Freedman's arguments seem to require that professional life take on a separate morality.

(It may be useful to emphasize that two kinds of argument are made for Freedman's premise: [a] survival of the fittest or "justice will out" or laissez-faire—all of which turn on a theory of justice that says justice inheres in a governmental system and, as I think, amount to the idolatry of statism; and [b] freedom—that is, the lawyer serves his client's freedom, and the physician serves his patient's freedom, when they give the client or patient information, professional assistance, and support, toward a moral decision the professional might not make for the community or in and for his own life. One of these theories seems to me rejected in Hebraic theology; the other is more interesting. I discuss it and try to show why I prefer the ethics of virtues to the ethics that focus on [such] decisions, in chapter 1.)

3. Medicine's development and acceptance of technology has come to the place where physicians can preserve or prolong life beyond what their patients or their patients' communities are willing to bear—to bear, I mean, in terms of emotion and patience and suffering, as well as cost. This fact, combined perhaps with a strain of mid-twentieth-century professional modesty and the U.S. Supreme Court's decisions on abortion, contraception, and the legal

independence of minors, produces the medical ethics of privacy. The moral decision is not the physician's. It is made by patients or parents or guardians—or, in extreme but recurrent situations, by judges. The physician becomes a medical version of the legal hired gun, as impersonal as a respirator.

4. Debates about intrusive journalism and about the purposes of business are similar. Journalists intrude, for example, into grieving families in furtherance of a "right to know" in other people; they intrude, as journalists, as Samuel Bowles said they should, where they would not intrude if they were not journalists. What they say about this otherwise immoral violation of other people is analogous to the manager in business who says that profit, not public welfare, is the purpose of business. It is, for example, the government's job to decide whether to drop napalm on children; business's job is to make napalm at a profit if the government wants it.

The Possibility of Influences between the Kingdoms

Despite appearances, these secular professional versions of the two kingdoms—Karl Barth, in medical metaphor, called them the syndrome of the two kingdoms—are not the same as the theology of the two kingdoms. It is tempting, but it is not fair, even as a matter of history, to associate the two. St. Augustine and Martin Luther thought that the result of their moral theology, in the life of the individual, would be that the Kingdom of Love would redeem the Kingdom of Law, or at least that the Kingdom of Love would redeem the believer from the Kingdom of Law. Luther told sixteenth-century Protestant princes to look to their motives. The doctrine that Caligula was God's minister might give moral comfort to those who are told to obey Caligula, but it cannot give moral comfort to Caligula himself. The Christian prince's power, Luther said, should be used for the benefit of the prince's neighbors, his sisters and brothers. "For cursed and condemned is every kind of life lived and sought for selfish profit and good; cursed are all works not done in love [and] . . . directed with all one's heart, not toward selfish pleasure, profit, honor, ease and salvation, but toward the profit, honor and salvation of others."

Luther said this to the prince. It may be that the prince, as prince, need not behave as one who turns the other cheek, walks the second mile, and gives up his cloak with his coat. But he must, in using the power of the state, use it with righteous motives. There is a distinction in Luther's teaching between the conduct of the office and the motives of the officer. In exercising the coercive power of the state, the Christian prince depends on the law and not on love, but what goes on in the officer's heart is not governed by the earthly kingdom. In his heart the officer is in his faith and in his books; he lives there in the Kingdom of Love.

Baepler expresses this point in an interesting comparison of the way love influences law and law influences love. Love, acting in and acting through people in the community, has and should have an influence on the same people when they act in the secular state, that is, in medical practice, journalism, business, law, or government. Professional life, when it interacts functionally with love, comes to understand its own limitations. When we act in the earthly kingdom we have power and legitimacy but we have a poor imagination. People in an institution (government, hospital, newspaper, law firm) tend not to imagine much of anything beyond the survival of the institution. The Kingdom of Love, because it knows that God is Lord of all, and that God loves His people, imagines a destiny in which the survival of institutions is not as important as obedience is.

Here political theology is entirely different from secular formulas such as the adversary ethic or the ethics of patient privacy. Defenders of the adversary ethic can say that the lawyer who helps a scoundrel be a scoundrel is not really serving the scoundrel but is instead serving the Constitution. Physicians involved in life-and-death decisions can claim a professional moral agency and say they act for—or even as—their patients, not for themselves. Reporters can say they have a job to do when they poke microphones at a grieving mother. But these are only grand ways of saying that professionals are serving power, and when it is put that way, one is likely to notice that if these arguments are ethics at all, they depend on the conviction that institutions can produce goodness.

It is even worse than that. This service-to-the-system argument depends, it seems to me, on the expectation that institutions such as the government *will* produce goodness. Luther knew better than that, and so might those of us who know about the Holocaust, Hiroshima, Dresden, Vietnam, and Selma; about American concentration camps of World War II; about the fugitive-slave laws and yellow-dog labor contracts; about syphilis experiments and the worship of science; and about the professional idolatry that says people have a right to know anything that will photograph well.

Luther's teaching had two important points to make about this, two points on humility. One deals with humility about living in the Kingdom of Law; the other deals with appropriate humility about oneself. In making the first point, Luther told the prince to remember that the Kingdom of Law cannot save. "It pleases the divine will that we should call his executioners noble lords, fall at their feet, and be subject to them with all humility," he said, "as long as they do not extend their task too far and seek to become shepherds instead of executioners." Or healers. Or sources of truth. Or providers of the credentials of wisdom. The believer will not find salvation in institutions. That is not only a sixteenth-century argument; it is also St. Augustine's argument against Eusebius of Caesarea. In worldly terms Augustine lost that argument. The medieval notion of civil society came over his objection. This is also the argument of Karl Barth against the Nazi regime, in 1935, in Germany. Barth was convinced that the deepest danger from Hitler was that Hitler claimed to be a shepherd. Barth confronted the regime, lost his academic appointment, left the country. He put on a Swiss sergeant's uniform and got ready to go to war.

In his second point, Luther explained that his two-moralities doctrine was not a way for the children of light to feel superior to the unenlightened; Luther taught that we are all unenlightened. "It is the nature of God that he makes something out of nothing. Consequently, if someone is not nothing, God can make nothing of him. Men make something into something else. But this is vain and useless work. Thus God accepts no one except the abandoned, makes no one healthy except the sick, gives no one sight except the blind, brings no one to life except the dead, makes no one pious except sinners, makes no one wise except the foolish, and, in short, has mercy upon no one except the wretched, and gives no one grace except those who have not grace." It is important not to be misled by Luther's teaching to suppose that the Kingdom of Love is where believers are and the Kingdom of Law is for the heathen. He is talking about our behavior: We are all heathen. His ethic is an ethic for accomplices.

Many modern Christian theologians, expanding on what Reinhold Niebuhr taught in the 1930s, would say that the moral life in the world is a life of finitude, of limitation, of coping with claims that are inevitably ambiguous, contradictory, from more than one righteous source. This seems painfully true in the specific and endlessly argued quandaries of professional ethics. The earthly city is a fallen city; it is a place of tension and discomfort, even for the faithful—or, maybe, especially for the faithful. But it is in the sinfulness of living in such a place that the believer is forgiven. That, I think, was Luther's point, too.

Politically, it is important to notice that Luther's position was similar to St. Paul's teaching about the Rome of Nero and Caligula, and similar to St. Augustine's teaching about the Roman Empire after Constantine. Paul's political problem was to make it clear to early Roman Christians (and, probably, Jews) that they were not called to be part of movements of terrorist subversion. Paul saw the same problem with the Zealots in Rome that Jesus had had with Judas Iscariot in Jerusalem. Augustine's political problem was to make it clear to Jews and Christians that they could not live outside the earthly city. Luther stood amidst turbulent cultural and political change in the sixteenth century. Some of the turmoil was of his own making, and some resulted from the other giants of the Reformation; but there would have been turmoil in any case and the medieval order would have come apart anyway. In the words of an old poem about Luther, "His mind was the battle-ground of two ages—I do not wonder that he saw demons!"

I am not saying here that St. Paul, St. Augustine, Luther, and

Karl Barth were putting fences around a believers' enclave. They were not doing that; nor were they being expedient—coming to terms with the world so that one sort of believer could be, for the moment, safe in it. Their argument is much grander than that: The City of God does not depend on the earthly city, but the earthly city depends on the City of God. Paul and Augustine and Luther and Barth were all interested in showing that the influence of faith on the earthly city is a necessary influence. Their arguments were arguments to the faithful, about what the faithful imply when they claim the freedom to be faithful—in, say, the practice of journalism or teaching or law or medicine. The Faithful, in being faithful, make a claim on the community.

Luther argued to believers who were rulers and to believers who were subjects; to both he said that faith requires believers to do the work of the earthly city. Scripture forbids the faithful from resigning from civil society, as much as it forbids them from using coercion in matters of faith. He stood against the Anabaptists on one side, against the Inquisition on the other. He made what today would be called an argument for the mainstream church. It is an old and distinctly Hebraic argument for the significance of action. Louis D. Brandeis's biographer (Vorspan) referred to it when he talked in modern America of "the peculiarly Jewish zeal for social justice."

Luther's political environment was one in which there were strong ecclesiastical parties for withdrawal and strong parties for suppression of conscience. He regarded each of those points of view as erroneous. He was pressed on one side by those who wanted to live apart and on the other side by those who wanted to use criminal punishment against heretics. (Thomas More, for example.) His political argument today says, to us—who enjoy a more elaborate freedom of conscience in the practice of our professions, but who live, perhaps, in what Michael Schudson calls a society, rather than a community—that the Kingdom of Love influences the Kingdom of Law—that it lifts it up—and that the Kingdom of Law would not survive and would not deserve to survive if it were not lifted up. This is also what the framers of our national Constitution had in mind when they separated church and state; their object was to protect the freedom of religion so that the influence of religion would be assured. They did not suppose that democratic government would be independent of the influence of religion, or that democratic government could deserve to survive if it were. The same theology of influence applies to hospitals, clinics, schools, newspapers, and business corporations.

The admonition to the faithful, to serve in the earthly city but to refuse there to use coercion against the human spirit, is illustrated, I think, in the political life of a modern giant of the earthly city, who was as well a giant among the faithful—Dag Hammarskjold. Hammarskjold's work for world peace was, for all that appeared, a secular enterprise. It was only after his death and the discovery of his secret diary, *Markings,* that the world learned that he was a deeply spiritual, committed believer. The world was surprised and embarrassed at that; but, from the standpoint of Lutheran teaching, it had nothing to be surprised about. As Bernhard Erling put it: "Hammarskjold's religious faith did not prescribe specific political answers to the world's problems—answers which those of other religious traditions might not have found acceptable. He may have been helped at this point by his Lutheran tradition, which is not theocratic in its approach to government; that is, it does not teach that the civil government should in all respects conform to a specially revealed divine will, but teaches that human beings should be able through the exercise of reason to negotiate a consensus as to how a government should be organized and managed. There are, according to Lutheran teaching, 'two kingdoms.' There is a kingdom ruled by law—a law that can be coercively enforced, but which should represent a consensus among those governed by it. And there is a kingdom ruled by love and persuasion, which can influence the kingdom ruled by law, but in this latter kingdom coercion is not used to enforce the way of life which love prompts."

But, still, love does prompt a way of life; it explains the ways of life of Hammarskjold, Atticus Finch, Fanny Holtzmann, Trollope's Dr. Thorne, Eliot's Dorothea Brooke, Thomas More, John Peter Zenger, Eleanor Roosevelt, and Louis D. Brandeis. The difference between Hebraic theology and modern professional ethics is that theology insists on this influence where modern professional ethics calls it merely private and treats it as irrelevant. The difference within theology has to do with the way in which the influence is applied. That theological difference distinguishes Hammarskjold as Erling describes him from More as Bolt describes him and from Fanny Holtzmann and the dissenter-lawyers I discuss in chapter 5.

American history—especially the history of the church in America—vindicates Luther's wariness at both undue contempt and undue optimism. The way American Christians thought of their country before the Civil War—as a righteous empire, to use Martin Marty's phrase, or as God's new Israel, to use Thomas Jefferson's phrase—was untruthful. And in its untruthfulness it was wicked. It was a society which in those days could glory in the blessed assurance of the Revival and at the same time nourish slavery, manifest destiny, the suppression of women, and the exploitation of immigrant children. Undue contempt and undue optimism. Reinhold Niebuhr called it the irony of American history.

The Morals of the Task

An argument that may trace to two-kingdoms reasoning, or at least that resembles it, is the argument that each of our jobs has a moral logic of its own, an inherent morality that is defined not by the person's status or order but by the nature of the work he is given to do. The government agent in the Mark Trail comic strip claims he is doing his job when he accuses Mark of theft. He acts there as government agent, and the logic of that job requires that he accuse an honest man of theft. Albert Speer, Hitler's architect, told himself he need not worry about Hitler's slave-labor camps because his job was to be an architect, and the logic of that job required single-minded devotion to the design of great buildings. Martin Luther told the Christian hangman that he may deliver death to his brother or sister because the punishment of evildoers is the job of the hangman. And a Christian, in doing his job, serves his neighbors—serves even the victim of his gallows. The law of love pertains in that case to the hangman's regard for the evildoer, not to what he does to the evildoer.

The moral logic of the task is familiar in doctors' defense of the ethics of privacy and in lawyers' defense of the adversary ethic. Carrying out parents' decisions to withhold treatment from mentally retarded babies, or assisting the perjurious client in his lie to the judge and jury, are familiar cases in the debate. Those who disagree with the morals of the task speak of systematic immorality and of a dubious professional dispensation from moral responsibility. But defenders speak of the professional job as the exercise of an assurance for patients and clients of privacy, autonomy, equality, and due process; they use words such as health and justice.

The morals of the task do require that one consider the legitimacy of the task to be done. It may be immoral to hang an innocent man, for example. But, if the task is legitimate, the worker may base his morals on the logic inherent in the task. The claim is not a claim for special orders of people—orders such as nobility, clergy, aristocracy, and so forth—so much as a claim based on the legitimacy of tasks—healing, preaching, administering the government, managing corporate business, pleading cases for those who have a civil right to a lawyer, seeing to the survival of institutions that appear to be useful. The lore of our professions provides familiar examples:

1. "The Lord said to Moses and Aaron, 'When a man has on the skin of his body a swelling or an eruption or a spot, and it turns into a leprous disease on the skin of his body, then he shall be brought to . . . the priest . . . and the priest shall examine the diseased spot . . . and if the hair in the diseased spot has turned white and the disease appears to be deeper than the skin . . . it is a leprous disease; when the priest has examined him he shall pronounce him unclean. . . . The leper who has the disease shall wear torn clothes and let the hair of his head hang loose, and he shall cover his upper lip and cry, "Unclean, unclean." He shall . . . dwell alone in a habitation outside' " (Leviticus 13:1–3, 45–46, R.S.V.). Aaron's sons were physicians; the result of their professional judgment was the patient's banishment, loneliness, and physical peril. They were, however, doing their jobs as they were told. If they needed a secular word for their teleology, the word would have been health. The argument that went on in the professional community was probably

like the argument we are hearing now, in American medicine, on the quarantine of people who carry the acquired immune deficiency syndrome virus.

2. A modern physician, dedicated to patient autonomy or to the ethics of privacy (and they are not necessarily the same thing), needs a careful protocol to assure that his moral judgment is not interfering with his patient's moral judgment. Gerald Dworkin prescribes (a) methods of influence that assure "the ability of individuals to reflect rationally on their own interests," (b) methods that turn on information rather than ignorance, and (c) participation by the patient and the application of his desires and beliefs. This implementation of the ethics of privacy describes a professional task; it assumes that the relevant conscience is not the doctor's but the patient's.

3. The American adversary ethic claims its ancestral analogue in the ideal of the English barrister, the courtroom lawyer who traveled around with the king's judge and took in court whatever side needed taking. The lawyer stepped forward where he was needed, when he was needed, and made sure the judge considered all of the facts and all of the law. It was a professional task based almost on hypotheses—as if I would say to you, "Please argue that the world is flat, so that we can be sure to be fair to the flat-earthers." That would be a useful thing to do, and you could in moral confidence do your job as you were asked to do it. You would not need to believe the world flat to argue, for the common good, that the world is flat. The English-barrister ideal was, in purest theory, like that.

The barrister was, as Geoffrey Hazard puts it, "not merely an 'officer' of the court but a member of it." When, for another example, a lawyer invents a legal fiction to conform present reality to past theory, we allow him a bit of righteous dishonesty because fiction is an inherent part of legal reasoning; it is all right, on behalf of the plaintiff who complains that his cow was stolen, to say that he lost it and that the defendant found it. It is implicit in the legitimate task of making law fit life. If the barrister needed a word for his teleology, the word was justice.

The morals of the task resemble the morals of the two kingdoms; and the principal complaint of critics of the morality of the task is that a moral agent cannot be divided up—cannot be a person one moment and a doer of jobs the next. In morals, according to these critics, only a person acts, always a person, always and only a single and whole person. If he acts to deny or to diminish his being a person, he acts immorally—this both as a matter of principle and as a matter of consequences.

John Noonan, commenting on the lawyer who bribed the judge, and quoting Charles Curtis, says, " 'You devote yourself to the interests of another at the peril of yourself. Vicarious action tempts a man away from himself. . . . ' While I understand the attractiveness and even the inescapability of the catch phrase, 'I'm doing it for my client' [or for the shareholders, or for my patient, or for people who have a right to know], I also see the phrase functioning as a kind of carapace. The phrase functions as a defense against various moral claims, a defense against responsibility. If a lawyer can utter this incantation and can take it seriously enough, responsibility and the feelings accompanying it are shifted to the client." The fault is like the one St. Augustine confessed from his days as a Manichean. "I very much preferred to excuse myself and to accuse some other thing that was in me but was not I." Noonan's argument is that one who reasons vicariously does not reason as a moral person at all. St. Augustine would have said the attempt is destructive. "My two wills . . . were in conflict and in their conflict wasted my soul."

The point is one that is fundamental in the understanding of the professional gentlemen who first formulated professional ethics for English-speaking doctors and lawyers. "A gentleman," Shirley Letwin says, is "the opposite of someone whose steadiness depends on conformity to something outside himself and, where such a support is missing, contradicts himself and fragments his life. When a man contradicts himself, he becomes an adversary of himself, and when he divides his life into separate compartments, he hides himself from himself and is only partly alive, like someone who walks in his sleep. . . . A gentleman is aware of himself as engaged in shaping a coherent self."

David Burrell and Stanley Hauerwas, meditating on Albert Speer's old age of regret, say, "He had no effective way to step back from himself, no place to stand. His self-deception began when he assumed that 'being above all an architect' was a story sufficient to constitute his self. He had to experience the solitude of prison to realize that becoming a human being requires stories and images a good deal richer than professional ones, if we are able to be equipped to deal with the powers of the world." The argument here is that Speer's thinking of himself as an architect—his thinking of himself in the third person, to use Robert Bolt's phrase—led to his inability to think of himself as anything else. Self-deception lies in that direction; vicarious morality leads to excuses for monumental horrors with phrases such as acting in a good cause, or acting as God's representative, with words such as justice and health. It excuses the exploitations of social prestige or honor or recognition or wealth by saying that one's task requires status. It led Speer to such a position, as master of the manpower apparatus of the Third Reich—that is, to the management of Hitler's slave-labor camps. Schizophrenia is not only a disease; it is also a metaphor for bad reasoning and bad consequences.

Those who argue against the morals of the task say that it is the business of a moral person to confront evil means as much as evil ends, and if evil means are inherent in a task, to confront the people in institutions who require the task to be done. It is the business of a moral person to live as one who defines himself and his community in terms broad enough and hopeful enough to honor the Law of Love in his jobs and in the way he does his jobs. There may be such a thing as necessary harm—the moral life is impossible without the risk of harm to oneself and to others—but there is no such thing as necessary evil.

The ethics of task resembles the ethics of the two kingdoms, but there is a difference that has to do with a fixation on work—with the sort of thing that is popularly celebrated by saying of someone, "He lives to work rather than works to live." Dorothy Sayers's fictional teacher Miss deVine makes the consequent ethical comment with reference to an academic colleague: "She's the kindest soul in the world, in things she's indifferent about. . . . But she hasn't the slightest mercy on the prosodical theories of Mr. Elkbottom. She wouldn't countenance those to save Mr. Elkbottom from hanging. She'd say she couldn't. And she couldn't, of course. If she actually saw Mr. Elkbottom writhing in humiliation, she'd be sorry, but she wouldn't alter a paragraph. That would be treason. One can't be pitiful [have pity] where one's own job is concerned. You'd lie cheerfully, I expect, about anything except—what?" And Harriet admits the point: "Except saying that somebody's beastly book is good when it isn't. I can't do that."

Not so, perhaps, the one-kingdom gentleman in a profession. His is a "sensitivity to the context of all the moments that make up one's life," Letwin says. This "appears in a gentleman's care to consider whether the meaning of what he does today is consistent with what he did yesterday or is likely to do tomorrow, and in his readiness to question whether he has accurately observed what should have been taken into account. A gentleman's self-awareness is, in other words, a delicate sense of responsibility for the coherence of all his thoughts, words, and actions." He might even say a beastly book is good, as when Atticus said to Mrs. Dubose that she was as pretty as a picture.

The social argument for the ethics of the task is that we serve our fellows by dividing up the work of the community and taking, each of us, part of it. That way, everyone's needs are met. There are a couple of difficulties. For one, the theory requires certain conditions in the community, conditions that may not be present. A second difficulty is self-deception.

The biblical basis for this ethic is that God gives each of us a calling ("Let every one lead the life which the Lord has assigned to him" [1 Cor. 7:17, R.S.V.]). The ethics of the task is therefore a way to serve other people, and because of the variety of tasks to which people are called, to serve people in a way that satisfies each person's responsibility to all others. These are grand and persuasive moral claims. But the fact that Miss deVine's colleague is willing to watch Mr. Elkbottom writhe in agony, because of loyalty to her calling, presents a difficulty. Service to the community seems to feed the useful psychology that says to each of us that his work is important. The result seems to be intellectually wrong, though, when the task becomes an idol, as it did for Speer, and wrong in effect, too, when we become immoral toward particular people.

"Humanity has been greatly enriched by the Protestant concept of a system of callings in which each finds his or her place. Whether individual lives have been enriched by it is another, and harder, question," Gilbert Meilaender says of this Sayers story.

Maybe the central difficulty with Miss deVine's colleague is after all a deeper theoretical difficulty, more than a difficulty of self-deception. Maybe the theory is wrong to begin with, or, if it is not, maybe the modern expression of it—which has been colored by the economics of complex communities in industrial society—is wrong. Meilaender says that the notion that we live to work is wrong because it conflicts with the love we have and want to have for specific other persons. It is wrong because it tries to "have work . . . as central in our sense of who we are as friendship was to [Aristotle]. . . . [See chapter 5.] Our modern notion—into which even so independent a thinker as Sayers could be lured—that the point of work is to give meaning, purpose, and fulfillment to life is a degradation of the biblical theory. . . . It is a degradation against which we should be guarded by both our experience and our theological tradition." That is, we know better and even if we didn't know better our religious tradition should have taught us better. Meilaender (like Martin Buber) resolves the conflict between work and love, between work and friendship, by giving priority to love. In this way he avoids what he sees as the central theoretical evil in loving to work, the evil of idolatry—the evil of making an idol of what one has to do, of putting work where God ought to be. He (like Martin Buber) argues that work cannot provide self-fulfillment, but love can.

One rarely sees in American professional ethics the argument that an accountant or a lawyer ought to love his clients—or try to. One often sees the argument that a professional ought to work hard for his clients. The implications of the two kinds of moral admonition are not as similar as one may at first think.

The Doctrine of One Kingdom

There are of course ethical thinkers in the professions who do not accept the theology of the two kingdoms—even though, I think, almost all of us have been influenced by it and have learned to take it into account. These dissenters say they believe and try to live as if there is only one kingdom and as if there can only be one morality in our lives, a single morality to govern both personal life and professional life. A wise elder in my profession (teaching law), Harry Jones of Columbia, reflects this point of view when he says, "The restraining influence that good lawyers have had on even their most avaricious clients is a significant story that should be told far more often than it is. . . . Men of large affairs do not select their legal advisers entirely or principally for ethical insensitivity." I found that to be so when I practiced law, as I will explain in the next chapter.

Ann Landers and Abigail Van Buren may know what they're doing when they refer their correspondents to physicians for moral advice, but only if and when, as Lewis Thomas puts it, the primary qualification for family medicine is friendship. Jones also argues that many of the modern American lawyers who defend the adversary ethic find it too cynical to be lived. Few gynecologists are, I think, as hardhearted as they sound when they argue the "pro-choice" position on abortion. Professional talk does not jibe with professional behavior. Behavior is better than talk.

The sources of the one-kingdom view are, like the sources of two-kingdoms ethics, deep and ancient. One source is in Judaism. In Judaism, to say that a person is just is to say that he is righteous, that he lives his life in conformity to the covenant that Israel has with God. In this view, love and justice are the same thing. If distinctions must be made between a person's life in institutions and his life with his family or his neighbors, they are distinctions based on the melancholy fact that we are not as put together (Buber would say, not as personal), in ourselves and among ourselves, as we should be. But with grace and with effort we find ways of communicating with one another, of mediating our unfortunate separateness. Health is a condition for such mediation and law is one of its means. Professionals preside over the conditions and means we use to work out what Richard McBrien calls our imperfect harmonies. And our imperfect harmonies express how difficult it is to love one another. This, I think, is the Jewish way of looking at the one kingdom. If the God of Israel takes the lands of other nations and gives them to Israel, God nonetheless acts for the good of the other nations. We may not understand how that is so, but we know that it is so, and we obey and praise God in Psalms for truthfulness and for justice.

Another ancient source of the one-kingdom view is Greek thought, and particularly the ethics of virtue in, say, Plato and Aristotle. The Greek word for virtue means a perfected power, which in turn suggests a moral life in which the creature behaves according to its nature. In this view of things, the purpose of law relates to the nature of human persons, and the moral universe that is implicit in nature is the source of the legal universe. All of this, both law and morals, flows from the law of nature—from what the American Declaration of Independence calls "the Laws of Nature and of Nature's God."

This view is consistent with the gentleman-professional's concern for coherence, integrity, and constancy. There, as Letwin describes it (and she could be describing professional forebears such as Percival, Hoffman, and Sharswood), the virtuous person tries in his morals to be all of a piece, here and there, yesterday and today, in town and at home. The Judaic teaching on faithfulness, like the Greek teaching on virtue, accepts such coherence as necessary to sound morals, but it adds to it a sense of goal—of teleology; and that sense of goal requires a consequent concern for moral priorities. It isn't enough simply to be all together, in this Jewish view of faithfulness or this Greek view of virtue; it is also necessary to know where I am going and what steps along the way lead to where I am going. An anecdote, from Lis Harris's study of Lubavicher Hasidism in New York City, makes the point:

Harris visited sexually separate parochial schools in the Hasidic neighborhood. She noticed that little girls get less education, they study less intensely, and they have shabbier facilities and less demanding teachers. She of course thought she was on to something (and maybe she was). "I asked an elfin, dark-skinned girl wearing Mary Janes and pearl earrings what she would like to be when she grew up. She pretended to think about the question, then grinned broadly: 'A mother.' A chorus of 'Me too's' echoed down the hallway. As it happened, I'd asked the same question of a kindergarten class at the boys' school. None of the boys wanted to be firemen, policemen, or astronauts. Their equally unanimous answer was, 'A father.' "

· § ·

The one-kingdom view of ethics in the professions is a monolithic theory, and since I here speak of it in a positive way maybe I will be excused for using a story that pokes a little fun at it. After one of William James's lectures on cosmology, a woman who had been listening came up and said to him, "Mr. James, you have it all wrong. The world is not as you say. The world rests on a giant turtle." He meditated on that for a respectful moment and then asked her, "If that is so, can you tell me what the giant turtle rests on?" Yes, she said, she could; it rests on a second and even larger turtle. And before he could say anything more, she interrupted him: "Wait, Mr. James. I know what you're going to say, but it's no use. I'm afraid it's turtles all the way down."

If the kingdom is one, and turtles all the way down, the questions of importance are how we know that and how we determine what it means. Critics of one-kingdom moral theology, or of this version of it, argue that such a theory rests on intuition, that it is not derived logically from moral principles. One way to answer that would be to cite William James again. So much the worse for logic. (See chapter 1.) Another way to answer it would be to claim the ability to formulate perceptions about human nature in codal propositions. The "natural law" is thus-and-so. (We older Roman Catholics remember how that worked.) On the whole I would rather admit to intuition, and avoid codes, but to say that is not to say that intuition is a weakness. (See chapter 5.) Intuition is not a bad way to know something; C. G. Jung called intuition the ability to see around corners, and that is not a bad ability to claim in a profession. But, having admitted to an intuitionist theory, I also claim empirical corroboration for what I learn by intuition.

It is therefore possible to leave the charge of intuitionism aside and see how the perception of turtles works. The procedure is to look at cases in which virtue, in a turtle's sense of the term, works. This may be to see how professionals in their office behavior, if not in their thought, deny the proposition that public and professional life has a separate morality.

Case One. My jurisprudence teacher at Notre Dame, Robert E. Rodes, told us a story about a young couple who got on a boat in China to come to the United States and settle here. While they were on the boat on the Pacific Ocean, the wife had a baby. When they landed and went through the immigration process in San Francisco, the baby was found to have no visa. He didn't even have a passport. Both of the parents had visas and passports. The immigration official involved cabled to Washington, asking what he should do. The answer he got by return wire was, "Don't be a damned fool." The bureaucracy need not have a separate morality, and therefore it need not have a rule for everything. An immigration official deals with what Justice Wilson, in a tax case, called the noblest work of God.

Case Two. In Benét's play, *The Devil and Daniel Webster,* Jabez Stone sold his soul to the Devil, and the Devil came to collect it. Stone resisted the claim and hired Webster to represent him. The Devil presided at the trial. Webster won the case by demanding a jury trial—even though the jury was made up of the greatest scoundrels in human history, all of them dredged up from the depths of hell. The Devil, who controlled the jury lists, thought these subjects of his would enjoy having Jabez Stone's company. Webster won because he invited these jurors to ignore the literal purport of St. Paul's direction to obey Caligula. He said to the jury, "Look, this Jabez Stone is a *man.* And you, too, are *men.* You are not devils."

"He was talking about the things that make a country a country, and a man a man."

"And he began with the simple things that everybody's known and felt—the freshness of a fine morning when you're young and the taste of food when you're hungry, and the new day that's every day when you're a child. He took them up and he turned them in his hands. They were good things for any man.

"Then he turned to Jabez Stone and showed him as he was—an

ordinary man who'd had hard luck and wanted to change it. And, because he'd wanted to change it, now he was going to be punished for all eternity. And yet there was good in Jabez Stone, and he showed them that good. He was hard and mean, in some ways, but he was a man. There was a sadness in being a man, but it was a proud thing too. And he showed what the pride of it was till you couldn't help feeling it. Yes, even in hell, if a man was a man, you'd know it. And he wasn't pleading for any one person any more, though his voice rang like an organ. He was telling the story and failures and the endless journeys of mankind. They got tricked and trapped and bamboozled, but it was a great journey. And no demon that was ever foaled could know the inwardness of it—it took a man to do that."

Case Three. In *Terminiello v. Chicago,* the Supreme Court held for a repulsive rabble-rouser whose speech was so objectionable that his listeners threatened to riot. The court said the police had to protect the speaker, not silence him. There are two ways to look at that decision. One—and the most popular just now—is to explain the case in a quantitative, utilitarian way, as a matter of the greatest good for the greatest number. Terminiello was allowed to speak because of the "marketplace of ideas," because a democratic state has to hear from everybody who wants to be heard from, even a scruffy anarchist. He is protected, not for himself, not because he is the noblest work of God, but as a means to a political end. The lawyers and judges who seem to serve Terminiello are acting for the Constitution, for democratic government, for the good of the state. This way of explaining the case is a public-square adversary ethic; it depends on a political Darwinism in which one expects that the best ideas will survive. Another way to explain the case is to say that Terminiello was a human being who needed to communicate with other people, as we all do, and that is one thing not even the welfare of the majority—not even civil peace—can interfere with. Theologically, Jews and Christians might say (Buber did say) that God speaks to us in the person of the other, who stands before us not just in her or his speech but as a self. It is a theory that should encourage journalists, especially the really creative ones.

Case Four. Or consider the rescue cases in tort. It is said to be a rule of the common law of tort that no one has a duty to rescue a stranger in peril. But it is also a rule that if one attempts rescue and is hurt, the author of the original peril is liable to the rescuer. "The risk of rescue, if only it be not wanton, is born of the occasion," in Benjamin Nathan Cardozo's phrase. It is also a rule that when one begins rescue, he can't give it up carelessly; he can't let the victim fall back into the river because it turns out that the victim is heavy. What the common law seems to say here is that it is a good thing to rescue a stranger in peril, even if the law hasn't enough spunk to make you do it. Here the law recognizes and accepts its failure to be separate. In this, as Cardozo demonstrated in a judicial opinion that is, I think, sly, common law followed rabbinical teaching.

Case Five. One of the curiosities of slaveholding America was that slaves were not subject to punishment by their masters for serious crimes. In such cases slaves were tried in the civil courts. Alabama provided defense counsel in such cases, at public expense, from the earliest days of its existence as a state. But for most other purposes the slave was a chattel, not a human being. One way to read this curiosity is that the legal tradition required it; if one could commit murder or arson, he was entitled, as a matter of deductive reasoning, to the processes developed in the common law of England for the treatment of murderers and arsonists. (Mr. Tutt, of the old *Saturday Evening Post* stories, once demonstrated that European law provided trials for animals [see chapter 5]; that custom was apparently not preserved in antebellum Alabama.) Another way to read the curiosity is that in some extreme situations it was impossible not to notice that the offending slave was a person, the noblest work of God. It was not so much a matter of having the culture's bluff called as it was of the happy fact that you cannot fool yourself forever. I think here also of the refusal of American doctors to preside over capital punishment by lethal injection.

Advice to doctors from Dr. C. G. Jung: "We must see whether we cannot learn something from the medical philosophers of a remote past when body and soul had not yet been torn asunder and handed over to separate faculties. . . . The personality of the patient demands the personality of the doctor. . . . The true physician never stands outside his work but is always in the thick of it. . . . If the doctor wishes to help a human being he must be able to accept him as he is. And he can do this in reality only when he has already seen and accepted himself as he is. . . . Wholeness is in fact a charisma which one can manufacture neither by art nor by cunning, which we can only grow into and whose reign we must simply endure. . . . Every illness is at the same time an unsuccessful attempt at healing. . . . Modern man has heard enough about guilt and sin. He is sorely enough beset by his own bad conscience, and wants rather to learn how he is to reconcile himself with his own nature—how he is to love the enemy in his own heart and call the wolf his brother."

A wrenching literary example of this insistence on the truth about who a person is is Robert Penn Warren's poem-story *Brother to Dragons,* which tells of the murder of a slave in Kentucky by two of Thomas Jefferson's nephews. What Warren did there was tell us, as Jung would, that we have to come to terms with the evil in ourselves by telling the truth about it, telling the truth to ourselves and in our communities:

> Fulfillment is only in the degree of recognition
> Of the common lot of our kind. And that is the death of vanity,
> And that is the beginning of virtue.
> The recognition of complicity is the beginning of innocence.

The Bible is full of stories about the death of vanity as the beginning of virtue. For example, the story of Jesus and the woman taken in adultery (John 8:1–11) is about an offender and the moral indignation of law professors. Or, perhaps, it would be better to overlook the moral indignation and say that the professors were trying to implement the law, in opposition to Jesus who was, as they saw it, a denigrator of the law. Their concern was justice. This story can be read as a one-kingdom story and as a story in which Jesus is a professional—a healer, certainly, and perhaps a lawyer. Jesus was able to express love without denigrating the law or separating love from the law as the professors understood the law. (The persons who threw the first stone had to be the witnesses to the woman's crime; their turning away left the case unproved. Acts 7:58 reports a case, St. Stephen's, in which the accusers were not reluctant to throw the first stones.) In this case, as in the case of the Roman coin, Jesus put the law and love together, without either overriding the other.

These stories illustrate that the one-kingdom view of professional and public morality depends less on a theory or a doctrine than on a perception, an intuition maybe, on what the Thomistic tradition calls "connaturality"—the human experience in which I look out from myself, as the jury in the case of *Stone v. Satan* did; as the other Pharisees did when the Pharisee Jesus told them that the one without sin should cast the first stone at the adulterous woman; as the immigration officer in San Francisco should have done—and see that this other is a creature like myself. These were what Martin Buber called I-and-Thou moments. These are not points of view that rest only on principles, and I tend to believe that they would be corrupted if limited to principles—as they were, I think, in Blackstone and, in a different way, by many "natural law" moralists in the Roman Catholic tradition. Shirley Letwin says the gentleman "understands himself as one among others like himself," and so "his integrity entails respecting the integrity of others. He will think of them in the same way as he thinks of himself. He will recognize them as personalities, as characters, whose distinctiveness he is obliged to respect, and whom he must treat as he wishes himself to be treated."

· § ·

I am conscious here that I may have set up a straw man. Is the doctrine of the two kingdoms really inconsistent with what I have called the one-kingdom view? Arguably not. One should notice that Martin Luther taught that the believer should exercise worldly power with motives formed in the kingdom of love. Luther spoke of the prince as a minister; and, certainly, it is possible to think of a modern American professional's life as a life of ministry—that, really, more than a life of technique or of advocacy or of administration. The average American lawyer spends about four-fifths of his time talking to people in his law office; the percentage is nearly that for doctors and the clergy, and should be for university teachers. If life is a matter of being sometimes shepherd and sometimes hangman, most of our professional lives are the lives of shepherds.

It is important to notice that there is a recurrent tendency in moral thought, a tendency that serves the deceptive way in which we excuse the evil we do, to find a special morality to govern each part of our ambiguous selves. The adversary ethic, the ethics of privacy, and the ethics of profit and of having to know, may not require or turn on that kind of thinking, but it is fair to say that these ethics tempt us to that kind of thinking. It is hard to live as a whole person. It is important to see that, I think, and to tell the truth about it. What I have identified as the one-kingdom view seems to me one sound intellectual discipline for telling the truth, for being responsible. It may not be important, as it may not be fair, to blame the error on those who have taught the moral theology of the two kingdoms. In any case, it is important to say of both sides of the argument that these theologians teach about a single person. That single person behaves in two prototypical ways—in institutions and out of them. He serves institutions much of his time, and some of the time he does not serve institutions. The debate is about how he should behave when he behaves institutionally. Traditional two-kingdoms reasoning would come much of the way with me in making some melancholy reflections about the way we behave when we behave institutionally—in government and in courts; in hospitals, businesses, and newspapers; in law firms; in schools and churches, universities, and Rotary Clubs:

1. We tend in institutions to suppress our best discoveries about human nature. People in institutions tend to take all human insight, all sound principles, and turn them into ways of insuring the institution's survival. Our life in institutions seems to be a life in which the noblest work of God is made subject to the noblest work of man. I think this fact explains the archetypal need we seem to have for a theology of two kingdoms. It is what makes the two kingdoms not so much a theology as a syndrome, and, finally, an idolatry.

2. When we act in institutions—and this is the reason it seems

good to act in institutions—we act in favor of stability and order. That was true of the government Martin Luther told to suppress revolt, and it is true of America's twentieth-century, wartime government that, for example, impounded an entire ethnic group among its citizens because members of that group reminded it of its enemies. Institutions tend to turn the noblest work of God into a fungible commodity and then to invent noble reasons for having done so. I think of the fact that the old American ethics of the gentleman—in, say, the case of Faulkner's Gavin Stevens—depended on the belief that most people have to be protected (and that tends to become only a nice way of saying that most people are inferior). As Gavin said, one begins protecting the weak, and he comes to the place where he protects the weak who aren't even weak—women, black people, and the Boo Radleys among us whom we call feeble minded. It isn't conscious evil and shoddy excuse you have to cope with when you study our professional history; it is deception caused by noble motives.

3. People in institutions have a way of acting, an official tendency to turn other people into commodities, and to excuse themselves with grand, official phrases such as health, justice, equality, due process, privacy, democracy, and the rule of law. But behind the phrases are hidden patterns of behavior that show, when brought into the light, that people in institutions usually do not have values strong enough for community life. (See chapter 5.) The institution is substantively empty when all it has is procedures. Lutheran two-kingdoms theory provides substantive values through the doctrine of love's influence on law. Martin Buber provided value through efforts to sustain the personal when one acts in the "It-world," as he called institutional life. Covenant, natural-law, and other one-kingdom theologies provide substantive values through denial of the distinction between law and morals. Without personal, substantive morals, people in legal institutions tend to forget, as both Luther and the medieval Scholastics would have said, that law is an ordinance of reason for the common good; that the human body is the temple of the Holy Spirit; that not even the best investigative reporter can know much about anybody.

One way to put this would be to say that our institutions benefit from the syndrome of the two kingdoms because, that way, there is always at least one kingdom for our institutions to control. Another way to put it would be to say that the moral theologians who have taught of the two kingdoms have been misused. They never supposed that the kingdoms were as separate as twentieth-century American professional perversion has made them. Luther closed his essay on obedience to law with an appeal to the justice that is written in our hearts, to love, and to the law of nature. He urged the prince to whom he sent the essay, the Duke of Saxony, to take account of these springs of justice, "and not make the spring dependent on its rivulets, nor take reason captive to the letter."

Chapter Four

· § ·

THE PROFESSION

That things are not so ill with you and me as they might have been, is half owing to the number who lived faithfully a hidden life, and rest in unvisited tombs.

—George Eliot

ONE of the things that happens to a young person who comes into a profession is that she or he encounters the profession as a moral teacher: The profession itself claims teaching authority. Thus the founder of modern medical ethics, Sir Thomas Percival, writing in 1791, demanded for the profession not only obedience but even reverence. "Every [one] who enters into a fraternity engages, by a tacit compact, not only to submit to the laws, but to promote the honor and interest of the association. . . . A physician, therefore, should continuously guard against whatever may injure the general representations . . . all general charges [of] . . . selfishness, improbity . . . [and] affected or jocular skepticism concerning the efficacy and utility of the healing art."

And Judge George Sharswood, originator of what are now official lawyers' ethics in the United States, said in 1854, "Nothing is more certain than that the practitioner will find, in the long run, the good opinion of his professional brethren of more importance than that of what is commonly called the public. The good opinion and confidence of members of the same profession, like the King's name on the field of battle, is a tower of strength . . . the title of legitimacy."

Another thing that happens to a young person entering a profession is that she or he returns home. I remember my first year in law practice, when September came and the air felt like football, that I noticed, as if discovering something, that I was not in school. I was in a town, with people who didn't take academic vacations. It was a place not of dormitories and blackboards but of families and churches and neighborhoods. The world around was more like the world of my childhood than the world I had been studying in for seven years. My wife and I bought a home, joined a church, got acquainted with our neighbors, became people—like our parents. The clients who came into the law office were more like the people I grew up with than like players in law-school casebooks.

Doctor and lawyer stories show both of these aspects of professional entrance—the profession's claim of moral authority and the return to the moral authorities that formed our characters. The best doctor story in English, George Eliot's *Middlemarch,* has the young physician Lydgate come to town and do the things my wife and I did, and encounter the wary influences of older practitioners. In Sinclair Lewis's doctor story, *Arrowsmith,* Martin goes to his wife's hometown, and Martin begins to learn, as Lydgate did, the threat and the comfort of practicing among country doctors. In Louis Auchincloss's big-firm lawyer story, *The Great World and Timothy Colt,* Timmy moves downtown when he finishes law school at Columbia, becomes Henry Knox's apprentice and the breadwinner of a family, in a neighborhood where young professionals and their wives think that getting ahead is fun. Some of the stories show how the moral authority and the return home are at war with one another. Thus, William Carlos Williams fled from the corruption of pediatrics in Hell's Kitchen and went to live with his parents in New Jersey—to practice medicine there.

Williams's story is unusual among twentieth-century American stories in that it shows the failure of the professional moral teacher and the triumph of character, as his character was formed in his parents' house. In the cases of Martin Arrowsmith and Timothy Colt, the professional teacher prevails and character fails. The nineteenth-century stories are in a third category. In them, character is determinative: The professional teacher cannot rescue a weak character. As the professional moral spokesmen put it then, the professions are for gentlemen. Nor can the profession damage strong character. Lydgate rejects his professional teachers, and suffers for it, but his character is strong; and for him, in a phrase that is characteristic of Eliot, the professional limit becomes a moral beginning. *Middlemarch* makes the point in medicine that William Dean Howells's American story *The Rise of Silas Lapham* makes about business, or Trollope's *Orley Farm* about the law.

My argument in this chapter turns on this distinction between professional teacher and culture, between code and character in professional ethics, and on two propositions: (1) sound ethical codes in the professions are those that depend on character, and (2) ethical codes in which that dependence is not understood are corrupt and corrupting.

The first proposition—that code depends on character—was fundamental and clear in the earliest codes in British and American law and medicine. Both professions came in the nineteenth century to take the dependence for granted, then to ignore it, then to betray it—so that modern codes in both professions are at least irrelevant to ethical reasoning and are often worse than irrelevant. They are often corrupting. And so the modern professional associations that purport to be the guardians of professional ethics are pressure groups more than anything else. The schools that these organized professions maintain and protect are not places of moral formation so much as places where moral issues are evaded by vocational redefinition. Morals in professional life are treated there as private if not eccentric, and moral outrages are excused by modern forms of licensed irresponsibility.

That is the situation in our official professional ethics, I think, but it is not yet, or not consistently, the situation in professional practice. The professions practice better than they preach. How do I, an aging academic, know that? I know it because our doctor and lawyer stories say so. In our stories code still depends on character, and, because I trust our stories, I take comfort as I see my friends and my children go out to practice in these two ancient callings. (When I use "code" in this context, I do not mean a document or a consensus statement so much as I mean the influence of the profession as moral teacher—the profession's claim that it is a moral teacher and the substance of its moral teaching.)

Medicine in Middlemarch

Tertius Lydgate came to Middlemarch with ideal training for the practice of medicine in a nineteenth-century country town. He didn't know anybody, but he had obtained a place. He had purchased Dr. Peacock's practice. He was ready. He had the most thorough medical education available (London, followed by Edinburgh and Paris); he had learned a disciplined, curious, and scientific approach to disease; his clinical training had been at the hands of doctors who were not afraid to innovate but who also respected the contributions of hidden and faithful professional forebears who rest in unvisited tombs.

Lydgate had optimism that he could cure and explore at the same time, "that the two purposes would illuminate each other: the careful observation and inference which was his daily work, the use of the [microscopic] lens to further his judgment in special cases, would further his thought as an instrument of larger inquiry. . . . He would be a Middlemarch doctor, and by that very means keep himself in the track of far-reaching investigation."

"He was but seven and twenty, an age at which many men are not quite common—at which they are hopeful of achievement, resolute in avoidance, thinking that Mammon shall never put a bit in their mouths and get astride their backs, but rather that Mammon, if they have anything to do with him, shall draw their chariot."

"[H]is scientific interest . . . took the form of a professional enthusiasm: he had a youthful belief in his bread-winning work . . . the conviction that the medical profession as it might be was the finest in the world; presenting the most perfect interchange between science and art; offering the most direct alliance between intellectual conquest and the social good." His personal and emotional equipment, trained in the virtues of the English gentleman and in liberal education, led him to seek this combination of mind and progress, and to seek as well human companionship with his neighbors and, perhaps, in his work. His "nature demanded this combination: he was an emotional creature, with a flesh and blood sense of fellowship which withstood all the abstractions of special study. He cared not only for 'cases,' but for John and Elizabeth."

Lydgate came with all this useful cultural equipment to a new town, among professional elders he had not met. He came without money from a good family; he was physically attractive, socially capable, personally charming. The town he came to was conventional in all the conventional ways. It had ordinary morality and a lively awareness of the religious tradition. It had its economic and moral elite—squires, baronets, and senior Anglican clergy. It had a respectable mercantile class, to which most professional people (lawyers, physicians, apothecaries, and lesser clergy) belonged. Lydgate's story is the story of how a beginning professional enters the professional and civic world, the world of code and character, and a world—Jane Austen described it best—in which code depends on character. Middlemarch provided surmountable and virtually insurmountable difficulties to him in his practice of medicine; it also provided support and training for him in his practice of the virtues.

Consider, for example, the case of Nancy Nash's tumor. Nancy was Mrs. Larcher's charwoman. Dr. Minchin, an established physician in Middlemarch, was called in by Mrs. Larcher when Nancy complained of "alarming symptoms," most notably a lump that was said by Nancy's neighbors to be "as large and hard as a duck's egg, but later in the day to be about the size of 'your fist.' " The neighbors thought, as Dr. Minchin did, that the lump was a tumor, and the view in the neighborhood was that it would have to be cut out by a surgeon, although "one [neighbor] had known of oil and another of 'squitchineal' as adequate to soften and reduce any lump in the body when taken enough of into the inside—the oil by gradually 'soopling,' the squitchineal by eating away."

People who could pay doctors in Middlemarch were treated in their homes, usually with drugs. People who could not pay doctors were referred to a charitable hospital. Hospitals in that time (1820s), in both Britain and America, were places where the poor went, usually to die. In Middlemarch, care at the hospital was given principally by Lydgate, assisted by surgeons, who were then a lesser species of medical practitioner. But all the physicians in the town were on the hospital's "medical board" or "faculty."

Dr. Minchin gave Nancy Nash a certificate for the hospital. After consulting her neighbors in Churchyard Lane, she went to the hospital and was seen by Tertius Lydgate. He examined her and said, to Nancy and to the house surgeon, " 'It's not tumour: it's cramp.' He ordered her a blister and some steel mixture, and told her to go home and rest, giving her at the same time a note to Mrs. Larcher, who, she said, was her best employer, to testify that she was in need of good food.

"But by-and-by Nancy, in her attic, became portentously worse, the supposed tumour having indeed given way to the blister, but only wandered to another region with angrier pain. The staymaker's wife went to fetch Lydgate, and he continued for a fortnight to attend Nancy in her own home, until under his treatment she got quite well and went to work again. But the case continued to be described as one of tumour in Churchyard Lane and other streets—nay, by Mrs. Larcher also; for when Lydgate's remarkable cure was mentioned to Dr. Minchin, he naturally did not like to say, 'The case was not one of tumour, and I was mistaken in describing it as such,' but answered, 'Indeed! ah! I saw it was a surgical case, not of a fatal kind.' "

Dr. Minchin was, though, annoyed at Lydgate's oral disagreement in the presence of Nancy and the surgeon. "He had been inwardly annoyed . . . when he has asked at the Infirmary about the woman he had recommended two days before, to hear from the house-surgeon, a youngster who was not sorry to vex Minchin with impunity, exactly what had occurred: he *privately* [emphasis added] pronounced that it was indecent in a general practitioner to contradict a physician's diagnosis in that open manner, and afterward agreed . . . that Lydgate was disagreeably inattentive to etiquette."

If Dr. Minchin had accused Lydgate of being unethical, he would have been on solid professional ground. The medical profession in Britain, and notable leaders in the American profession, had adopted by that time the medical ethics of Sir Thomas Percival, physician and teacher at the Manchester Infirmary, who laid down professional principles for cases of disagreement in diagnosis. One, directly applicable, said, "When a physician or surgeon is called to a patient, who has been before under the care of another gentleman of the faculty, a consultation with him should be proposed, even though he may have discontinued his visits. His practice, also, should be treated with candor and justified, so far as probity and truth will permit. For the want of success, in the primary treatment of a case, is no impeachment of professional skill or knowledge, and it often serves to throw light on the nature of a disease, and to suggest to the subsequent practitioner more appropriate means of relief."

If Lydgate disagreed with the diagnosis written by Dr. Minchin on Nancy's certificate, he should have consulted Dr. Minchin—both as a matter of courtesy (which was important for the preservation of public trust in healers, then as now) and as a matter of education. Lydgate might have learned something from his older and more experienced colleague. Dr. Minchin was right to be offended; his and Lydgate's profession gave him justification.

Lydgate would have admitted he had been inattentive to etiquette. But he did not value etiquette as highly as he valued technique and science. He "did not make the affair a ground for valuing himself or (very particularly) despising Minchin, such rectification of misjudgments often happening among men of equal qualifications. But report took up this amazing case of tumour, not clearly distinguished from cancer, and considered the more awful for being of the wandering sort; till much prejudice against Lydgate's method . . . was overcome by the proof of his marvellous skill in the speedy restoration of Nancy Nash after she had been rolling and rolling in agonies from the presence of a tumour both hard and obstinate, but nevertheless compelled to yield." The public approval made Dr. Minchin uncomfortable, and it did not give Lydgate as much satisfaction as it might have. "He had to wince under a promise of success given by that ignorant praise which misses every valid quality." If Lydgate had thought more about his behavior, he might have seen more serious reason than he did for respecting professional propriety in the case. The probability of ignorant blame and praise is one good reason for a group of professionals to keep its esoteric disagreements to itself.

Lydgate had similar success with Fred Vincy, member of a merchant's family whose medical care was paid for and given at home. Fred was seriously ill with typhoid fever. He was at first under the care of Mr. Wrench, one of Middlemarch's two apothecaries. Mr. Wrench thought that Fred had a slight derangement. But Fred was in the pink-skinned stage of typhoid fever and became so ill, during one of Mr. Wrench's absences from town, that Fred's parents called in Lydgate, who diagnosed the disease correctly and, with great difficulty, finally cured it. Lydgate did not consult Mr. Wrench and thus offended two of Sir Thomas Percival's principles of medical ethics—the one quoted above, and another that dealt more directly with a general practitioner who was called in to see the patient of an apothecary: "Physicians are sometimes requested to visit the patients of the apothecary, in his absence.

"Compliance, in such cases, should always be refused, when it is likely to interfere with the consultation of the medical gentleman ordinarily employed by the sick person, or his family. . . . Physicians are the only proper substitutes for physicians; surgeons for surgeons; and apothecaries for apothecaries."

Mr. Wrench, like Dr. Minchin, was annoyed at Lydgate, as he had every right to be. So devoted was the profession to respect for the first healer that it had made it a matter of patient duty, so that Mr. and Mrs. Vincy also violated professional ethics when they called Lydgate in to see to their son. The American Medical Association adapted Percival's principle in its first code of ethics (1847): "A patient should, if possible, avoid even the friendly visits of a physician who is not attending him—and when he does receive them, he should never converse on the subject of his disease, as an observation may be made, without any intention of interference, which may destroy his confidence in the course he is pursuing, and induce him to neglect the directions prescribed to him. A patient should never send for a consulting physician without the express consent of his medical attendant. It is of great importance that physicians should act in concert; for although their modes of treatment may be attended with equal success when employed singly, yet conjointly they are very likely to be productive of disastrous results."

Lydgate could have consulted Dr. Minchin about Nancy Nash's tumor without difficulty and without jeopardizing what he saw as correct care for her. He could at least have applied the blister and steel and kept his mouth shut. He could—even within Percival's careful separation of subcategories in the profession as it was then—

have discussed Fred's case with Mr. Wrench, and probably have persuaded Mr. Wrench that the case was more serious than Mr. Wrench at first thought. The likely reason Lydgate failed at these two easy and obvious observances of professional ethics was not zeal for healing but contempt for his elders. He did not regard his elders as his teachers; his teachers were in Edinburgh and Paris. "With our present rules and education, one must be satisfied now and then to meet with a fair practitioner," he told Mr. Bulstrode, the town banker, when he first met him. "As to all the higher questions which determine the starting-point of a diagnosis—as to the philosophy of medical evidence—any glimmering of these can only come from a scientific culture of which country practitioners have usually no more notion than the man in the moon."

Mr. Bulstrode was embarrassed to hear this criticism of the town's other doctors. He changed the subject, but for his own reasons he remained committed to getting Lydgate appointed as physician at the hospital, and to a longer-range project for a new and more scientific fever hospital under Lydgate's direction. Lydgate was later ungracious enough to hint in a dinner conversation that he was the only person qualified for either job. "Sometimes, if you wanted to get a reform, your only way would be to pension off the good fellows whom everybody is fond of, and put them out of the question."

The hospital board, and particularly Mr. Bulstrode, supported Lydgate in his medical objectives, but not because they accepted his superiority as a scientific physician. They did it to get his support for the appointment of an evangelical clergyman to be chaplain at the hospital, a political project that involved other professions and other objectives. Lydgate's devotion to science, as he saw it, led him to alienate his professional colleagues and to make bad political alliances, and those two factors in turn contributed to early failure in his practice of the profession in Middlemarch.

He should have moved more sensibly than he did in setting up practice in a strange town. The conventional way to have done that was to pay attention to his professional elders, not so much in technical matters as in moral matters. "For character too is a process and an unfolding. The man was still in the making, as much as the Middlemarch doctor and immortal discoverer, and there were both virtues and faults capable of shrinking or expanding." His faults were ordinary in the sense that any bright young doctor could have been expected to have them. His "conceit was of the arrogant sort, never simpering, never impertinent, but massive in its claims and benevolently contemptuous. . . . Lydgate's spots of commonness lay in the complexion of his prejudices, which, in spite of noble intentions and sympathy, were half of them such as are found in ordinary men of the world." The usual way for such a young person to be made better in a conventional world is for him to listen to and learn from his professional elders. For young doctors who come home to practice medicine, this part of professional education is made easier because they return to their towns and their families and find it comfortable, or at least customary, to learn there how to practice, as they have learned there how to behave in church, how to court or be courted by those they want to marry, and how to say good morning to their neighbors.

Lydgate was offered an inkling of how this professional training might work, but didn't pay attention to it, in a dinner conversation about the office of coroner in Middlemarch. The incumbent coroner was a lawyer, Mr. Chinchely. He said to Lydgate, "You never hear of a reform, but it means some trick to put in new men. I hope you are not one of the Lancet's men, Mr. Lydgate—wanting to take the coronership out of the hands of the legal profession." Mr. Chinchely was worried about his job, and Dr. Sprague, an elder physician, saw that and was sensitive to it, but Lydgate was not. Dr. Sprague supported his young colleague for a while, as doctors should support one another in public. He said he could think of a point or two on which the reformers were right.

Mr. Chinchely said, "I should like to know how a coroner is to judge of evidence if he has not had a legal training," and, of course, Lydgate said that only a doctor knew medical evidence when he saw it. "A lawyer is no better than an old woman at a *post-mortem* examination. . . . You might as well say that scanning verse will teach you to scan the potato crops." The argument then took on some heat for a while, although Mr. Vincy, the host, tried to deflect it with the opinion that a coroner should be a man who enjoys hunting. Finally, Dr. Sprague gave his young colleague a lesson in how to be gracious, a lesson that was, though, lost on Lydgate: "I hope it will be long before this part of the country loses the services of my friend Chinchely, even though it might get the best man in our profession to succeed him."

Lydgate also offended medical convention—and, probably, medical ethics as well—by seeking to do autopsies on the bodies of patients who died under his care or in the hospital. "Mrs. Dollop became more and more convinced . . . that Doctor Lydgate meant to let the people die in the Hospital, if not to poison them, for the sake of cutting them up without saying by your leave or with your leave; for it was . . . known . . . that he had wanted to cut up Mrs. Goby, as respectable a woman as any in Parley Street, who had money in trust before her marriage—a poor tale for a doctor, who if he was good for anything should know what was the matter with you before you died, and not want to pry into your inside after you were gone."

This propensity for the postmortem was in the interest of science. If Lydgate had been coroner, he would in his postmortems have been after discoveries for pathology and anatomy more than after medical evidence for the case at hand. His hero, he said, was Versalius (1514–1564), "a great fellow, who was about as old as I am. . . . And the only way he could get to know about anatomy as he did, was by going to snatch bodies at night, from graveyards and places of execution." This interest, and Lydgate's use of new methods of diagnosis such as the stethoscope, the microscope, and (the then uncommon) physical observation of patients, were subtle matters within the medical fraternity in Middlemarch. Lydgate's professional elders would probably have admitted that there was something to his preferences, or at least would have put the preferences down to youthful enthusiasm, and their dislike for them to habit and taste. They probably respected science as much as Lydgate did—or, at least, they respected his respect for science.

In one final particular, Lydgate offended virtually everyone in the professional fraternity, and all but a few in the town; and that one particular was probably as delicate as any he could have chosen if he had set out to offend. It had to do with the economics of practice. He did not charge for the drugs he dispensed and did not receive any part of the price of drugs he prescribed when they were dispensed by Mr. Dibbitts, the druggist. This was a radical enough departure from custom to be the sort of issue that could not be contained within the professional fraternity of Middlemarch. It was bound to end up in the ordinary gossip of the town, particularly because of Lydgate's unprofessional behavior.

"He did not mean to imitate those philanthropic models who make a profit out of poisonous pickles to support themselves while they are exposing adulteration, or hold shares in a gambling-hell that they may have leisure to represent the cause of public morality. He intended to begin in his own case some particular reforms which were quite certainly within his reach, and much less of a problem than the demonstrating of an anatomical conception. One of these reforms was to . . . simply prescribe, without dispensing drugs or taking percentage from druggists. This was an innovation for one who had chosen to adopt the style of general practitioner in a country town, and would be felt as offensive criticism by his professional brethren. But Lydgate meant to innovate in his treatment also, and he was wise enough to see that the best security for his practising honestly according to his belief was to get rid of systematic temptations to the contrary."

Maybe so. And maybe this seems a particularly admirable reform in this story, written about half a century after its own time. In Lydgate's day, though, the best professional guidance was that professional income from dispensing drugs was orderly, appropriate, and even admirable. "This apparent profit," said Sir Thomas Percival, quoting an unidentified "political and moral writer of great authority" (William Paley perhaps), "is frequently no more than the reasonable wages of labour. The skill of an apothecary is a much nicer and more delicate matter than that of any artificer whatever; and the trust which is reposed in him is of much greater importance. He is the physician of the poor in all cases, and of the rich when the distress or danger is not very great. His reward, therefore, ought to be suitable to his skill and his trust, and it arises generally from the price at which he sells his drugs. . . . The whole drugs which the best employed apothecary, in a large market town, will sell in a year . . . may not perhaps cost him above thirty or forty pounds.

Though he should sell them, therefore, for three or four hundred, or a thousand percent profit, this may frequently be no more than the reasonable wages of his labour charged, in the only way he can charge them." "A physician, who knows the education, skill, and persevering attention, as well as the sacrifice of ease, health, and sometimes even of life, which this profession requires," Sir Thomas said, speaking of apothecaries, and not quoting anybody, "should regard it as a duty not to withdraw, from those who exercise it, any sources of reasonable profit, or the honorable means of advancement in fortune. Two practices prevail in some places injurious to the interest of this branch of the faculty, and which ought to be discouraged. One consists in suffering prescriptions to be sent to the druggist, for the sake of a small saving in expense. The other in receiving [a] . . . stipend . . . for being consulted on the slighter indispositions to which all families are incident."

Lydgate's practice thus offended professional ethics, a system of ethics that was observed in the British medical community then, and was adopted by the American Medical Association within Lydgate's lifetime. That fact, coupled with what was seen as criticism of the way the elder medical men in Middlemarch made their living, led to the strongest possible local moral indignation. Lydgate's so-called reform "was offensive both to the physicians whose exclusive distinction seemed infringed on, and to the surgeon-apothecaries with whom he ranged himself; and only a little while before, they might have counted on having the law on their side against a man who without calling himself a London-made M.D. dared to ask for pay except as a charge on drugs." (Lydgate had his medical education in Scotland and France and did not have the M.D. degree. The allusion to the law is to judicial construction of the Apothecaries Act of 1815.)

This was exactly the sort of distracting debate that Sir Thomas Percival's medical ethics was designed to keep within the professional fraternity, which has, since Lydgate's day, managed to work the issue out so that, if modern professional ethics were applicable, none of the doctors in Middlemarch would make their income from selling drugs. Percival, who first wrote his ethics as a referee in an intraprofessional squabble at Manchester, knew as well as anyone the harm that could come from open professional quarrels. "A diversity of opinion and opposition of interest may in the medical, as in other professions, sometimes occasion *controversy,* and even *contention.*" He recommended arbitration within the fraternity—that is, with doctors as arbitrators. "Neither the subject matter of such references, nor the adjudication, should be communicated to the public; as they may be personally injurious to the individuals concerned, and can hardly fail to hurt the general credit of the faculty." Lydgate would say, of course, that no arbitral settlement of the fee matter could have occurred under Percival's procedures, since Lydgate could not have succeeded in reforming the profession in Middlemarch, which had Percival's ethical principles in its support, and since he could not have avoided disapproval by minding his own business. The other doctors noticed his practice of not charging for drugs, of charging only for his professional time, and they took Lydgate's procedure as a criticism of what they did. Here again, though, Lydgate could have been careful, and he was not. Differing practices were not new to the Middlemarch medical fraternity. Dr. Sprague "had weight, and might be expected to grapple with a disease and throw it; while Dr. Minchin might be better able to detect it lurking and to circumvent it. They enjoyed about equally the mysterious privilege of medical reputation, and concealed with much etiquette their contempt for each other's skill."

The result of Lydgate's indiscretion (as distinguished from his following his own conscience about fees) was that the debate became a debate in the town, a debate that provoked the other members of the medical fraternity to speak in public about their fees. It was a thoroughly bad case of dirty professional linen being washed in public, and Lydgate was more to blame for it than the other doctors were. It was Lydgate who started the public debate, in reckless remarks made to Mr. Mawmsey, a grocer. "It is in that way that hard-working medical men may come to be almost as mischievous as quacks," Lydgate said. "To get their own bread they must overdose the king's lieges; and that's a bad sort of treason, Mr. Mawmsey—undermines the constitution in a fatal way. . . .

. . . Mr. Mawmsey laughed more than he would have done if he had known who the king's lieges were, giving his 'Good morning, sir, good morning, sir' with the air of one who saw everything clearly enough. But in truth his views were perturbed. For years he had been paying bills with strictly-made items, so that for every half-crown and eighteenpence he was certain something measurable had been delivered. He had done this with satisfaction, including it among his responsibilities as a husband and father, and regarding a longer bill than usual as a dignity worth mentioning. Moreover, in addition to the massive benefit of the drugs to 'self and family,' he had enjoyed the pleasure of forming an acute judgment as to their immediate effects, so as to give an intelligent statement for the guidance of Mr. Gambit." Mr. Gambit was one of Middlemarch's apothecaries.

" 'Does this Mr. Lydgate mean to say there is no use in taking medicine?' said Mrs. Mawmsey. . . . 'I should like him to tell me how I could bear up at Fair time, if I didn't take strengthening medicine for a month beforehand. . . . I should have told him at once that I knew a little better than that.' " She discussed the matter with Mr. Gambit, who was carefully professional and tried to keep the professional dispute out of a public arena, but who was personally annoyed by what Lydgate said. Mr. Gambit thought of the uncompensated hours he spent talking with his patients. But Mr. Gambit said only, "Well, Lydgate is a good-looking young fellow, you know." Nonetheless, "Mr. Gambit [went] away from the chief grocer's . . . [with] a sense that Lydgate was one of those hypocrites who try to discredit others by advertising their own honesty, and that it might be worth some people's while to show him up. Mr. Gambit, however . . . did not think it worth his while to show Lydgate up until he knew how." It was perilous for Lydgate to have a professional elder bent on learning how to show him up. The point of the professional tradition—of Percival's ethics—was that this situation was also perilous for sound morals in professional practice.

Mr. Toller and Mr. Wrench were also apothecaries. Both of them were at first restrained in what they said about fees, as Mr. Gambit was, and as Lydgate was not. Mr. Toller made a good-natured joke about the inventory of the druggist to whom Lydgate sent his prescriptions: "Dibbitts will get rid of his stale drugs, then. I'm fond of little Dibbitts—I'm glad he's in luck." He was provoked into a little pique and some economic inaccuracy on the question of whether what Lydgate was doing was a professional reform. "The question is, whether the profit on the drugs is paid to the medical man . . . or by the patient, and whether there shall be extra pay under the name of attendance." Mr. Wrench was finally even less restrained, but only after he drank wine at a party. "What I contend against is the way medical men are fouling their own nest, and setting up a cry about the country as if a general practitioner who dispenses drugs couldn't be a gentleman. . . . I say, the most ungentlemanly trick a man can be guilty of is to come among the members of his profession with innovations which are a libel on their time-honored procedure."

The professional context in *Middlemarch* is a trifle quaint—not because healing was any quainter then than it is now, but because Eliot, writing half a century after the events she described, was able to make it appear quaint when she wanted to. The story is meant to sound at first like an account of professional hypocrisy. But only at first. Lydgate was a young man of learning, character, and courage—just the sort of young professional who can be prophetic against corruption in a profession. But he was also reckless, thoughtless, and unfair to those whom convention would expect him to honor as his elders in the profession. And he violated the ethics his medical counterparts in Britain and America, then and now, have agreed on—particularly about the two most delicate of intraprofessional matters: seeing a patient who has been under another doctor's care, and taking exception to the arrangements under which doctors earn their bread. The precepts Lydgate seemed most interested in violating—and not only violating, but scoffing at—came about because of an ugly, harmful, intraprofessional quarrel at the Manchester Infirmary, a quarrel that was recent enough to be within Lydgate's sense of his profession; it had occurred within forty years of the time he began practice. What it comes down to, I think, is that Lydgate had good intentions and good character but was in the wrong. He set himself up for the most common of all complaints by professionals against professionals—the callous ignorance of the young.

· § ·

My favorite legal example of contempt for the profession as moral teacher occurred a couple of generations after Lydgate's, in Trollope's *Orley Farm.* A barrister named Thomas Furnival, who had a general practice, sought to retain as counsel for the defense of Lady Mason, on a charge of forgery, a more specialized barrister named Mr. Chaffanbrass. Mr. Chaffanbrass was a professional forebear of Horace Rumpole; both served as defense lawyers in London's Old Bailey, the central criminal court. Mr. Chaffanbrass was willing to be retained, but he and Mr. Furnival wanted a third and more junior lawyer to join them, and Mr. Furnival suggested a young barrister named Felix Graham. Graham was known at the Bar for having been influenced by German jurisprudence, and particularly for his disagreement with the settled professional principle that a criminal-defense lawyer should serve his client faithfully whether he thinks the client is guilty or not.

Mr. Furnival told Mr. Chaffanbrass that Graham was interested and that Graham believed in Lady Mason's innocence. " 'Ah,' said Mr. Chaffanbrass. 'But what if he should happen to change his opinion about his own client?'

" 'We could prevent that, I think.'

" 'I'm not so sure. And then he'd throw her over as sure as your name's Furnival.'

" 'I hardly think he'd do that.'

" 'I believe he'd do anything.' And Mr. Chaffanbrass was quite moved to enthusiasm. 'I've heard that man talk more nonsense about the profession in one hour, than I ever heard before or since I first put a cotton gown on my back. He does not understand the nature of the duty which a professional man owes to his client.' "

Code before Character

Both professions cherish the tradition that says the young doctors' and young lawyers' best moral teachers are their professional elders. Both professions invoke metaphors of family or monastery or military colleagueship to express this tradition and to characterize relations among professionals. These metaphors suggest intraprofessional morals based on philosophical and theological concepts such as covenant, commitment, and faithfulness, rather than codal rules of behavior. That is, in these doctor and lawyer stories, code depends—expressly—on character. The metaphors for the profession as moral teacher are more like the morals of behavior in a family than like a civic polity. "The *espirit du Corps* is a principle of action founded in human nature, and when duly regulated, is both rational and laudable," Sir Thomas Percival said.

Percival pursued this professional fealty only "so far as . . . consistent with morality, and the general good of mankind," and Judge Sharswood probably would have agreed with that limitation. Not so the modern professions. Virtually no ethical instruction reaches modern lawyers and law students except that prepared and dispensed by the organized profession. In teaching hospitals, where the principle of scientific discipline is probably stronger *as an ethic* than anywhere else in practicing medicine, even science is subject to the judgment of elders. "There are two competing systems of legitimation for medical authority: clinical expertise and scientific evidence," Charles Bosk says. "These systems are not of equal importance: in the case of discrepant opinions, arguments based on clinical expertise override those based on scientific evidence; in some specific cases the attending [physician] is literally the last word on a subject."

Bosk reports such an example, from a discussion between senior (attending) and junior physicians on a surgical service. "Mr. Darnell . . . had a proctocolectomy the day before. As Arthur [attending] was surveying the wound, Ernest [junior] asked him about a new technique developed by Dr. Stanley and reported in a recent journal article. According to Ernest, Stanley reported that on a series of patients using this new technique, he had no instances of a particular complication. Arthur replied: 'I've tried that technique and I've seen patients on whom it was used, and I'm convinced it's not a bit better.' Ernest repeated: 'But in a large series, there were no complications.' Arthur answered: 'Then Stanley has a poor memory, or he didn't include in his series at least six of his patients I treated for that complication.' Ernest asked: 'Doesn't that call for a letter to the editor, sir?' Arthur answered: 'I don't think it would do much good. Dr. Stanley is the editor.' "

The same primacy of the judgment of elders is applied to moral matters—is applied even more stringently when the issue is integrity rather than technical competence—and in both cases the judgment of senior physicians is final. In Bosk's study, a resident was denied promotion, for example, despite a flawless clinical record, because his behavior caused "public embarrassment to the department." He had perhaps ignored etiquette in the ways Lydgate did in Middlemarch.

But modern professionals find it uncomfortable to live with the arrangement, when the arrangement is described as one in which the moral judgment of elders is not argued with. That way of accounting for the power of elders leads to resistance among the young. It is more effective for the profession to describe the power of elders in terms of technical skill—that is, to define the medical issue as one involving clinical judgment rather than moral judgment. Wendy Carlton, in a study of teaching hospitals similar to Bosk's, found that moral issues in medical education are not taken on directly; they are defined as clinical whenever possible, and when they cannot be defined as clinical they are ignored.

Carlton describes, in a chapter she titled "Being Female," the case of Joan Spoon, an eleven-year-old Down's Syndrome patient. Her parents wanted their doctor, Ralph Hodge, to get a hysterectomy done on Joan—so that Joan could not become pregnant and would not menstruate. That is what her parents wanted; nobody asked Joan.

The moral problem presented in that situation is one doctors and lawyers and judges have fretted over extensively since about 1970. It tends to remind us of Justice Holmes's opinion in *Buck v. Bell*: "Three generations of imbeciles are enough." All the young physicians and medical students in the surgical service Carlton studied were aware of the moral problem and, in cryptic phrases, they discussed it among themselves. They did not discuss it officially as a moral problem, though. The best they could do collectively—meeting together about it in the absence of the attending physician, Dr. Fine—was to define the problem as clinical: Joan might have a weak heart (Down's Syndrome patients often do). Her heart might not withstand the trauma of major surgery. No one was willing to call Dr. Fine and put this clinical problem to him, though; they were all afraid he would take an inquiry of this sort as reflecting on his clinical judgment. And no one was willing to describe the issue as moral, not to Dr. Fine, not even to himself. One resident asked Dr. Hodge if he had discussed the clinical risk with Joan's parents, and he said he had not. "It turns people off," he said, "and they go elsewhere to get it done."

The issue that could have been put to Dr. Fine was a clinical issue—risk to Joan by reason of her weak heart. The moral issue was not put to him, and not clearly discussed among the junior doctors. "The invisibility of ethical issues is supported by the absence of questions," Carlton says. Learning to rearrange moral questions, so that they are clinical, is one of the first things the profession teaches young doctors, she says. "The first year of significant clinical responsibility is also the year of gradual extinction of the ethical perspective. . . . The clinical perspective is held out as the mainstay of . . . professional identity. The student actively works to internalize the behavior, vocabulary, and manner of thinking of the physician."

It is important to notice that the modern surveillance of old over young, and of collective profession over individual professional, is more Olympian than it was for Tertius Lydgate or Felix Graham. If Lydgate had been working in the surgical service of the hospitals Bosk and Carlton studied, his progress toward surgical credentials could have been stopped because of his defiance of professional norms. If Felix Graham had been employed by a modern large law firm, he could have been denied advancement and thrown out of the firm.

It is not altogether comforting that modern arrangements, in both professions, move the violator to a less prestigious, less profitable, but still licensed and responsible professional position. In the hospital Bosk studied, one young physician who was found to lack integrity and another who was found to lack technical skill were moved to the minor leagues—the less competent surgeon to another form of medical practice, the less moral surgeon to a less illustrious surgical residency. On the other hand, the tendency to collective practice, in both professions, and particularly in the most attractive parts of both professions (large law firms, teaching hospitals, and specialized clinics), gives power to professional elders that

Dr. Sprague or Mr. Chaffanbrass would never have imagined they could have.

It is likely that the arrangement for collective practice that has occurred, say, in the legal profession in the United States, *is* the profession. At any rate, the moral teacher Percival and Sharswood described as local and focused now has not only the authority of older and wiser practitioners but also the power to promote, cast out, and fix pay. The situation that beginners in the medical and legal professions now face, when they consider the profession as moral teacher, is more tyrannical than those which Tertius Lydgate and Felix Graham faced and may be less vulnerable to gentle persuasion or prophetic witness. The issues these old English stories present are more acute now than they were then. (See chapter 6 for further discussion of medical education as Bosk describes it.)

The Law Firm as Moral Teacher

Louis Auchincloss describes this world for modern lawyers in America. In the story of the young lawyer Timothy Colt, Auchincloss called it a "great world." The country and the profession most broadly considered have largely lost the moral and religious consensus that Middlemarch had, and that America once had. The profession broadly considered now operates on what Emile Durkheim called a market morality; it has come to terms with robber barons of various sorts so thoroughly that it no longer attempts to be a moral teacher. What it calls ethics are traffic regulations that make professional intercourse efficient and keep professional practice at least (and often at most) within the boundaries set by the criminal law. The nationally organized legal profession in the United States has lately and clearly dropped even the attempt at moral admonition for its younger members.

The profession *narrowly* considered—as the young lawyer meets it intensely—is then the more interesting source of the professional ethics Lydgate and Graham might meet if they came along today with their new licenses. A local bar association in a smaller city might be, still, very like the medical fraternity Lydgate found in Middlemarch. But in the urban practice of the law, which is what most young lawyers now do, the profession as moral teacher is not a local bar association, or a specialized bar association (patent lawyers, trial lawyers, or whatever); it is the *law firm.* The profession as Timothy Colt met it, and the profession in the only manifestation he cared about, was the law firm. If the profession is, to such a lawyer today, a moral teacher, it is because the profession has become the law firm. Otherwise the profession is not a moral teacher; otherwise it has given up the office Judge Sharswood claimed for it.

The legal profession in America, when I came into it in 1961, was, in this way, a moral teacher. When I later left my law firm to become a full-time teacher, I could say—I did say—that the lawyers with whom I had practiced law there were persons of character who taught their junior colleagues how to practice the virtues in their practice of law. One of the most ordinary of these lessons—and the one I have found it most difficult to persuade my students of—is that the lawyer in modern business practice in the United States is a source of moral guidance for his clients.

I had come from law school with the certainty that (to use the phrase of one of my teachers), "the American businessman is the biggest sonofabitch in the world." I expected (as my students usually do) that the business clients I would meet would threaten my morals. They would ask me to do things that offended conscience, a particularly perilous matter because the organized legal profession—the American profession considered broadly—has largely given up concern for the conscience of lawyers. One of the first small cases I worked on involved a young husband and father who made a life-insurance claim on a policy insuring his recently dead wife. She died of cancer. The insurance policy was a group policy, insuring the employees of a factory; it had a thirty-day claim clause. That is, the beneficiary had to let the insurance company (our client) know, within thirty days, of the insured person's death. And this young husband and father had not done that. I was asked to determine whether the company could avoid the claim; and the answer the law gave was that it could.

I was working under the guidance of a partner. That is the way the law-firm-as-profession functions in modern America, in teams, and usually in hierarchical teams that are like the medical services

Bosk and Carlton described in the teaching hospital. I reported my findings to the partner, and added that I thought it would be bad (my phrase was "pretty crappy") for the company to deny the claim, even if the law let them do it. He agreed with me and said we should advise our client, the insurance company, of what the law said, and say that we thought the company should pay the claim. If they did not pay the claim, he said, our law firm would consider whether it should continue to represent that company. He was the lawyer who relayed our advice to the insurance company, and I suspect he did not hint at what we might do if they denied the claim. (That point was for my benefit.) In any event, the company paid the claim. An early lesson of my law practice was that business clients follow the moral advice of their lawyers.

The first large job I had involved President Kennedy's executive order on equal employment opportunity. This (1961 and 1962) was before the days of modern federal civil rights legislation. There was no clear federal law prohibiting racial discrimination in employment, and our clients in several parts of the country maintained racially segregated factories. One of our best clients had factories that were segregated according to the procedures of the Old South—separate jobs, separate areas of work, separate rest rooms, separate cafeterias. That corporate client, through its secretary, wanted to know what President Kennedy's order would require of it. The client was one we gave especially good service to. It had become large enough to have set up its own internal legal department, but had not taken that step, and we, of course, did not want it to take that step. We acted, and were happy to act, as if we were the internal legal department, and we thought we did a better job than an "in-house" set of lawyers could have done. There was folklore in the firm that said one of our senior partners had got up from a treatment table in the hospital to take a phone call involving this client's business. We young lawyers heard and heeded the lessons in that sort of folklore. In our youthful skepticism, though, we gave the lessons an economic, rather than a moral, explanation.

President Kennedy's executive order required that government contractors integrate their work forces. It bore most directly on contractors that sold to the federal government. Our client had virtually no business with the federal government. If the executive order was inconvenient for it, it could drop the government business without serious harm. But the order also had provisions covering second and third and fourth tier government contractors—companies that sold to companies that sold to the government, and so on. The regulations grew weaker as the chain grew longer. Our client, which did business mostly in the third or fourth link of the chain, was required to do little integrating, and even then it was unlikely that the regulations would be enforced on a company that was so peripheral to the federal enterprise. It was unlikely, really, that President Kennedy and his advisors had companies like our client in mind. The "bottom line," as we came later to call terse conclusions in business, was that our client had to do nothing.

I reported this in elaborate detail to the partner I worked under. He heard me out, asked some questions, and said he understood. He said he would call the corporate secretary of our client, who had referred the question to us, and asked me to stay in his office while he did that—on a "squawk box" telephone that would allow me to join in the conversation from across the partner's desk. I sat there while the partner and the secretary and I worked through my arcane analysis, and they came to understand that the law was not a threat to our client's segregated factories.

The secretary said, at the end of all this, "Well, what do you think we ought to do?" My senior in the practice of law said, "Oh, I don't think there's much doubt about what you ought to do; I think you ought to integrate those factories." The secretary said, "All right," and hung up his telephone. I did some other work for this client, at its factories in the South, about a year later. They were well into the integration of the factories, and well into the social, political, and business turmoil that accompanied such decisions in 1962.

Those two stories involved two different partners in the firm—men who were philosophically and temperamentally different and who practiced law in different ways. That they were so much alike in these moral matters said something about their personal character, of course, but, because of their personal differences, it also said something about the way the firm practiced law—about the way the firm functioned as the profession (for me) and, as the profession, functioned (for me) as a moral teacher. It was not, that is, an apprenticeship, in which I was learning my craft, and the morals of my craft, from a master—or at least it didn't seem then that it was. It was the profession (the law firm) that was the moral teacher. There was a consensus at work within the profession (the law firm) that was somewhat like the professional code as Lydgate and Graham experienced it. Except that it wasn't a code; it wasn't explicated as a code. It was in some ways like a covenant (as that term is used in Jewish and Calvinist theology). It was even more like the moral formation a person gets from family, town, and church. Which is to say that, here, code depended on character.

One of the jobs young lawyers in big firms get is the job of searching through the files of corporate clients for documents that somebody wants. The somebody is often the other side in an antitrust action—either a civil plaintiff who has demanded the client's documents under discovery procedures, or a criminal-justice or administrative authority seeking ammunition for an indictment or a punitive administrative order. I spent many tedious weeks going though file cabinets in corporate offices to comply with such orders. I think our law firm's theory was that it was worth the cost to the client to have a lawyer who understood generally what was in the files and who could report to the court or administrative agency that a lawyer had selected the papers it wanted.

These were also the days when one or two federal district judges were sending corporate executives to jail for violations of the federal antitrust laws. There had been several cases (my memory says they were in Michigan) in the news at that time. I was asked to go through a corporate client's files in response to a subpoena from a federal antitrust grand jury. I was doing this alone, but under the guidance of a partner, a third partner, not one of those I worked for in the insurance-company or segregated-factory cases. After a couple of weeks at it, I had assembled a formidable, ominous pile of papers for the grand jury and I had two sales executives passing by the desk I was using, several times a day, looking at that pile and asking me how I was doing. They were worried. I reported to the partner that they were worried, and he did three things.

First, he gave his attention to the worried executives. He asked me to invite those two businessmen to come in and talk to him—which I did. They came in on a Saturday morning and they and I sat with the partner for most of an hour. When they left, they were a lot less worried, even though he didn't give them any assurances about what was going to happen to them or to their company. We say that such lawyers have "good bedside manner," but I have found since that it is the rarest and likely the most valuable of all skills for lawyers who see worried people—as business lawyers often do—and I have tried to write and talk about it, at tedious length, for students. I wish I had that bedside skill, and, even more, I wish I knew how to teach it.

Second, he suggested that I bring the incriminating documents into the law office as I gathered them, rather than leaving them on the desk in the client's offices. "You never know when a fire might break out or something," he said—with a wink. And, third, he told me a story to guide me in a later step in this file-search process, the step in which we lawyers would compare the language of the subpoena with the papers we had (incriminating papers, by hypothesis) and see which ones we had to turn in. He said he and another partner in the firm, when they were young lawyers, had a job like mine. The day came for them, as it would for me, when they sat down at a conference table in the law office to go through the incriminating papers and decide which ones had to go in. One of these papers, he said, was particularly damning; it was hard for them to see how the client could avoid serious trouble if that paper went in. It was not a paper that would have been missed by the prosecutors; it should not have been filed in the first place. (This is true of most such incriminating papers; they tend to have scrawled on them, at the top, "Destroy this.") There was, near the conference table, a wastebasket. Either lawyer could have disposed of his client's trouble with a flick of his finger. My mentor said he looked at the other lawyer, and the other lawyer at him, and each understood what the other was thinking, and then they silently agreed on what they should do, and they put that incriminating paper in the pile that had to go in.

Does the profession still appear that way to young lawyers entering it in law firms? (It has been fewer than twenty-five years since these things happened to me, less than a generation.) I have talked to friends in and out of teaching who are in or are newly arrived from large law firms—firms that would find it difficult to function as my firm did, by reason of differences in size. Some of them are now approaching a thousand lawyers; my firm had fewer than fifty. My friends say that law firms do, by and large, function in the ways I discovered—as profession and as moral teacher—although, they say, the group in which that function occurs may not be the firm any more. It may be a department in a firm, or some other working team of lawyers within a firm, who are together intensely and frequently.

I hope my friends are right; not all the evidence says they are. Others of my friends say that competition, shopping for lawyers by corporate clients, and, perhaps, more ambiguous forms of moral entropy, make my stories from the sixties sound quaint.

In James B. Stewart's recent study of large law firms, *The Partners* (1983), there is little evidence of what I found—and Stewart is an acute observer. His picture of the associate in a large firm is the picture of a lawyer who feels exploited by an amoral if not corrupt institution. The young lawyer is a person who at first thinks she or he is overworked and well paid and then comes to realize that, however well paid, the young lawyer makes much more money for older lawyers than he makes for himself. The older lawyers take the credit for what the younger lawyers do. One, who left to become an in-house corporate lawyer, said "you had to wait 25 years to get a real share of the money. . . . Where was my pot at the end of the rainbow?" He did not seem to have any significant personal relationship with the partner he worked for—and therefore there was no significant possibility of moral influence from elder to younger. If Stewart is right, and the moral influence I claim to have found is disappearing in law firms, my memory of it is still fresh enough, and my hope for it clear enough, that I am willing to say it will show up again, somewhere.

Louis Auchincloss describes what I found in *The Great World and Timothy Colt* (1960), a novel that was once used by interviewers in Wall Street law firms to acquaint law students with the world of big-firm, urban practice. In that novel, the firm claims collective, organic moral character. This moral character is described as "the ideals of old Mr. Sheffield," named for an elderly partner whose years in the practice reach back to the firm's earliest days. These ideals carry a certain grandness of style, the sort of thing that shows up in the tasteful furnishings and the restrained elegance in discourse that are familiar to anyone who has dealt with an old Wall Street firm.

In Auchincloss's case the firm was Sullivan and Cromwell: "A visitor had the impression of wandering through the bright, clean avenues of an ordered city. . . . The whole great hushed interior, with its hum of muted typewriters, its discreet scurrying of office boys and the distant, silvery bong of the endlessly repeated autocall, summoning the absent to their telephones, gave an impression of efficiency but not, as in some firms, of an efficiency that was ruthless or even harsh."

Our firm had an autocall, too; it sounded like the door bells I heard when I was a boy, in houses of the well-to-do. The autocall meant that no one was summoned by a human voice; the tone of the office was restrained civility. We weren't allowed to come into the halls without our suit jackets on. (There were no women lawyers there.) The main waiting room was paneled in dark wood and had a white marble bust of George Washington over leather-bound copies of the *English Reports.* "If things were neat and ordered, they were still not over-regimented. . . . Oh, we can be grand, if it's grandness you want, the long corridors seemed . . . to echo, but who are *you* to want it?"

I first read that novel when I was in law school. It was probably part of what made it possible for a poor boy from rural Colorado to think about joining a large urban law firm. I read it again years after I had left the practice to become a teacher, and what I decided then was that it was no accident that my firm had an elegant style; a tradition of and insistence on careful, thorough work; and the moral teaching authority I had learned from when I was a lawyer there. It was no accident. It was the result of the influence of a moral spokesman, a mentor, a contemporary, specific, and influential person.

In Auchincloss's story the person was Henry Knox, a regal figure with white hair, an expert on securities law, the son and grandson of

Calvinist clergymen. Old New York gave him his manners, his style, and many of his clients; his family and religious tradition gave him his morals; and an amiable and finally paternal concern, coupled with years of astute law-firm politics, gave him his influence. Most law firms have such a person in their hierarchy, and those that don't have such a person tend to disintegrate over quarrels such as Sir Thomas Percival found in the Manchester Infirmary—fees, turf, division of profits, selection of employees. The essential difference for present purposes is that the firms that have a moral leader function, as my firm and Henry Knox's did, as moral teachers for young lawyers. Law firms have become, as a result of the implacable forces of history, I guess, the profession. As the profession they may or may not be moral teachers, but most of them are, I think, moral teachers. Still. Even now. Those of us who have hope for legal ethics in the United States had best depend on them, if only because there is no one else to depend on.

Our firm's Henry Knox was a grand old Hoosier lawyer named Kurt F. Pantzer. When I read the Auchincloss novel the second time I thought of Mr. Pantzer. He had been a founder of the firm; he presided at weekly firm meetings (elegant affairs held in a dining room at his club). He talked to us about the firm's public responsibility and its high standards of professional service. He conducted evening sessions on legal skills—sessions to which he sometimes invited other denizens of the law, such as the late Professor Karl Llewellyn. He selected the art for the hallways in the firm's offices, which included handsomely framed etchings of each of Indiana's ninety-some county courthouses. It was he who decided that the firm's new conference room should be paneled in sycamore (as in "Back Home Again in Indiana"). And it was he, I think, who symbolized for the firm both its style and its moral tone. Both Knox's firm and the one I worked for have now passed into other hands. Mr. Pantzer's will soon be a hidden life. He rests in an unvisited tomb. I don't know who sets the moral tone now. I doubt that she or he is as good at it as Mr. Pantzer was.

What Henry Knox had done (and what Mr. Pantzer may have done—I don't know), was to seize control of the law firm, at a turbulent and propitious time, with the force of his personal leadership—his charisma, as we say of a president who is a movie actor—*and* with a coherent moral claim. The moral claim in Knox's case was that lawyers are in practice to serve clients and to serve the public interest. Serving clients means competence and diligence, as I found out in the cases I have described, and it means moral leadership—the sort of moral leadership I saw exhibited in the cases I worked on. In those cases I was working with lawyers who had learned their craft, and how to practice it, from Mr. Pantzer.

As a tactic in closed politics, Henry Knox's claim (coupled with his personality) had been successful for Knox and he had continued to use it to maintain control of the firm for some twenty years before Timothy Colt came from law school. It was a claim Knox appeared to take seriously, after it had been successful for him in firm politics, and therefore—because he took it seriously—it gave him something to use when he became the mentor of younger lawyers. His use of it gave these younger lawyers a sense of purpose in their practice of law, and it also enlisted them among those who supported Knox's continued leadership.

As Auchincloss described it, and as he and I both experienced it, this was (and perhaps is) the way a law firm *is* the profession and, as such, the way it carries out the profession's office as moral teacher. Similar dynamics take place in medical residencies of the sort Bosk and Carlton describe; they are evident among the doctors, young and old, on "St. Elsewhere." And, I suspect, the medical profession as moral teacher tends to be personified in attending physicians in residency programs, and then, beyond personification, their style tends to become the ethos of a place, of a group of professionals, of a collectivity that uses monastic or familial or military metaphors to describe itself. Mr. Pantzer called us "the collegium." We chuckled over that—when he wasn't looking—but we liked it, too, and I think we all remember it.

Failure to Teach

Professions fail as moral teachers. They fail at least as often as other moral teachers, and probably oftener. This was part of the story in *Middlemarch,* and part of the fate of the professional moral instruction that came to the doctors of Manchester from Sir Thomas Percival. It was certainly true of the legal profession in late nineteenth-century America. By Durkheim's (and Michael Schudson's) account, what had happened was that morals in big business, and by that I mean the broad political and economic enterprise that set out to exploit the resources of the North American continent, had come to separate the making of profit from the making of character. Durkheim described this as the development of a "market morality." Nancy Woloch suggests it came about because the advertent and focused part of moral formation was assigned to the "woman's sphere," turned over almost exclusively to women (mothers), so that those who *manned* the machinery of exploiting North America were able to ignore moral education, as not part of *their* sphere.

However this happened in business, it happened in the legal profession derivatively, as those who were exploiting North America found they needed legal help—both because their business behavior got them into trouble and because the legal forms for transactions, for raising money, and for insulating commercial behavior from the influence of government were not adequate to what the business barons wanted to do. And this, of course, produced a professional moral agenda: On what terms would lawyers be enlisted in the business enterprise?

This way of describing the chain of events is, of course, wrong. Lawyers were naturally involved in the behavior that raised the issue for lawyers. But my inaccuracy makes it possible to state the issue the way, I think, it arose. That is, complicity with the robber barons became an issue for the *organized* legal profession in such a way as to account not only for the moral issue and the answer to the moral issue, but also for the existence of the organizations that considered the issue and formulated principles to deal with it. Until this issue about complicity became prominent, there was not an organized legal profession in anything like the sense in which lawyers talk about the organized bar today. Bar associations were formed around the issue of what bar associations should say about the lawyers who both formed the bar associations and served the robber barons.

Until the issue of complicity with rapacious business surfaced, two things were true about the legal profession in America: (1) it was almost *un*organized, more like the medical profession in Middlemarch than like the bar associations I met when I became a Hoosier lawyer in 1961; and (2) the general position among vocal American lawyers (who, in such a professional world, were the profession as moral teacher) was "republican"; that is, a lawyer felt himself responsible for what his clients did with his advice and assistance. After the change I am describing, those who referred to the legal profession in America usually meant, one, some, or all of the bar associations, and two, lawyers in America proclaimed the adversary ethic, our version of market morality, which said that probity in business was not the responsibility of the lawyers who were employed to advise and represent business.

"The Bar" in America did not have a clear corporate existence until it defined itself as not responsible for what clients do. Until then it was more like a neighborhood than a company or a fraternal organization. The legal profession as Judge Sharswood knew it was like the medical profession in Middlemarch. Lawyers did not claim or exercise the power of a fictional person. The moment in which the profession began to exercise the power of a fictional person was also the moment in which it formulated moral answers based more in the market than in the professional tradition. Such moral answers were, from the first creation of modern bar associations, inadequate. The bar association was, from the first, a compromised moral teacher. The persistence or appearance of less corporate, more organic professional moral teachers was to be expected, because lawyers, or most lawyers, were better people than their associations expected them to be. Bar associations and medical societies do not have hidden virtuous lives. They do not rest in unvisited tombs. They do not rest in tombs at all; they do not rest at all. But neighborhoods and families have hidden lives; they have forebears who rest in unvisited tombs. The profession in its modern manifestation separates code and character. The profession in its old, organic sense, which did not separate code from character, showed its moral self more in associations like neighborhoods than in corporate associations that commissioned rules of professional conduct.

· § ·

I speak, then, for the rest of this chapter, as if the term "profession" refers more to the association that is like a neighborhood than like a bar association or a medical society—more like Middlemarch than the AMA.

The failure of a profession to be a moral teacher seems to show up in one of two ways—as a failure to aspire and as self-deception. James Stewart's description of large law firms in America is the description of moral teachers who fail to aspire, as is Edward Tivnan's melancholy story of the demise of the large New York City law firm of Marshall, Bratter, Greene, Allison, and Tucker. These are stories of organizations of people who work together intensely but who suffer under the moral dispensations that the market morality gave them. Their coming together is a set of trade negotiations. And sometimes considerations of trade and political power so dominate the lives of those in the profession that their common enterprise falls apart, as the law firm did in this story Mr. Tivnan told, and as the medical profession sometimes seemed about to do in William Carlos Williams's account of his life as a young doctor. But that disintegration is not the ordinary result of the collective failure to aspire; the ordinary result is survival, as Stewart's book describes it and as it appears in Auchincloss's novel about Knox's law firm. The stories that Stewart tells are banal stories; they don't describe even the whimpering disintegration that Tivnan's story shows. And they don't have the remembered story of decline and moral rescue that Knox's story had.

In any event, the first failure one finds in professional stories is the story in which the profession fails to aspire. My point about it is that usually the profession survives in such stories, and, if you are hopeful, it waits for a moral renewal—as Israel waited for the prophets—and, meanwhile, it is still able to be a moral teacher. Its failure to aspire is continuous. It fails every day. I suspect that is about the situation many law firms in the United States are in today.

The other way the profession fails to be a moral teacher is in self-deception. These professionals do not fail to aspire—they make grand, collective, moral claims, but they deceive themselves. George Bernard Shaw described the medical profession in such a state in his play *The Doctor's Dilemma.* You hear a profession preening itself in this way annually, on Law Day, in the United States. It is not that lawyers don't mean it when they talk at luncheons and citizenship ceremonies about the rule of law and principles of equality. It is not even that they choose to be unfaithful to these grand moral claims. It is not that they are hypocrites. It is that they deceive themselves.

Williams and Arrowsmith

Failure to aspire and self-deception are losses of the connection between code and character. The difference between them is the difference between the hospital staff that William Carlos Williams described from his internship at Nursery and Child's Hospital in Hell's Kitchen and the medical elders Sinclair Lewis described, from about the same time and in the same country, in his novel *Arrowsmith.*

Williams describes the failure to aspire. He did his internship in a hospital for poor children and poor pregnant women. That hospital, in the 1930s in New York, and the hospital Lydgate presided over in Middlemarch, were mostly alike; the difference between them was the discovery of sanitation. Because of asepsis, there was a chance that Williams's patients could stay in the hospital for a while and survive. But Williams's hospital was otherwise a miserable and professionally neglected place, the sort of place in which an intern could, as Williams did, become the resident surgeon while he was an intern. Williams found that one job of the resident surgeon was to certify to the public authorities how many patients the hospital had and how long each of them stayed.

"The hospital . . . was in part state-supported, though it had its separate Board of Governors, headed by one of the most distinguished figures in Wall Street banking circles. Each month we received funds from Albany commensurate with the admissions and discharges for that month." His job was to take treatment statistics from the hospital administrator, copy them on to Albany's form, and sign the form. With a stubborn and youthful integrity reminiscent of Lydgate's, Williams refused to accept the administrator's figures; he wanted to see the admission and discharge records, which were on blue and salmon cards. The administrator wouldn't let Williams see the cards and Williams wouldn't sign the form without them. "So the report went to Albany without my signature. Then all hell broke out. . . . But my back was up and there it was to stay. . . . The doctors took their turn. They were some of the leading men in the East. . . . Kerley was one of the worst, all this at a bad time for me because Kerley had asked me what I intended to do after I had finished at Nursery and Child's. When I told him that I had no plans, he asked me if I would not come into his office for the first year. What an opportunity! A New York specialist. I was practically made, I thought."

Kerley said to Williams, "Look . . . why don't you sign that report? This is just a routine matter. It's been going on for years. . . . Sign the damned thing and forget it."

"Williams, we all like you in this place," another doctor said. "Your work has been excellent, outstanding. You have a brilliant future before you either in pediatrics or obstetrics. I know you're young and a stickler for your principles. But look, we doctors can't go against the business of an institution like this. Our business is to cure patients, not to worry over where the money comes from. You're actually doing everyone an injury by this eccentric conduct." He knew, as Kerley knew, and as Williams found out, how the administrator had the power to bring the enterprise to a standoff. The administrator was blackmailing the chairman of the hospital board, not because of fraud but because of an illicit sexual affair. It was a miserable situation, but not one that is unusual in stories about institutions. The point for present purposes is that the profession, as young Dr. Williams met it in Hell's Kitchen, did not aspire to the ordinary regularity that makes it possible to develop and support integrity in one of its young members.

"How can we afford to fight it? And with some of the leading specialists of New York too cowardly to back me, afraid of big money and what their stinking little hides might have to take for it. . . . I resigned. I didn't tell anyone about it, but I wrote a letter to the board giving them a piece of my mind and started to close up shop. . . . I didn't give a damn. I felt better in fact than I had felt in two months, unhappy as I must have been internally. I couldn't work with that gang any longer. . . . I packed and said good-bye and went home. . . . Not a single doctor of the attending staff had stood by me. To hell with them all, I thought." Williams went into his own practice in New Jersey, a practice among poor immigrant families. There was no further discussion of being a specialist in New York City. He opened his first office in his parents' house. He lived there a hidden life, and, but for the fact that he also wrote poetry, he would today rest in an unvisited tomb.

The elder doctors in Hell's Kitchen did not aspire. That was not true of the elder doctors in *Arrowsmith.* It was their aspiration that disgusted Sinclair Lewis, and that his doctor, Martin Arrowsmith, was repeatedly fooled by and then disgusted at. Arrowsmith's is a story of self-deception. He first went into practice in Wheatsylvania, his first wife's home town in the Midwest, in much the way Lydgate went to Middlemarch—full of scientific idealism, hopeful of caring for his patients and pursuing his science at the same time. He was driven from Wheatsylvania because he was as careless in what he said aloud as Lydgate was. Arrowsmith then went to work as a public-health administrator. He was the understudy of a flamboyant, political doctor who made speeches about the elimination of disease through public leadership. This was Dr. Almus Pickerbaugh, who "had the personal touchiness of most propagandists; he believed that because he was sincere, therefore his opinions must always be correct." It turned out that Dr. Pickerbaugh was interested only in politically popular diseases and in being elected to Congress.

Arrowsmith then retreated to science and joined the staff of the Rouncefield Clinic in Chicago, there to work as a pathologist, relatively unconcerned about the principles of healing on which the clinic claimed to operate. There he found, for the first time, prosperous professionals: "Men with limousines and social positions and the offensive briskness of the man who has numerous engagements, or the yet more offensive quietness of the person who is amused by his inferiors; master technicians, readers of papers at medical congresses . . . unafraid to operate before a hundred peering doctors, or to give well-bred and exceedingly final orders . . . never doubting themselves . . . men mature and wise and careful and blandly cordial." Martin's scientific mentor, Dr. Max Gottlieb, called such physicians "men of measured merriment." Arrowsmith's classmate, Dr. Angus Duer, was in training for this kind of eminence; he "would not fail to arrive precisely on time, precisely well dressed, absolutely sober, very cool, and appallingly unpleasant to any nurse who made a mistake or looked for a smile."

Arrowsmith later found a job with the McGurk Institute in New York, a scientific laboratory at which his teacher, Dr. Gottlieb, worked—a place where each medical scientist was free to pursue, for good pay, whatever he thought important. There Arrowsmith hoped to find the moral security of science; he even prayed for it. "God give me unclouded eyes and freedom from haste. God give me a quiet and relentless anger against all pretense and all pretentious work and all work left slack and unfinished. God give me a restlessness whereby I may neither sleep nor accept praise till my observed results equal my calculated results or in pious glee I discover and assault my error. God give me strength not to trust to God!" He said of a colleague that his moral integrity rested in his failure to be charming. "Stokes is hard—thank God!—and probably he's rude. Why not? He's fighting a world that bellows for fake charm. No scientist can go through his grind and not come out more or less rude."

What finally tripped Arrowsmith up was that this distinction between honest science and pretentious healing did not work. For all his contempt for the pretense of healers, he wanted to heal. He might even have ended up, as Williams did and as Lydgate did, in unpretentious healing. He might have been the sort of country doctor the dean of his medical school, "Dad" Silva, spoke about to his students—"physician . . . dentist . . . priest, divorce lawyer, blacksmith, chauffeur, and road engineer . . . out of sight of trolley line and beauty parlor." Arrowsmith didn't end up that way. The pretense of medical practice drove him from the promise of medical practice, and because he was duped by the pretense that science was without pretense. He had learned the lesson his profession taught him, about healing, so well that he could neither own up to it as Williams did, nor violate it as Lydgate did.

Working at McGurk, with the independence that had been promised to him, he came up with what he thought was a treatment for plague—a serum. And then plague broke out on a Caribbean island, St. Hubert's, and Martin went there to try out his serum. Before he left New York, science, and his scientific mentor and model, Dr. Gottlieb, demanded of him that he be a scientist and *not* a healer. If the serum was to be established scientifically, it had to be given to some patients and denied to others; both sets of patients had to be otherwise in the same condition; and those who did not receive the serum had to receive a placebo instead—and they had to be lied to. Martin could not deny treatment to sick people; he gave his serum to everyone who came to him. Then, because the institute demanded his support in making himself famous as both a heroic and a scientific doctor—in circumstances in which the moral choice was between being heroic and being scientific—he lied about his experimental procedures. (My friend Stanley Hauerwas would say that Arrowsmith never figured out the truth that healing is tragic.)

Arrowsmith's world was a world in which the profession failed as a moral teacher because it was self-deceived. Even the nearest moral hero in the story, Dr. Gottlieb, was self-deceived. He was duped into taking over the administration of the McGurk Institute, and was destroyed by the demands of that job and by his own abandonment of science; he ended up isolated, ill, and inactive. The reason the profession was not a moral teacher was that it was pretentious. Pretentious—that is, self-deceived—in both its healing and its science. Sinclair Lewis could not find a way for a profession not to be pretentious. He could not find a way for America not to be pretentious. He never found a neighborhood in America—and he was too clear-sighted to believe or to show how a self-deceived, pretentious group of people could be a source of morals.

The practice of science is as close as Martin Arrowsmith came to an unpretentious life, and that life was finally pathetic. He deserted his wife and their son, gave up all claim to being a healer, and went into the woods in Vermont to be alone with his scientific apparatus, an insular world that was "enchanting sometimes and tragic always." The difference between the profession Williams found in

Hell's Kitchen and the profession Arrowsmith found in small town, public-health clinic, and scientific institute, was that Williams's profession failed to aspire when it could have, and Arrowsmith's profession (in its science and in its healing) pretended to aspire and was not truthful.

I suspect that the difference between the failure to aspire and self-deception is one of tone and change and cycle more than a difference of category. What seems to happen to aggregations of professional people (clinics, law firms, and the organic grouping that occurred in Middlemarch), where people are doing the same work in the same place at the same time, is that failure of aspiration (Williams's slum hospital) becomes halting aspiration (Middlemarch and *Arrowsmith* when Martin first came to the McGurk Institute), becomes pretense and self-deception (Dr. Pickerbaugh's public-health office, and the modern American legal profession on Law Day), becomes something else, or starts all over again.

Auchincloss's law-firm stories show how this works, and how individual moral leaders fit into it and make it work. Henry Knox made a clear-headed moral claim in his firm at a time when it lacked leadership and had become unable to aspire to anything more than income. The firm listened to Knox and began to aspire. It gathered around Knox's claim, a claim about which Knox was serious and that he taught seriously to the young lawyers who come into the firm as his novices. And then, gradually, because of the demands his partners made on him for continued prosperity, and the pressures and satisfactions of eminence, which let him hide from the facts of his life, he no longer talked to his clients. He began to assume that he knew what their interests were.

Professional people do this, not so much because they are parental and think they know what is best for their clients, as because they assume that their clients do not want to be good. Knox came to a place where he still made the claims of his youth about serving clients, but hid from the truth that he was serving their worst instincts, and even serving instincts he imagined were in his clients when they weren't. "Your client wants to do something grasping and selfish. But quite within the law." Or you imagine that he does; or he says he does and you don't talk to him about it, as my mentors in the practice talked to their clients about insurance claims, segregated factories, and turning their incriminating memoranda over to the authorities. "As a lawyer you're not his conscience, are you? You advise him that he can do it. So he does it and tells his victim: 'My lawyer made me!' You're satisfied and so is he."

The Issue: Work

The more I have thought about this development, to and fro, in law firms, the more it has seemed to me that Auchincloss had it right when he made *work* the central moral issue in *The Great World and Timothy Colt.* The fact is that success in a profession requires lots of hard work. The moral issue between young and old—the central issue on the question of how (or how well) a law firm or a teaching hospital functions as a moral teacher—has to do with how it talks about work.

What does the profession (the teaching hospital or the law firm as profession) make of work? The religious tradition (which was alive in Knox's law firm and is alive in Dr. Mark Craig's "St. Elsewhere," because it was alive in Knox and is alive in Dr. Craig) teaches that work is a theatre for the glory of God. (That's John Calvin's image, but I find it in the rabbis, too, especially the Hasidic rabbis, and in other Christian traditions.) Work is service, or, better, servanthood. It is (as Milner S. Ball says law is, or should be) a medium, since the glory of God becomes clearer when you learn to love His creatures.

Often the religious tradition does not talk about work in metaphors at all. It uses the word servant, for example, advertently and literally. The religious tradition and Martin Arrowsmith and Timothy Colt are alike in this. Neither wants to locate a metaphor for work; both want to face work head on, on its own terms, seeing work for what it is. Arrowsmith wants to work as a scientist so literally that he rejects scientific metaphors for work as progress. Dr. Gottlieb tells him that the verb *succeed* "is a word that liddle schoolboys use at the University. . . . It means passing examinations." "The ultimate lesson of science . . . is to wait and doubt."

Timothy Colt said, "What makes a good lawyer is hard, digging work."

Arrowsmith and Colt thought there was a correlation between work and rudeness. In their lives the only human relationship that could be borne while a person worked was one of uncritical loyalty. Arrowsmith got uncritical loyalty from his first wife and he abandoned his second wife because she would not give it to him. Colt's experience with women was much the same; his wife Ann is the picture of a 1950s lawyer's wife.

"Pure" work, work without pretense, was as close as Sinclair Lewis could come to defining professional honesty, and loyalty was as close as he could come to defining virtue. "Angry, indignant . . . sick in his heart of the false standards of success, of the empty worship of pecuniary ambition and of the blatant, raucous monster that emerged from the pioneering efforts of his grandfathers on the various frontiers of American life," William Soskin says of Lewis, he "poured his wrath down upon the heads of his neighbors."

There is purity in such wrath; the purity probably explained Lewis's popularity in his own generation, as it might have explained the irreverent lawyer stories of Arthur Train (which I discuss in the next chapter). Whether the wrath is pure or not, it will not sustain aspiration; and it fails, even in Arrowsmith's story, to sustain the idealism that makes it possible for a profession—however conceived of—to be a moral teacher. When you have swept away the pretense, Lewis leaves you nothing to teach with.

Auchincloss is, by comparison, a poet. His Henry Knox developed metaphors for work. Timothy Colt was a tireless (and, as it turned out, compulsive) worker. Knox told himself that he admired this in Colt, and that Knox's support of Colt's tireless work was good for Colt and good for the law firm (i.e., the profession). Those claims showed up in the metaphor of art. What Colt did, his colleagues told him, was painting or a symphony. The problem with that metaphor is that the work-as-art is justified with its own integrity. If the metaphor is a truthful one, a good argument, a comprehensive trust agreement, or a creative charter for business stands on its own as something to be admired—and that is rarely a truthful view of such things. There is a certain, sound craftsmanship in legal work, as there is in medical work; but integrity rests on the effect of such work *in lives* and particularly in what it causes or encourages people who are not lawyers or doctors to do to one another. Art as a metaphor for work let Colt excuse himself for ignoring his clients. To the extent that Knox deceived himself with the art metaphor for work, he hid from his responsibility both for what Colt was doing to himself and his family and what he was doing or failing to do in the lives of his and Knox's business clients and their communities.

Knox and Colt were friends in and around all this work. They thought of that interpersonal dimension in metaphors for work that were like the ones other professional people use to justify their faithfulness to one another. Such intraprofessional metaphors justified such things as the ethical principles with which Sir Thomas Percival and the physicians and apothecaries of Middlemarch turned fee arrangements into a principled morality. The intraprofessional metaphors I am thinking about are those that describe the relationship among the members of a profession—things such as Mr. Pantzer's "collegium," or Percival's reference to the medical fraternity as a "corps," or almost any profession's tendency to define itself as a band of brothers and sisters.

Knox and Colt thought of their relationship with one another in words suggesting the keenest of these metaphors: they related to one another in *love,* the love of parent for child and child for parent. It is possible that love may not be a metaphor at all. Scriptural use of that word is not usually metaphorical. Theological use of it tends more to synonym and simile (love of God is like love of neighbor) and to analytical distinction than to metaphor—as, say, in C. S. Lewis's analysis of love as the erotic, the friendly, the affectionate, and the charitable.

Knox and Colt worked together in such a way that, whatever they made of their care for one another, they had to come to terms with work. And so they also used the word love, or (in their masculine world) some word meaning love, as a metaphor for work. The work that Colt did (tiresome days, weeks without weekends, years without vacations) was love—love for Knox. And the support that Knox gave Colt was not exploitation (as in Stewart's accounting of the gain that elder lawyers have from young lawyers in law firms) but love. Because it was love, it was good for Colt, good for Colt's family, good for clients, good for the community. It had to be. Whatever we may think of work, who can be against love?

Love as a metaphor for work fails because, as Colt's story shows, it is self-deceptive on the issue of what professionals do to their clients and in the community. Work as love of one professional for another is finally as solipsistic as art is. Love of professional colleagues for one another does not deal with the claim on which Knox's law-firm idealism rested—service to clients and responsibility in the community. Work as love hid from Knox the waning of the honest idealism he had once used to sustain the law firm, that brought Colt to the firm, that brought Knox to power in the firm, and that made it possible for the law firm, as the profession, to be a moral teacher.

Character before Code

The medical profession as Tertius Lydgate came on it in Middlemarch might not have been much of a moral teacher, but Lydgate did not find out whether it was or not. He rejected his profession as a moral teacher before he found out whether it was a moral teacher. He was, though, honest and virtuous and sharp enough to see that he needed moral teachers. He wanted them, as Arrowsmith and Colt did not. The second and more important half of Lydgate's story as a doctor is the story of his finding moral teachers—of his success at that, and of his moral success as a doctor because of it.

The story is an important one for people in the professions in modern America because—and to the extent that—our professions have failed as moral teachers. While we wait, as Israel waited for the prophets, for the professions to find their way back to a substantial claim to moral authority, we need stories such as Lydgate's. And that is because Lydgate found in the sources of character what he did not find in the profession. Because code depends on character, character could sustain him when code did not.

In Lydgate's story the young professional found his teachers within the moral culture that sustained and empowered both him and the profession. The moral culture of the community was a broader thing than the professional moral culture, but it had the same substance. Code depended on character. Lydgate found his moral teachers beneath his profession; he and his teachers and his profession were in concord with the morals of the town and the church, the families in the town and the families in the church. Lydgate is a creature of his dominant moral culture, and he is faithful to it, as George Eliot, for all of her irregularity, was a creature of the same culture, and was faithful to it. Lydgate might have found, within the dominant moral culture of Middlemarch, that his profession could be his teacher. He refused to do that—and perhaps that was a mistake—but his finding his teachers elsewhere in Middlemarch was not so much a turning away as it was a resort to the moral lessons his profession might have taught him if he had been willing to listen. Lydgate changed teachers; he didn't change lessons. The lessons were the same because in that world—Jane Austen's world—code depends on character.

Lydgate's trouble was a woman—the beautiful Rosamond Vincy, sister of the Fred Vincy whom Lydgate saved from typhoid fever. Lydgate and Rosamond nursed Fred together, and they fell in love. They got married sooner than was prudent for a couple in Jane Austen's rural England. Neither of them had money. Lydgate should not have married until he was better established as a doctor—not unless he married a woman with money. And Rosamond, by the standards of the marriage market, should have used her beauty to land a squire. These economic facts brought Lydgate's practice down, finally, because Rosamond was empty-headed and reckless with what little money Lydgate earned. Lydgate fell back on his banker and political ally Mr. Bulstrode, who had seen to Lydgate's appointment to the hospital and had thereby obtained Lydgate's support for the appointment of an evangelical clergyman as hospital chaplain. Mr. Bulstrode loaned him money, but he did it in circumstances that were public and that created the impression that Lydgate was in complicity with Mr. Bulstrode in killing a blackmailer named Raffles.

Bulstrode was a hypocrite with fervent and intolerant religious opinions and a dark past. He was being persecuted by Raffles.

Raffles finally showed up, ill, in Bulstrode's country house, and Lydgate was called in to treat him. Lydgate left instructions for Raffles's care, which Bulstrode connived to neglect, and Raffles died. This went on at the time Lydgate was borrowing money from Bulstrode—and, of course, there are no secrets in a small town. Bulstrode was so thoroughly disgraced that he had to leave, although his role in the death of Raffles was never established. Lydgate was left without money, in debt, with an impossibly rebellious wife and a great (though probably surmountable) obstacle to prosperity in his medical practice. He gave up his practice and moved to a seaside town, where he spent the rest of a short life treating the wealthy and writing a treatise on gout. These events follow an important theme in George Eliot's stories—that, as she put it, every limit is a beginning. The point of Lydgate's story turns, though, on the facts that Lydgate was a person of character who stayed with and supported his difficult wife, and that he was able to do so because his moral teachers in Middlemarch sustained his character and supported him in the difficulties of the virtuous life.

Lydgate's move from Middlemarch was necessary because Rosamond could not bear both the disgrace of Lydgate's association with Bulstrode and the continued poverty of his practice among the poor. He moved to a seaside practice to secure Rosamond's emotional and moral well being. He could, but for her, have worked out his professional life in Middlemarch. Marital endurance is conventional morality in nineteenth-century English stories. Scores of them show devoted wives surrendering all to stand by their caddish husbands. Lydgate's behavior was much like that of the husband in Trollope's novels about Plantagenet and Glencora Palliser. Glencora was the victim of an arranged marriage; she was forced to turn away from her (in the Victorian sense) lover when she married Plantagenet. But she continued to be in love with Burgo Fitzgerald—so much so that she nearly eloped with him to France. Plantagenet slowly understood this (Lydgate would have been quicker); but, when he did understand, he was heavily occupied in politics and about to become Chancellor of the Exchequer and to gain thereby the power he needed to achieve his dream of a decimal coinage for the United Kingdom. Despite such an important personal and professional agenda, when Plantagenet found out that Glencora's character was in peril, he dropped everything and took her to Europe to recover, which she did. As Lydgate, when he found out about everything, took Rosamond to the seaside, got patients who could pay him enough to support her, and confined his scientific research to an ailment of well-to-do men. In both stories the triumph is a triumph of character. In both the moral limit is a moral beginning. If code depends on character, both stories are stories of professional success.

In any case, in both stories, marital stability was conventional; divorce was conventionally unthinkable. Lydgate never thought of it. (Similar and roughly contemporary circumstances in Thomas Mann's story of Antonie Buddenbrook turned out differently. She went through two divorces and her daughter through one. But it did not happen that way in English stories.) Lydgate had to remain with Rosamond; the moral issue in the story is how he sustained his character in doing it. It is a case of virtue as living with the rules more than in obeying them. It is one of two issues I want to talk about. The other issue is how he continued to be a virtuous doctor.

W. J. Harvey, the editor of the modern edition of *Middlemarch*, says that Lydgate failed as a doctor. "His story is in large part the defeat of the man of the future by the stubborn conservatism of the present." That, I think, is wrong. Lydgate's moving to the seaside, treating the wealthy, and writing the treatise on gout is rather, in my view, an example of the limit as a beginning, and, since life is a thing of limits, his was a successful professional life. Lydgate was occasionally bitter about the way things turned out. He groaned under the burden. The moral lesson is that he bore this, not as a mandate but as a circumstance. It was a matter of leading a decent life. The inquiry is *how* he bore it.

It is important, I think, to read through the obvious political point that conventional marital faithfulness was, for an English gentleman such as Lydgate, the price men paid for their subjection of women in marriage. That, too, was a circumstance. There is some irony in Eliot's writing a story in which the husband is the victim of the circumstance, but, irony aside, the setting for the moral lesson in the story is that Lydgate accepted the price his generation of English husbands had agreed to pay.

My inquiry is how he went about paying the price—living through it—as a doctor. Eliot's conviction on that score, a principle she insisted on in her literature and in her life, is that the best chance any of us has for happiness lies in making others happy. She knew about the subjection of women and about the price a virtuous husband had occasionally to pay for the benefits of that subjection. What she insisted on was that a married person could pay that price, and pay it virtuously, and lead a useful life—in this case a useful professional life. It is just there that I think Harvey misunderstands the story; Lydgate did not fail as a doctor.

Eliot's memorial stone in Poets' Corner in Westminster Abbey says, "The first condition of human goodness is something to love: the second something to reverence." Phyllis Rose says of her, "She understood . . . thoroughly the failure of most people to see their lives as analogous to anyone else's . . . this was the greatest failure of the imagination." Lydgate was bound to stand by Rosamond; he would not otherwise have been Lydgate. That is almost a matter of course, although it is probably useful here to look at an American doctor story and notice that this sort of conventional faithfulness is exactly what the American doctor, Martin Arrowsmith, could *not* manage. He abandoned his wife.

The point of Eliot's story is not that conventional result, but in how Lydgate lives his limited life, both as a gentleman and as a doctor. Harvey's observation is wrong in that it leaves out the doctor part of the inquiry. And that includes the question of how he worked out a professional morality for himself.

I argue that Lydgate lived well, and lived well as a doctor, within the conventional morality that required him to remain with and support Rosamond (in all senses of support), and that the way he lived well was that he was virtuous (i.e., he had the habits or dispositions or moral skills that make it possible for a person to live with conventional rules), and that his virtue rested on his ability to learn from and be supported by the moral teachers he found and listened to in the entirely, tiresomely conventional world of Middlemarch. And then, I want to argue, his virtuous life, so lived, was successful professionally—that his locating moral teachers worked out for him professionally. I think this educational result occurred because of convention, because of friendship, and because of fraternity.

Convention. Lydgate came to Middlemarch trained in the morals of the English gentleman; and by that I mean that he had developed habits that were virtues, that he had habits that were just habits, and that he figured out the difference.

He was well bred and was therefore accustomed to comfort many of his patients never experienced. "He would have behaved perfectly at a table where the sauce was served in a jug with the handle off. . . . But it never occurred to him that he should live in any other than what he would have called an ordinary way, with green glasses for hock, and excellent waiting at table. . . . We may handle even extreme opinions with impunity while our furniture, our dinner-giving, and preference for armorial bearings in our own case, link us indissolubly with the established order. . . . [He] walked by hereditary habit." He had habits that were just habits. He didn't think much about them; but, as he was willing to be served from a jug with a handle off, he was able—and he did—sacrifice his comfort when there was a reason to do so.

On the other hand, Lydgate had an easy and even democratic approachability; he was not a haughty man. "That distinction of mind which belonged to his intellectual armor did not penetrate . . . the desirability of its being known (without his telling) that he was better born than other country surgeons." He did not flaunt his good taste. He tried to avoid community entanglements that would distract him from his work; he tried even to avoid being annoyed at popular opinion on his skill as a physician, "where danger was extreme, and when the smallest hope was worth a guinea." He was impetuous but he had the virtue of that tendency, a "chivalrous kindness which helped to make him morally lovable."

"I should never have been happy," he said to Rosamond, "in any profession that did not call forth the highest intellectual strain, and yet keep me in good warm contact with my neighbors. There is nothing like the medical profession for that: one can have the exclusive scientific life that touches the distance and befriend the old fogies in the parish too."

"He was an ardent fellow. . . . His ardor was absorbed in love of his work and in the ambition of making his life recognized as a factor in the better life of mankind—like other heroes of science who had nothing but an obscure country practice to begin with."

He was tolerant with the pretentious auctioneer, Mr. Turnbull, who wanted to appear before his neighbors as sophisticated about his own disease "by learning many new words which seemed suited to the dignity of his secretions." He taught Mr. Turnbull some medical terms to use for ammunition. The ordinary and important human connections were important to Lydgate, important enough that he had little theory of professional distance. He was willing to be a friend to his patients. He told people what was wrong with them. He responded to a patient's interest in plain speech, even to the point of referring to and explaining the state of medical research on the matter at hand.

The importance of this approachability is not bedside manner or Lydgate's consciousness that he needed to build a practice. The point is that maintaining conventional connections is how he learned to be truthful, and truthfulness is essential to virtue. The argument is, as another English novelist, Iris Murdoch, puts it, that *seeing* is a moral art; and seeing with our fellows is ordinarily how we see. Lydgate failed to do that with his professional elders, but he made up for the failure by *being with* his patients.

When the other principal character in this story, Dorothea Brooke, was widowed and wanted to live alone, the wonderfully ordinary Mrs. Cadwallader, wife of the vicar, gave her ordinary advice that incidentally says something about the spirit of Lydgate's practice of medicine in the seaside town. "We have all got to exert ourselves a little to keep sane, and call things by the same names as other people call them by," Mrs. Cadwallader said. "What a bore you might become yourself to your fellow-creatures if you were always playing tragedy queen and taking things sublimely. Sitting alone in that library at Lowick you may fancy yourself ruling the weather; you must get a few people round who wouldn't believe you if you told them."

The backdrop for this conventional moral world was the ethos of the English country gentleman. It was a moral world probably better described in Jane Austen's *Emma* than in this story, but it is clearly present here and important to the moral growth of Lydgate as a country doctor. " 'I do wish people would behave like gentlemen,' " said Sir James Chettam, "feeling that this was a simple and comprehensive programme for social well-being." The alliances one makes in such a world are habitual, routine, and human; they rarely come about from conscious political or economic design.

The country gentleman, for all of his faults, had an ability to detect falseness. Much of Dorothea Brooke's story involved the careful pretense and self-deception of her first husband, Edward Casaubon, who lived a life of such careful rectitude that he was not able to be fair even to the members of his own family. "He has got no red blood in his body," Sir James said. Casaubon saw himself as involved in a great scholarly work. Work for him, as for Timothy Colt, was art. "When a man has great studies and is writing a great work, he must of course give up seeing much of the world. How can he go about making acquaintances?" But Sir James understood, as Eliot says, that "there is no general doctrine which is not capable of eating out our morality if unchecked by the deep-seated habit of direct fellow-feeling with individual fellow-men." Arrowsmith and Colt never learned that lesson. Lydgate learned it in a conventional way, from conventional country gentlemen. Here is an example from the conventional Sir James.

The complexities of English law and Casaubon's will had it turn out that when Dorothea married a second time it was possible for Sir James to gain Casaubon's property and to thereby disinherit Dorothea's children. All that was needed was that Dorothea's uncle, Mr. Brooke, dock the entail on the property. That arcane but simple legal procedure by Mr. Brooke would have been flattering to Sir James, partly because Mr. Brooke's regard for him was important, and partly because Sir James disapproved of Dorothea's second marriage anyway—and it would have benefited Sir James's son. Sir James felt these emotions most strongly when Dorothea's uncle mentioned the prospect to him. "There was a stoppage in his throat; he even blushed," but his country gentleman's morals told him that this was an unacceptable emotion, and, when Mr. Brooke asked him for advice, Sir James said, "For my part, I would let that alone.

I would let things remain as they are." His disapproval of Dorothea's marriage was snobbish and inexcusable—but he would not take personal advantage of the fact that Mr. Brooke also disapproved of the marriage.

Lydgate lived in this world and he learned from it. These people were his patients and Dorothea became his friend. It was the world of what Disraeli called "muscular Christians," like Rosamond's father, Walter Vincy, who said he was "a plain Churchman. . . . I take the world as I find it, in trade and everything else. I'm contented to be no worse than my neighbors." But, as Mrs. Cadwallader showed in her unsolicited advice to Dorothea, convention contains and communicates wisdom. It harbors a surprising modesty underneath its pretensions, a modesty that makes it possible to respond to individual people—and that response was a necessary part of Lydgate's character, a part that the conventional moral world in which he worked supported him in better than Martin Arrowsmith's world would have. Mr. Brooke, a country magistrate, for example, endured criticism from his neighbors because he was not more severe in sentencing poachers. "You know, Chettam, when you are a magistrate," he replied, "you'll not find it so easy to commit. Severity is all very well, but it's a great deal easier when you've got somebody to do it for you. You have a soft place in your heart yourself, you know."

Friendship. The conventional moral teacher is not, however, the same thing as a friend. (I explore the difference at length in chapter 5.) Friendship in this story is rarer and more precious than the easy amiability that Lydgate has been brought up to and finds among country gentlefolk. Friendship is in this story a moral alliance. It is not an alliance toward autonomy, as it was for Colt and Arrowsmith, and as it was represented to be in the posters we used to see in the 1960s that said a friend is someone who leaves you with your freedom. Friendship in George Eliot's (as in Aristotle's) moral world is an alliance toward goodness. A friend is someone who supports you in the difficulties of living a virtuous life.

The principal friendship in *Middlemarch* was between Lydgate and Dorothea Brooke. Dorothea was a fiercely idealistic and evangelical Christian who, like Lydgate, made an unfortunate marriage (to Edward Casaubon). Lydgate was called in to treat Casaubon for what, as it turned out, was a terminal illness. Dorothea was left a wealthy widow, able to help support the hospital in Middlemarch and therefore to be a patron of Lydgate's professional practice. She was also his patient and she became his friend. When the days were darkest for Lydgate—impoverished by Rosamond's extravagance, disgraced by the gossip about Raffles's strange death, disapproved of by his professional colleagues—he turned to Dorothea. She was the only person in Middlemarch who penetrated his pride enough to hear him describe his troubles. She stood by him in his decision to risk his professional dream in faithfulness to his wife—not so much in making the decision, which was a matter of course, but in having the character to live with the decision, and to live with it as a doctor.

Lydgate had thought, early in his difficulties with Rosamond, that his profession would sustain him. "He tossed his head and thrust his hands deep into his pockets with a sort of vengeance. There was still science—there were still good objects to work for. He must give a tug still—and the stronger because other satisfactions were going." He had thought, as Edward Casaubon did, that he could turn away from other people and find comfort in his work; and he did not talk to anybody, then, about his troubles. But Dorothea heard of his troubles and asked him to come to Lowick and talk to her. There was, of course, a polite "cover" for this visit; she asked him to come and talk to her about financial matters at the hospital. This was conventional; convention and friendship are not the same, but in a good story they work together.

It turned out, as Dorothea foresaw it would, that Lydgate came to Lowick to make a friend. "Lydgate turned, remembering where he was, and saw Dorothea's face looking up at him with a sweet trustful gravity. The presence of a noble nature, generous in its wishes, ardent in its charity, changes the lights for us: we begin to see things again in their larger, quieter masses, and to believe that we too can be seen and judged in the wholeness of our character. That influence was beginning to act on Lydgate, who had for many days been seeing all life as one who is dragged and struggling amid the throng. He sat down again, and felt that he was recovering his old self in the consciousness that he was with one who believed in it." The friend here is not one who buttresses freedom—freedom is assumed—but one who buttresses goodness.

"He gave himself up, for the first time in his life, to the exquisite sense of leaning entirely on a generous sympathy, without any check of proud reserve. And he told her everything." What Lydgate found at Lowick, Eliot said, was "an equivalent center of self." He got back a calm awareness of his own character, which, simply because of who he was, could not sustain the lonely life Casaubon had imposed on himself, that Colt and Arrowsmith tried and failed at. With the support of this friend, Lydgate could bear the limit that faithfulness put on his life as a doctor and could make of that limit a beginning. In that way, his practice of medicine at the seaside was a professional fulfillment, because profession cannot be fulfilled unless character is fulfilled.

Dorothea taught Lydgate how to live with conventional morals, partly by being an empathic listener, but mostly by being the virtuous person she was. (Or, better, her empathy was a virtue, the virtue of friendship, rather than a technique.) "She seems to have what I never saw in any woman before—a fountain of friendship toward men—a man can make a friend of her." They were not lovers. Few novelists of Eliot's day could have described a relationship between a virile man and a beautiful woman as friendly love and not erotic love; but Eliot is insistent on the difference. It occurred to Lydgate that Dorothea would, when she married again, make her new husband her friend. "Her love might help a man more than her money," he said. But even that point was part of her being a good moral teacher—a good moral teacher because she was a friend. Dorothea had lived well within the conventional marital life her society gave her, with her unfortunate first husband, Casaubon; and she lived well again in a second conventional marriage, with Will Ladislaw. She was a Victorian woman, and marriage was the only profession available to her. But she lived faithfully in her hidden life, and she was therefore able to help Lydgate live faithfully in his hidden life. Because of such people things have been not so ill with us as they might have been.

The moral lessons from this friend as a moral teacher were the importance of holding onto oneself in a conventional professional world, and the consequent importance of maintaining a connection with the past, of putting one's life together, of being constant. Lydgate figured out at Lowick that he had to be who he was, to be faithful to his own character, and that that was a lot *more* than being free. Dorothea helped him do it. It may be possible to state this in several ethical propositions:

Wit is subject to character. Dorothea was an intelligent woman and was attracted to Edward Casaubon because she thought of him as engaged in a great scholarly project, a project in which she could be helpful. "It would be a great mistake to suppose that Dorothea would have cared about any share in Mr. Casaubon's learning as mere accomplishment; for though opinion in the neighborhood pronounced her clever, that epithet would not have described her to circles in whose more precise vocabulary cleverness implies mere aptitude for knowing and doing, apart from character." Dorothea had the ability a professional career would have required, but the limits put on women in her conventional world denied to her any profession except marriage. The moral trick was to live in that world without being destroyed by it, as a merely clever woman might have been. She shows our modern and liberated generation how much we owe to our grandmothers.

The virtues are products of training. "In marriage"—in Dorothea's marriage and therefore, by virtue of her being Lydgate's teacher, in Lydgate's marriage—"the certainty, 'She will never love me much,' is easier to bear than the fear, 'I shall love her no more.' " Love here is not a metaphor or a means, as it was for Henry Knox and Timothy Colt. Dorothea and Lydgate are people who learn to be skillful at loving.

Faithfulness depends on integrity. As long as Casaubon was alive, and more intensely as he grew more ill, Dorothea was devoted to his scholarly work, even though she had come to see it as a useless pretense. But she did not promise him that she would continue it after his death, and, despite his clear wish that she do so, she did not. By definition, faithfulness cannot require a loss of self; only a self can be faithful. Lydgate was Dorothea's doctor as she went through this refusal, and he learned from her. That is why he could not let himself stop loving Rosamond; if he did that, he could not be faithful and be himself, and if he could not be himself he could not be faithful. Faithfulness is not a matter of being *right;* it is a matter of being *good.*

Character is the product of effort among people. It ebbs and flows, of course, as success in training always does. "The painful struggle to break free from the prison of egoism into a life of sympathy," the discovery of "an equivalent center of self whence the lights and shadows must always fall with a certain difference," that is, friendship, was the means, in this story, for training in character. "Character is not cut in marble," the parson, Camden Farebrother, told Lydgate. "It is something living and changing, and may become diseased as our bodies do." It needs other people, particularly those who are nearby. "People glorify all sorts of bravery," Dorothea said, "except the bravery that they might show on behalf of their nearest neighbors." Lydgate tried for the rest of his life to build this sort of friendship with Rosamond. He failed to do it, but his trying was the necessary means for maintaining his own character, and the means as well, I think, for his maintaining his morals as a doctor.

Memory preserves and revives character. Memory as a way to maintain the self over time is shown most poignantly in this story in the sad fate of Lydgate's sometime political ally, the banker Mr. Bulstrode. Bulstrode had a dark and shameful past, the facts of which were the basis of Raffles's blackmail. Bulstrode conspired to defeat Raffles and to preserve his rectitude as an evangelical Christian, even to the point of (at best) allowing Raffles to die when Raffles was under his care. Bulstrode came to such disgrace that he had to leave Middlemarch, but his story (in a way like Lydgate's story) was at last an acceptance of who he was, by a recognition of the importance of remembering who he had been. "Even without memory, the life is bound into one by a zone of dependence in growth and decay: but intense memory forces a man to own his blameworthy past. With memory set smarting like a reopened wound, a man's past is not simply a dead history, an outworn preparation of the present: it is not a repented error shaken loose from the life: it is a still quivering part of himself, bringing shudders and bitter flavours and the tinglings of a merited shame." Connecting with the past in this way made it possible for Bulstrode to be just at last to those he had wronged, and even to be generous. He left Middlemarch with the possibility that his limit might be a beginning, too. His presence in Lydgate's story helps us students of Eliot understand how Lydgate's professional life at the seaside was fashioned out of the reality of his life with Rosamond, and the fact that his being true to himself meant being faithful to her. The importance of this for his life as a doctor is that the fulfillment of his professional life could not be broader than the fulfillment of his life at home. (Cooper translates Aristotle so that the word for this is "flourishing"; see chapter 5.) It seems an obvious lesson, but it is not one that Martin Arrowsmith could understand. It is a lesson Timothy Colt learned only through bitterness much greater than Lydgate's, and it is a lesson that even Henry Knox too often neglected as he got older.

Fraternity. The profession as moral teacher expects that a practitioner will make friends among his professional colleagues. (The traditional word, hidden in the Latin, is stronger than friends; it is *brothers.*) When this idea is advanced in professional ethics, rhetoric usually connects professional fraternity with public good. No doubt that connection was present when Middlemarch's medical fraternity offered to be Lydgate's moral teacher. (It was clear in Percival's medical ethic.) Lydgate rejected the offer, but, in my reading, he nonetheless learned the fraternal lessons he might have learned from the Middlemarch doctors. Again, the story is important to us who labor with (or as) weakened professional teachers. Lydgate rejected his profession as moral teacher but he located an alternative fraternity—a fraternity shown to him by Camden Farebrother, a parish priest.

Farebrother was a bachelor by circumstance—his small income and the need to support his mother, his aunt, and his sister. He was a professional man whose limit had been a beginning. He was so chronically short of money that he had taken to playing whist and billiards, and playing well, and gambling on his skill, to supplement his income. Lydgate learned many professional lessons from Farebrother, among which two seem to me illustrative—the importance of self-denial (a routine and almost definitional professional lesson) and the importance of integrity. The latter lesson is similar to the lesson Lydgate learned from Dorothea Brooke, but Lydgate's association with Camden Farebrother gave the lesson a professional focus. Farebrother supported Lydgate in the appointment to be physician to the hospital. Farebrother then became a candidate, along with the evangelical clergyman Mr. Tyke, for the post of chaplain at the hospital. Farebrother could probably have given up whist and billiards if he had gained the income from the chaplain's post; he therefore wanted the job. But Lydgate owed a political debt to Bulstrode, and Mr. Tyke was Bulstrode's candidate to be chaplain. Lydgate paid his debt and voted for Mr. Tyke, who won. Farebrother forgave Lydgate that bit of ingratitude—even forgave in advance, which is the hardest way to forgive. That was what first attracted Lydgate to Farebrother and made Farebrother his professional (fraternal) teacher.

The next lesson Lydgate got from Farebrother was to avoid any further alliance with Bulstrode. "Don't get tied," Farebrother said. In this, Farebrother showed how the best professional counsel is personal, but that the personal is trustworthy only if a person is truthful about what it is. Farebrother admitted that his only reason for giving the advice was intuitive, and might have been colored by his distrust of evangelicals. "Perhaps it seems like personal feeling in me to say so—and there's a good deal of that, I own—but personal feeling is not always in the wrong if you boil it down to the impressions which make it simply an opinion."

In a similar and poignant way, Farebrother warned Lydgate off gambling. "Try and keep clear of wanting small sums that you haven't got," he said. "I am perhaps talking rather superficially, but a man likes to assume superiority over himself, by holding up his bad example and sermonizing on it." Lydgate lived to regret not taking these pieces of advice on alliances and gambling, of course. The deeper lesson in professional morals is that he learned a bit about being honest with himself. That lesson might have come differently if he had accepted his own professional elders as his fraternity—Percival set great store by a physician's ability to assess the effects of his treatment after a case was concluded, for example—but the moral lesson Lydgate learned from Farebrother was, in any case, the same lesson.

Part of Farebrother's lesson on self-denial is that the core of professional satisfaction is competence. Lydgate knew some of that lesson already—he had, after all, been trained in Paris—but he knew less well than he should have the importance of taking satisfaction from competence. (I remember my own learning of this lesson at the hands of Mr. Pantzer and his partners.) Farebrother worked hard on his plainspoken sermons. He disciplined himself in the regard for others that is at the heart of pastoral counseling. He was aware of who he was (that is, he was integrated and constant), a skill Lydgate kept keen with the help of Dorothea Brooke, and so he knew when to be concerned about the gossip of the town and when not to be concerned.

Lydgate had, late in the story, the opportunity to recommend Farebrother for the lucrative parish appointment at Lowick, which was in Dorothea's gift. He said to her, of Farebrother, "He has at least achieved a reasonably honest compromise with the world and quietly makes the best of a bad job. A good shepherd, he contrasts with the doctrinal barrenness of Tyke and the pastoral indifference of Cadwallader." Farebrother got the new appointment, but did not give up the old one. He hired a curate for his old parish and kept the power in Middlemarch affairs that he had by being vicar there. He retained both incomes, and suffered the gossip and political censure that came from his petty participation in multiple patronage—just as he suffered gossip from making money at his card playing. "I shall be too busy for whist; I shall have two parishes. . . . It is protest enough against the pluralism they want to reform if I give somebody else most of the money. The stronger thing is not to give up power, but to use it well." He trusted himself to use power well. "Looking at him as a whole," Lydgate said to Dorothea, "I think he is one of the most blameless men I ever knew. He has neither venom nor doubleness in him, and those often go with a more correct outside."

Farebrother had a large role in the romance and marriage of Fred Vincy (Rosamond's brother) and Mary Garth. Fred thought of himself as a gentleman, because he went to a university at his father's expense; but he had no money. He therefore proposed to become a clergyman himself, that apparently being the only way an impecunious gentleman might make enough money to afford a wife without working with his hands. But Mary would not marry Fred as long as he wanted to be a clergyman, and in this she was gently supported by Farebrother. This bit of the story tells a lot about how Farebrother regards his professional work, and it, too, is a lesson for Lydgate on professionalism.

Mary's objection to Fred's being a clergyman was that the clergy would require him to deny who he was; it would be a "caricature," she said. This was not to deny Fred's character, and it was not to demean clergymen such as Farebrother either. Mary was, after all, otherwise willing to marry Fred, and she was a faithful churchwoman. But, she said, "His being a clergyman would be only for gentility's sake, and I think there is nothing more contemptible than such imbecile gentility. . . . He would be a piece of professional affectation." When Farebrother relayed these sentiments from Mary to Fred, he added, "Men outlive their love, but they don't outlive the consequences of their recklessness."

Fred eventually went to work with his hands, for Mary's father, who managed farms. Fred learned, as Timothy Colt did not, that there is a metaphor-free congruence between work and character. "You must be sure of two things," said Caleb Garth to Fred. "You must love your work, and not be always looking over the edge of it, wanting your play to begin. And the other is, you must not be ashamed of your work, and think it would be more honorable to you to be doing something else. . . . No matter what a man is—I wouldn't give twopence for him—whether he was the prime minister or the rickthatcher, if he didn't do well what he undertook to do."

Lydgate also learned from Farebrother the importance of truthfulness in professional life. Eliot has a little fun on this point, by contrasting Farebrother's professionalism with that of Mr. Bambridge, the horse trader. "Some people who had lost by him called him a vicious man; but he regarded horse-dealing as the finest of the arts, and might have argued plausibly that it had nothing to do with morality. He was undeniably a prosperous man, bore his drinking better than others bore their moderation, and, on the whole, flourished like the green bay tree."

Farebrother taught, as all good professional teachers do, more by the exhibition of his own character than by admonition. He had "unusual delicacy and generosity . . . [and] other points of conduct . . . which . . . made his character resemble those southern landscapes that seem divided between natural grandeur and social slovenliness. . . . [He was] filial and chivalrous . . . to the mother, aunt, and sister, whose dependence on him had in many ways shaped his life . . . few men who feel the pressure of small needs are so nobly resolute not to dress up their inevitably self-interested desires in a pretext of better motives. In these matters he was conscious that his life would bear the closest scrutiny; and perhaps the consciousness encouraged a little defiance toward the critical strictness of persons whose celestial intimacies seemed not to improve their domestic manners, and whose lofty aims were not needed to account for their actions."

There is an affinity between that observation about Farebrother and Percival's justification of the practice among apothecaries of selling drugs, at a profit, to their patients. These are useful professional lessons, about "the pressure of small needs," about celestial intimacies and domestic manners. Lydgate, who was later able to support Rosamond from his seaside practice, learned the lesson from Farebrother that he might have learned from Percival and the apothecaries of Middlemarch.

The final and greatest lesson in integrity that Lydgate learned from Farebrother was the difference between honor and virtue, between shame and vice. It was an important lesson in a professional gentleman's culture, because the surest corruption of the gentleman's ethic comes when it is turned into an ethic of honor and shame. Honor is not a virtue because it depends on the opinions of others, on the gossip of the town and the judgment of circumstantial elites, rather than on character and fidelity to self. Shame is not a vice, as Farebrother showed in his own choices regarding whist, billiards, and the retention of two clerical livings, because it turns on the disapproval of others, and particularly of influential others, rather than on the truly vicious failure to be truthful, courageous, and loving.

The lesson about honor was important to Lydgate as a gentleman, but even more important to him as a professional person. Professions tend to proclaim honor as a professional credential; this was evident to Lydgate's generation of British doctors in the ethics of Sir Thomas Percival. Professions glorify themselves. We lawyers and doctors torture virtue into congruence with dominant fraternal opinion. We insist that professional honor is equivalent to public good. Our pretenses drive poets such as Shaw and Sinclair Lewis into acetic anger, and cause poets such as Auchincloss and David Hilfiker to write tragedies about us.

Lydgate showed that he had learned the lesson about honor, late in the story, when Bulstrode, exposed as a scoundrel, was drummed off the hospital board. Bulstrode stood to leave the boardroom, tottering in his agony. Lydgate stood with him, and helped Bulstrode to remain on his feet, and left the room with him. "This act, which might have been one of gentle duty and pure compassion, was at this moment unspeakably bitter to [Lydgate]. It seemed as if he were putting his sign-manual to that association of himself with Bulstrode, of which he now saw the full meaning as it must have presented itself to other minds. He now felt the conviction that this man who was leaning tremblingly on his arm, had given him the thousand pounds as a bribe. . . . [T]he town knew of the loan, believed it to be a bribe, and believed that he took it as a bribe." An honorable doctor would have kept his seat.

In these ways, Lydgate the doctor learned his professional lessons from a parson, as he learned from a pious widow that a doctor needs a friend, and from conventional country gentlefolk that seeing is a moral art. The substantive morality, the moral and religious tradition that carried the lessons to Lydgate, were the same substance, morality, and religion that carried professional lessons to and through codifiers such as Sir Thomas Percival. Code depended on character. It could be that Lydgate learned his moral lessons better and more clearly from Dorothea and Camden Farebrother and the country gentlefolk of his community than he would have learned them from his spurned medical colleagues. But they were, in any case, the same moral lessons. The story shows how character might help us survive the corruption of our codes.

Chapter Five

· § ·

DISSENT

No one would choose to live without friends,
even if he had all the other goods.

—Aristotle

PART ONE: DISSENT

ETHICS is a characteristic activity in the modern, organized professions. Legal and medical ethics are academic disciplines and courses of study in American medical and law schools. But in both of these manifestations, professional ethics is a creature of the establishment; it comes to us from the old boys who run things. As ethics, it is and has always been the study of what the "better" doctors and lawyers do. As professional regulation, it has for about a century been what the better lawyers and doctors impose on their colleagues and on the country—a negative matter, mostly, of what better professionals try to keep lesser professionals from doing.

The first systematic presentation of ethics for lawyers in the English-speaking profession was devised by a prosperous, social-climbing, Andrew-Jackson-hating, utilitarian, Baltimore lawyer and law teacher named David Hoffman. Baltimore lawyers were, in Hoffman's generation, the best in the country; they practiced with remarkable prosperity in the most affluent of America's mercantile cities, and they charged the highest fees. Medical ethics for Britain and America were devised by a referee, Sir Thomas Percival, called in to soften a quarrel in the Manchester Infirmary in the 1790s. He wrote for gentlemen, he said. Percival's ethics became influential because the better doctors, who were gentlemen, most of them, adopted Percival's view of what a doctor should be.

Legal ethics was propounded for later generations of American business lawyers by a law teacher and judge in Philadelphia, George Sharswood, whose original lectures on the subject were given in 1854, the year David Hoffman died. In the generation after Sharswood's, legal ethics was codified for the first time by a federal judge, Thomas Goode Jones of Alabama. Judge Jones was a Confederate war hero, a legislative leader, a trial judge, and the governor of Alabama.

American medical ethics was first systematically propounded in Hoffman's Baltimore. The doctors' project there was published in 1832, the lawyers' in 1836; and it is at least amusing that, at the time, Professor Hoffman had a bitter, rancorous quarrel going with the medical faculty. Medical ethics in America became an official subject in 1847, when the American Medical Association codified Percival's ethics.

The medical and legal projects both reflected the popular ethical system of William Paley, which was a theological ethic for the successful. "The rights of the poor," Paley said, "are not so important or intricate, as their contentions are violent and ruinous. . . . [S]omething may be done, amongst the lower orders of mankind, towards the regulation of their conduct, and the satisfaction of their thoughts." The profession he recommended for the task was the lowest end of the Anglican clergy, the ill-paid curates who were as poor as their parishioners (Trollope's Josiah Crawley, for example, or the prolific Mr. Quiverfull). Percival and Hoffman brought Paley's view on the lower orders to medicine and to the law.

If you review the membership of the commissions and committees appointed since then to revise regulatory rules for doctors and lawyers, you will find many Percivals, many Sharswoods and Joneses. You won't find lawyers who do title opinions in the county seat or doctors who make house calls. You may find professors on these commissions, but not any who are awaiting tenure.

Retail Justice

Considering only legal ethics for a moment: I have wondered what sort of official ethics we lawyers would have in America if the creators of the subject had been frontier lawyers and urban defenders of street criminals, and what sort of revisions we would be making if the committees and commissioners of revision were made up of the flamboyant, the irreverent, and those who do their interviewing and counseling in prison cells. Hoffman, Sharswood, and Jones mostly ignored such lawyers, and when they did notice such lawyers, they disapproved of them. They are the objects of the enduring words of professional disapproval—"disreputable . . . unworthy . . . unseemly . . . unscrupulous . . . immoral . . . embarrassing . . . offensive . . . objectionable . . . scandalous . . . wholly unprofessional."

Frontier lawyers and urban defenders of street criminals have not used such words, of course. Which suggests that they might have a language of their own—an ethic of their own—that we might provisionally identify as the American legal ethics of dissent. Here, from one of the most popular of professional renegades, is a text, spoken about the representation of criminals:

"There is a distinct relationship between crime and progress. . . . Those who advocate progress are essentially criminally minded, and if they attempt to secure progress by openly refusing to obey the law, they are actual criminals. Then if they prevail, and from being in the minority come into power, they are taken out of jail, banquets are given in their honor, and they are called patriots and heroes. . . . The criminal laws are administered, interpreted and construed in favor of the rich, as against the liberties of the poor, for the simple reason that the administrators of the criminal law desire to curry favor with the powers that be."

This renegade was Ephraim Tutt. During the generation between World War I and World War II, Mr. Tutt was the hero in some 120 short stories in *The Saturday Evening Post.* He was the creation of a New York lawyer named Arthur Train. His long popularity was at least the equivalent of "Hill Street Blues," which did not run for nearly as long and whose lawyers were not nearly as grumpy as Mr.

Tutt was about his profession and about the law. (I will have to refer to him as Mr. Tutt, not because I have been reading the *Wall Street Journal,* but to distinguish him from his law partner, also named Tutt, who was not a relative and who has to be referred to as Tutt.)

Arthur Train published *The Autobiography of Ephraim Tutt* in 1943. It was to all appearances a legitimate autobiography; no authorship other than Mr. Tutt's appears in it. The center section of the book is a set of photographs of Mr. Tutt as a child, and of his parents, and of the house he was born in. The *Autobiography* was welcomed in the loftiest professional places, including law reviews published in Cambridge, Massachusetts, and New Haven, Connecticut. Train wrote the review in the *Yale Law Journal*—of his own book. He almost succeeded in getting Mr. Tutt into *Who's Who in America.* The review in the *Harvard Law Review* was written by Professor John M. McGuire, eminent teacher and scholar in the law of evidence, and was in content the story of Mr. Tutt's—Major Tutt's—service in the Army in World War I, possibly the only Mr. Tutt story not written by Arthur Train.

There is something significant about the popularity of a lawyer such as this among the readers of the *Saturday Evening Post.* The *Post* was, I think, the most ubiquitous magazine in the golden era of American magazines, a time with no television but with reliable mail service. You could subscribe to it, but many people got it from children who delivered it or sold it on the street for a nickel a copy. Readers of Russell Baker's recent autobiography *Growing Up* may remember that he got his start in journalism by peddling the *Saturday Evening Post.* It is probably important that, in such a magazine, the enduring lawyer character was someone who dissented from the dominant professional myths—both from the myth of the rule of law and from the pretense that the legal profession is a monkish brotherhood devoted to the common good. "The fact of the matter is," he said, "that honor and law haven't anything to do with one another."

Mr. Tutt was also popular among American lawyers. One of several modern anthologies of the stories was edited, when I was in law school, by a federal judge, Harold R. Medina, and there have been several other anthologies edited by lawyers. Judge Medina said that Mr. Tutt was his hero when he was studying law, and that there were then "thousands of . . . young lawyers eager to believe that justice was not necessarily at the mercy of prosecutors who wanted convictions . . . or of the large number of unscrupulous persons in various categories . . . who seemed so often in real life to prevail over the righteous and the just."

Mr. Tutt was popular among older and more settled lawyers, too—lawyers who were in the situation the judge was in when he compiled the 1961 anthology. Judge Medina did not relate this curious but general popularity to Mr. Tutt's truculent jurisprudence. "The law," said Mr. Tutt, "has inevitably been used for the benefit and aggrandizement of those in power." Inevitably! It would be hard for a federal judge to reconcile that point of view with the fact that everybody—even the judge—loved the lawyer who said it. But the fact that the judge loved the Mr. Tutt stories is ethically indicative.

Mr. Tutt dissented from the law, and from the legal profession. He refused the leadership and aristocracy that Tocqueville said come with being a lawyer in America. He avoided the possibility of increasing the power he had from his license to practice and his wit. He declined appointment to the bench. He accepted a wartime commission in the army, but he devoted himself to technical jobs rather than to command. He distrusted the profession's definition of the lawyer-client relationship, its rules on conflicts of interest, its notions about confidentiality, its idea of professional detachment, and the judgmental words with which it characterized lawyers who did not agree with the bar-association codes. He dissented from the codal principle that a responsible lawyer works within the system to make things better:

"No doubt," he said, "it is unsound charity to give a bleary-eyed old souse a dime for a cup of coffee, but when I look at his blistered feet bursting through the soles of his ragged shoes I haven't the heart to tell him to walk two miles to a wood yard. It is bad philanthropy but it is good for the arteries. . . . Let John Rockefeller deal in wholesale charity—I'm a retailer."

Mr. Tutt was not an all-purpose curmudgeon. He was a retailer. He was generous and selectively loving. He had a sense of humor and more than ordinary wisdom. He adhered to conventional morals—was what his generation called a gentleman, both in the sense that his personal morals were admirable and in the sense that he could have had rank and position in the establishment, for the asking, if he had wanted them. His Yankee credentials were clean and bright. Calvin Coolidge was his neighbor and friend and he studied at Harvard, even if he was not content with the law he learned there nor the profession he joined there.

Mr. Tutt was not a revolutionary. He did not propose alternative political or economic systems—probably because he had no faith in systems. He did not propose an alternative social or professional ethic, either. He was a dissenter. He dissented from the proposition, common in his generation of lawyers and in the better law schools, that the practice of law was a school for virtue—that practicing law and following the leadership of prosperous lawyers was the way for a lawyer to become a good person. He dissented even more radically from the notion that the United States of America was, to use Jefferson's phrase, "God's new Israel," a righteous empire, a city on a hill. He dissented from the older and more English notion of the rule of law. The peculiar and vaunted boast of the Anglo-American system, the jury, was, he said, "trained militiamen of the gibbet." The law, to Mr. Tutt, was a device to be used in his practice of retail justice. He did not share the view of his sometime ally, Miss Althea Beckman, who "prided herself equally on her adherence to religious principle and the Acts of Congress." As a social and political phenomenon, American law was, in his view, something used by the "better" lawyers to make sure weak Americans remained weak. A practitioner of retail justice can use the law, but he does not revere it, and he cannot live with it unless he has a sense of humor.

Mr. Tutt's retail justice is one kind of dissent among American professionals. It is *male WASP discontent*—individualistic, the eastern law-office version of the American frontier spirit. You get a contemporary and similar expression of dissent in medicine in Sinclair Lewis's young doctor, Martin Arrowsmith (chapter 4).

Dissent as Friendship

A different sort of dissent is in the stories of Mr. Tutt's contemporary, the entertainment lawyer Fanny Holtzmann, of the New York and California bars, and in George V. Higgins's modern stories about Jeremiah Francis Kennedy of the Boston criminal-defense bar. Neither Holtzmann nor Kennedy has Yankee credentials. Neither is a WASP; only one of them is male. Holtzmann's career as a lawyer is the story of a small, pretty, unmarried, Jewish woman from Brooklyn, the child of immigrants, the favorite granddaughter of a splendid, widowed Hasidic rabbi. Kennedy is a resolute Irish Catholic whose forebears worked with their hands, crossed themselves, went to church in Latin, and cursed the Protestant Brahmins of Boston. Miss Holtzmann studied law in the old Fordham night law school, on the twenty-eighth floor of the Woolworth Building. Jerry Kennedy went to Boston College. Both lawyers learned their law in urban Jesuit law schools, whose mission was to offer vertical mobility to the children of immigrants. Mr. Tutt's is an individualistic ethic of dissent as retail justice; Holtzmann's and Kennedy's is an immigrant's communal ethic, an ethic of dissent and friendship.

Fanny Holtzmann was the first woman to get an office in the new Bar Building, at 36 West 44th Street. That building already housed some of the gray eminences of her day, including Benjamin Nathan Cardozo, who helped her get an office there. The headquarters of the bar association was next door, but Fanny did not join it because it refused membership to women and admitted only a few safe Jews. She became a lawyer in 1923, at the age of 21. The day she passed the bar examination she had more than a hundred show-business clients waiting for her to get her license; she had retainers from them. She argued for prompt admission so she could see to these clients—an argument she took all the way to the New York Court of Appeals, and won. She had already bought her office furniture, furniture for a one-woman law office on the ninth floor. She had no partners. Some of what she did in practice was disapproved of in the more conventional law firm of her older brother, Jacob. She did, later, allow her younger brother, David, to practice with her as an associate—that is, on a salary.

Holtzmann was a magnificent, glittering success in life—both as a lawyer and as a leader. Her friends included the king and queen of England, Justice Cardozo, Chief Justice Taft, Eleanor Roosevelt, and Winston Churchill—but not many practicing lawyers. Her clients included Noel Coward, Clifton Webb, Rudyard Kipling, George Bernard Shaw, John Galsworthy, the royal family of Russia, Tex Austin's rodeo, Gertrude Lawrence, and Fred Astaire. She was probably the first film copyright expert in the American profession and the only lawyer in her generation who was objective about Hollywood. She was a brilliant negotiator, a consummate manipulator, a wise counselor, and a scholarly advocate.

There were virtually no women in practice in New York City then. Fanny did much of her professional work in England. (There were not many women lawyers there, either.) She suffered because of her sex. She never married; her only serious fiancé expected her to give up her law practice if she became his wife. The *London Daily Mail* published an interview with her that said, among other things, that "seen from behind, she is reminiscent of Janet Gaynor." Another London newspaper said that King George of Greece was a friend of hers and that she frequently broiled chops for the king in her Knightsbridge flat. Fanny said, "I didn't go to London to broil chops for anybody. The King of Greece knew where the saucepans were; when he came to see me, he broiled his own chops."

Those were the days when solicitation, advertising, and engineered publicity were mortal sins in legal ethics: "Disreputable . . . unworthy . . . unseemly . . . embarrassing." When I became a lawyer, some forty years later, the bar association still gave more attention to the size of the sign in the window than to what we did in the office. In the 1960s Hoosier lawyers got a loose-leaf volume called *The Indiana Code of Professional Responsibility Annotated.* At least a third of it was devoted to rules and rulings against advertising and solicitation. As late as 1977 the *ABA Journal* thrice called lawyer advertising "the issue of the decade."

This was the ethical climate in which Fanny Holtzmann practiced law. But she got into the newspapers regularly, and she went after any legal business that came to her attention. Before she became a lawyer, she was a sort of law-firm paralegal, with her own branch office in the theater district. In that capacity, she got clients by writing collection letters for her law firm's client, a newspaper. She asked the debtors to come in and talk to her, without being specific about her capacity in the law firm. When they came, she signed them up as clients—her clients, even though they had to wait a year or two for her to get her license. This is the way she met Edmund Goulding, Hollywood actor, writer, and director, and her lifelong friend and client:

Goulding owed the newspaper for a quarter-page Christmas ad. Fanny wrote him a collection letter, which was not answered. A year later, she wrote him again. She said she had heard many wonderful things about him, that the advertising bill was, she was sure, only an oversight, and that if he would come in and talk to her he would be able in the future to avoid such "quite unnecessary irritants." He came, brought her a bouquet of flowers he had bought on credit, and told her the story of his tangled professional and financial affairs.

"You're a man of imagination, Mr. Goulding," Fanny said. "You shouldn't be troubled with business matters."

"Who's going to handle them for me?"

"I will, if you wish."

"I wish," he said.

Later, after she had her license, she got wind of the fact that a Broadway review called *Jubilee* made fun of the British royal family. She called the Lord Chamberlain and offered to quietly "wangle something," which she did. One reason she got that job was that the Lord Chamberlain had declined a similar offer from her, two years earlier, to wangle something regarding the motion picture *As Thousands Cheer,* which also was distasteful to the Royal Family. In the earlier case the Lord Chamberlain declined her offer and made a public protest instead; the publicity over the protest sold thousands of tickets.

What Miss Holtzmann said, by the way, to the producer of *Jubilee,* was "Listen, dear, what are you trying to do, buck the British government? Maybe you don't want to put on a show in London ever again. Listen. . ." The revue was rewritten. Fanny did not get a fee for her work, but, as Mary Case Harriman's sketch in the *New Yorker* said, "The good will was worth thousands."

Fanny got bad will, too, especially from her male elders in the profession. The barrister who defended the libel claim she brought for the Russian royal family against Metro-Goldwyn-Mayer called her a charlatan and a publicity hound. Fanny learned of the libel case at a cocktail party, after other New York lawyers had turned it down. She recovered judgments and settlements running into the hundreds of thousands, about half of which she took as her fee. Louis B. Mayer, the principal defendant, was, before long, Fanny's friend and became her confidante, although she represented people who had claims against his company.

Fanny Holtzmann did not follow the professional rules. She may even have engaged in what lawyers then called barratry, maintenance, champerty, self-laudation, and solicitation. She sometimes, apparently, charged excessive fees. I suspect the reason she stayed out of trouble was that the old boys in the bar association did not want to prosecute a small, pretty, Jewish woman—not unless and until she did something really terrible, which she never did. Old boys and their ethics aside, Fanny Holtzmann was a good lawyer. Her clients became her friends. She was faithful to them and they were faithful to her, professionally and socially, and much of her success was due to her ability to call on the show-business fraternity to help her work her cases out. Justice Cardozo said to her, as she began practice, "Your true education will come from your clients. . . . You will be a good lawyer because you have infinite curiosity."

She also became a significant force in American Zionism and in the creation of the state of Israel. She worked tirelessly, sometimes with the young brothers, Joseph, Jr., and John F. Kennedy, to get Jews out of Nazi Germany. She led a simple personal life, lived at home and was the support of her aging parents, and was generous to the poor and the homeless. A nice Jewish girl, to whom the faith and moral tradition of Israel were not only important but definitional. But for her disregard of professional propriety—or maybe because of it—she would be remembered as a heroine of the profession. I teach with stories of American lawyers, and it is of course important that some of the stories I use be stories about women. Fanny's is the best such story I have found—and the students love her.

Dr. Carole Horn, internist and professor of medicine at George Washington University, could be Fanny's medical parallel. Dr.

Horn—like Dr. Fiscus of "St. Elsewhere"—is regularly criticized because she doesn't wear a white coat. "Psychologically," she says, "it seems to separate me from those who have asked me to participate in their care. Some people expect it, but for me it's a distancing mechanism, and that's not something I like."

"Occasionally, however, the absence of a white coat pays off in an unexpected way. One wizened little gentleman, charming but demented, was convinced that his social worker and I, since we do not wear those official-looking coats, were around the hospital for no better reason than to keep him company in bed. Regularly, he invited us to climb in and cuddle up. He wouldn't hear anything about 'doctor,' and by the time he finally left we were all a bit relieved.

"But four days later there was a frantic call from the daughter-in-law who had kindly agreed to care for him at home, so he wouldn't need to be institutionalized. He was trying to get her twelve-year-old daughter into bed with him, she sobbed.

" 'Did he touch her?' I asked, immediately concerned.

" 'No, never. Only kept talkin' to her to come in.'

" 'Oh,' I replied, relieved, 'That's no problem, he always does that with me, too.' An audible gasp at the other end of the line. Then we talked about the confusion that sometimes affects elderly people, and I explained that he seemed to be confusing women around him with his late wife. He had never pressed an invitation, I reassured her, and after his recent stroke I didn't think he ever could. She was able to tell her child that Grandpa just mistook her for someone he had once cared about, and she should ignore him.

"Had he remained troublesome, I suppose we could have gotten the young woman a white coat."

Dissent without Friendship

Calvin Trillin's story about immigration lawyers in Houston begins in a line outside the offices of the Immigration and Naturalization Service. The line leads to a waiting room that is, he says, like a bus station. This line is only for lawyers. The lawyers who wait in it are waiting for a seat in the waiting room, where they will wait to be heard by the low-level bureaucrats who decide the fate (and sometimes the life or death) of thousands of people who want to remain in America. The lawyers' line is the product of organized professional pressure. It does not assure a prompt or adequate or fair hearing in the bureaucracy. Some of the lawyers waiting there hope to provoke sympathy from the bureaucrats they finally reach, but the more urgent business is to get the bureaucrats' attention. Another rule for lawyers in that office is that each of them is permitted to bring five exceptionally old cases to the attention of the deputy director. There, too, the objective is attention, the hope is capricious sympathy.

That office is not a manifestation of the American dream or the rule of law. If it is by some analogy a court, the lawyers who seek there to serve client interests do not think of themselves as officers of the court. The rule of practice, one of them says, is, "Don't let those bastards get you." The reason behind the caprice in such a governmental operation, he says, is that "the bosses don't want strict enforcement; immigrants represent cheap labor." Many of the cases these lawyers argue there fall under an administrative rule extending permanent status to aliens who have resided in America for seven years and can show both good moral character and extreme hardship. "Some poor bastard has been here eleven years. His wife's a permanent resident. You ought to hear them down there rank gradations of hardship! The bastards! I could tear them apart!"

Not all of them adjust to their law practice with such anger; not all of them are Mr. Tutts. Some of them become as bureaucratic as the bureaucrats. One such lawyer "takes only cases that do not disrupt the system [of forms and files] he has worked out for processing applications." Another, who handles immigration cases involving corporate officials moving between countries, says, "A blueprint of the building is the key to the practice of immigration law." Another says, "I beg to differ. The key to the practice of immigration law is knowing that an immigration examiner who wants to go to the bathroom has to pass through the waiting room to get there." Most of the clients of these lawyers are immigrants from countries other than Mexico, because Mexicans have their own way of adjusting to the rule of law in American immigration practice. "Posting bond and going through a deportation hearing is expensive and difficult; coming back across the border in a few days usually isn't." The Mexicans are, therefore, for the most part, beneath professional notice.

The strongest hope these lawyers hold out to their clients is that the bureaucratic process will defeat its own purposes—that it will remain in lethargic motion, without being able to deport the client, until the client either grows old and dies in America or the law is changed. "Any immigration lawyer worth his salt would say, 'Get here first!' "

The first adjustment for an immigration lawyer is an acceptance of this legal world—sometimes with irony and sometimes with the resignation that says such a law practice is a way to make money that can then be spent doing something worthwhile or pleasant. A lawyer from the its's-a-living school says, "Immigration lawyers are people who have an interest in seeing that some folders are on the top of the pile and some folders are on the bottom of the pile." The ironic school is more creative—as, for example, in the part of the practice in which an immigrant is shown to be able to do something that an American employer cannot find a citizen to do. The professional task in that case is to draft a job description that sounds abstract but in fact describes abilities only the client has. It involves collaboration by client, employer, and lawyer. It is cynical about the law and takes its joy in verbal creativity. "Immigration law is taking a short-order cook and making him into an executive chef. What we're talking about here is a matter of focus."

Mr. Tutt would have enjoyed that. It was, I think, said with a smile, by a lawyer named Pete Williamson. He and his father Sam are immigration lawyers who react to their legal order with anger and irony rather than bureaucratic conformity. Sam Williamson is the lawyer who says "Don't let the bastards get you." His son Pete began law practice as counsel for the farm workers' union. Sam Williamson is the son of Jewish immigrants; his name was originally Wishneweski. He says, "It comes natural for a Jew to become an immigration lawyer. There's something vestigial, something in your blood. We've been strangers so long we resent it."

"When he is angry," Trillin says, "he punches the air with his index finger. He is usually angry." Sam Williamson was heard by Trillin, shouting from the lawyers' line outside the immigration office, "If Jesus tried to get into this country, they'd exclude him on a 212(a)(15)." That section of the Immigration and Nationality Act bars immigrants who are likely to become public charges. Another member of that small and informal professional association (thirty lawyers) says that it is characteristic of the rule of law in immigration that the people who are excluded from America are "the people who need the most help." These include refugees from Central America whose home governments want to kill them. "The United States is not an innocent party." Sam Williamson explained to Trillin why he is an immigration lawyer: "It's a competent, involved, technical job in which, if you're successful, you can see the consequences of your actions. Also, I don't like the government."

This is the practice of law as dissent and without friendship. It produces a professional fraternity that is mutually supporting and probably more truthful than most professional fraternities are but their consensus is sustained largely by dissent. They do not propose an ethic that can be an alternative to notions of the rule of law and civic responsibility that they scoff at. They do not make friends of their clients. This fraternity in some ways joins the bureaucracy in oppressing the poor. The creation of the lawyers' line to the waiting room means that people without lawyers wait longer. "Old people and women with babies remain outside in the cold."

Lawyers in the lawyers' line can apparently keep their clients with them. One such case involved a couple seeking permanent status for the husband, a waiter and a Turk. The law being invoked in that case permits permanent status for the spouse of a citizen, provided the bureaucrat in the case finds the marriage is not a sham. Much of the lawyer's art there is in anticipating the arbitrary bureaucratic categories that will be applied on the issue of sham marriage. Professional folklore says that marriages across racial lines are suspicious. The Turkish waiter in the case I am talking about was married to a black woman. A colleague of their lawyer came to their place in the line and struck up a terse conversation with their lawyer. "Three dollars," he said. That was the amount he was betting counsel on the outcome of the case. He was betting three dollars that the union of an American black woman and a Turkish waiter was, as we say in the law, presumptively a sham.

It is hard to imagine that Mr. Tutt or Fanny Holtzmann or Dr. Horn would have engaged in this esoteric transaction about clients, particularly when the clients were standing close by. Dr. Horn speaks of patients inviting her to participate in their healing, and I think her notion would have appealed to Fanny Holtzmann. The point suggests a distinction in the stories of professional dissenters. Some of them dissent with anger or irony. Some of them dissent and see an alternative moral vision—a vision such as the Horn theory of professional as participator. From the alternative moral vision comes an alternative ethic. The alternative ethic is a second step, a step beyond the dissent that is evident among the Houston immigration lawyers. I am suggesting that the alternative ethic is friendship.

Dissent as Coming Home

The strongest alternative-ethic stories in the American professions are stories of immigrants. Calvin Trillin reported some evidence of an alternative ethic in the Williamsons—son and grandson of Jewish immigrants. I notice the alternative ethic in the stories of Fanny Holtzmann and Jerry Kennedy. These dissenters look with disgust, as Mr. Tutt would, or at least with disagreement, at the legal world of the Immigration and Naturalization Service in Houston, or the medical world that prescribes white coats; but then they turn to another ethic, an ethic they bring with them to their profession and find better than the ethic the profession offers them. Michael Novak says this turning is "not so much an individual awakening as an individual's conscious and deliberate joining of a community" other than the professional community, a community "extended in time and space and into eternity. It is less like starting a new life, more like coming home."

Coming home makes it possible for the dissenters to practice the virtues as they practice medicine and law, and to offer something useful to the rest of us. The story of the immigration lawyers is mostly a story of professional contempt—even of contempt as an ethic. Mr. Tutt and his medical counterparts suggest an ethic that says clients are more important than institutions. Patients and clients are more important than science or the rule of law, than the ideal of an American doctor or lawyer as a moral and political leader, than the claim that being a lawyer is a way to become a good person.

The claim that clients are more important than institutions is less than I want to show with these dissenter stories, though—first because it is a negative argument, and second because it is not remarkable. I should be able to say something more, and to say something positive. I should be able to do more than to compare people whose lights are interpersonal with people whose lights are collective and social. I should, especially, be able to say something positive about the view of professional relationship that some of these dissenting doctors and lawyers have. I think I can do that with the story of Jerry Kennedy, who, I think, combines Mr. Tutt's retail justice with Fanny Holtzmann's understanding of friendship.

Jerry is the principal lawyer in George V. Higgins's two recent crime novels, *Kennedy for the Defense* (1980) and *Penance for Jerry Kennedy* (1985). Jerry is, according to his wife Mack, "the classiest sleazy criminal lawyer in Boston." His creator is himself a Boston criminal-defense lawyer. Both Kennedy and George Higgins are Irish Catholics who went to law school at Boston College. Both are passionate about the Red Sox.

Anybody who knows Jerry Kennedy would say that he is a good friend. Friendship is both the secret of his moral life as a lawyer and the source of what his friends call his innocence. His best friend is his wife Joan McManus (he calls her Mack), and, in violation of professional propriety, he discusses his cases with her. "Any man who had the brains . . . to marry Joan McManus probably shouldn't go badgering God about 'what have You done for me lately,' " he says. "A stupid mistake is one thing—ingratitude is something else again, and I'll be damned if I'll put myself in a position where I have to cop a plea to St. Peter for having been ungrateful. Mack is my life."

Mack and Jerry have been married for 20 years. They have one child, a daughter named Heather, whom they call Saigon, because her timely birth kept Jerry in law school and out of Vietnam. Mack is in the real-estate business and will this year make more money than Jerry makes from his law practice. She understands his law practice better than he understands her business. Mack says of Jerry's style as an advocate, "You sound different when you're saying something that you really think, and something you just hope maybe you can get somebody else to think." She does not understand the adversary ethic.

After Mack, Jerry Kennedy's closest friends are clients. He blusters about the adversary ethic and says that the only thing criminal defendants mean to him is fees, but this is an instance of his trying to get somebody else to think what he doesn't think. Maybe it's a way to live with the fact that he helps keep brutal pimps and loan sharks in business. Not all his clients are friends, but those he does the best work for are. Here is what he says about one of them, a man who has been a client nearly as long as Mack has been Jerry's wife, and who is known in his trade as Cadillac Teddy.

"Teddy . . . is . . . one of the best car thieves on the eastern Seaboard . . . so good that he is able to support himself as a car thief. He has been arrested repeatedly, which is how he made my acquaintance, but he has never done time. That is because I am so good. It is also because Teddy is so good. . . . I . . . bill Teddy . . . for my travel time, just like any other plumber working door-to-door, and since he categorically refuses to substitute a lawyer living closer to the scene of his most recent infraction, I figure he wants me. . . . Teddy pays me with some of the money he gets from stealing cars."

Jerry helps Teddy when Teddy gets into trouble—as, for example, when a police officer, who failed to catch Teddy with a hot Cadillac, ate Teddy's driver's license and then arrested Teddy for driving without it. Teddy also helps Jerry when Jerry is in trouble. When Jerry's family was being harassed by a thug, and Jerry told Teddy about it, Teddy said, "I know a guy that knows that area." Teddy put the wheels of justice—retail justice perhaps—in motion. When Jerry offended the government and got into tax trouble, and needed the best tax lawyer in Boston, and could not get an interview with this lawyer, Teddy called on a race-course friend and got Jerry his interview. The race-course friend was named Buddy Belcher. Jerry said, "Who the hell is Belcher . . . why should this guy help me out?" Teddy said, "Simple. I did him a favor." Maybe Teddy got Belcher a Cadillac.

Jerry's story teaches lessons about friendship that Paley, Percival, and Sharswood, with their talk of professional fraternity (chapter 4), did not know and did not think they needed. Jerry does not describe these lessons; often he does not have his own story straight. He says, "I go to my office to make a living, not to make a life. My life is at home." But that is one of those things he hopes other people will think—that he doesn't really think himself. The fact is that his friends are at and around his office and on the telephone as much as they are in his life at home.

Much of the worldly threat he hopes to save his wife and daughter from is at home, and not at the office. He does not put pictures of Mack and Saigon on his desk, lest some violent client get the wrong idea about influence or revenge. But that attempt at protection doesn't work. It doesn't protect them from the violence of his work, because Jerry, who has covered pretty well the risks he takes in practicing law, is unable to protect his family from the risks he takes in his practice of the virtue of friendship. He takes the risks of friendship home. He talks to Mack about them. He in fact makes his life in his office as well as in his home, and he in fact takes his office home. He mixes the two together. He comes home for his professional ethics, as you might expect a healthy, busy, threatened Irish Catholic to do. An interesting comparison here, a businessman who did not practice the virtue of friendship in his work, and who did not take his risks home, is Thomas Mann's stoic German Protestant businessman Thomas Buddenbrook, who suffered the burdens of a divided life, never said a word, and died young.

Jerry hasn't divided himself in two, the way Buddenbrook and the old boys' adversary ethic says he should. The more cases he loses, as he grows older, the more he realizes that there is a relationship between his work and his practice of the virtue of friendship—that, for him, to practice law well is to practice friendship. Cadillac

Teddy said to Jerry recently, "You're only good when you really mean it," and Jerry agreed. He would not have agreed when he first met Teddy, and Teddy would not have said such a thing then. But Teddy and Jerry have moved into the second half of life, and they have begun to realize that they are participating in one another's lives. They may not yet know what the score is, but they have begun to learn what it is not, and they try to be honest with one another. They have come home together.

In the 1985 story, Jerry defended Lou Schwartz, an accountant who grew rich by doing tax returns for organized crime. Lou and Jerry first became friends when Lou did Jerry's tax work. Jerry was Lou's client then. Lou has been as careful as Cadillac Teddy, but he has not been able to do anything about the fact that he is attractive as a potential informer for the federal government. The U.S. attorney came after Lou, on a technical tax charge, and tried to force Lou to inform on his Mafia clients. Jerry thinks this is an abuse of civil liberties. The prosecutor, he said, "was willing to do with an indictment what the cops used to do with truncheons . . . before the Supreme Court decided citizens have rights."

Lou and Jerry are friends. For that reason, Mack urged Jerry not to take the case. Her argument was instinctive and protective, but the words she used were words of professional detachment, the argument for wearing a white coat. They were words Mack could have got from the old boys who invented American professional ethics. Jerry uses those words, too, but not when he's serious. "Lou has done good work for me, and kept me out of trouble," Jerry said. "Now Lou is in the gravy. I'll see if I can get him out. Nothing wrong with that. . . . That is what I do. Do that sort of thing for lots of people. . . . It's something that I have to do, something I wish I didn't. The only problem with the sense it makes is that I wish it didn't." The first part of the speech is abstract professionalism, but the latter part, which sounds like Gary Cooper in *High Noon,* is friendship.

Jerry *feels* too much; that is Mack's argument. It, like the argument of our professional elders, says that feeling and professional work should be kept separate. Lou Schwartz, the client, made a similar argument. He knew that the case was a loser, and was resigned to that fact. "What you did was all I asked," he told Jerry, after the trial, "all any man could do . . . do the best you can. Miracles I don't expect. I'm not a Catholic." Lou called Jerry a hopeless innocent, a hopelessly nice guy.

Lou could have had a more experienced lawyer, at Mafia expense, but he wanted Jerry. The Mafia boss, Nunzio, was afraid of Jerry. He wanted a lawyer for Lou who would make sure Lou did not become an informer. If Lou becomes an informer, or seems about to, the boss will kill him. Selection of counsel is a sober decision for Lou. Lou argued for Jerry, though, rather than a retained Mafia lawyer. "He's tough and I trust him. He will go in and try the case, and he will hate to lose it. *But he will not ham it up*" (emphasis added). Lou wanted a friend to help him—someone who would not smother Lou's integrity and who would respect Lou's settled determination to go to prison rather than to inform—would respect that determination in *Lou,* rather than in the Mafia's professional code. Lou wanted his integrity taken seriously, and he therefore wanted a lawyer who had integrity of his own. He knows that Jerry is such a lawyer because Jerry is his friend.

Notice who is the advocate here. Jerry Kennedy had not done much work in federal court, and the little he had done involved heroin and sawed-off shotguns, not income taxes. Jerry, in the cases he knows, claims that he is like a person who can fix television sets. "What counts is not how long I spend turning screws and humming, but knowing which one is the right one when I open up the set." Jerry could not offer that sort of help to Lou Schwartz. But Lou did not want a lawyer, however expert, who would hide Lou's dignity behind technique and hypocrisy. He wanted a lawyer who had integrity, and who knew how important Lou's integrity was.

"This is my case," Lou said to the Mafia boss, "and my hide. This is my time I'll be doing. Jerry knows me, I know Jerry. I am comfortable with him." He won his argument with the boss. He got Jerry for his lawyer, and later he wanted Jerry to know how much he had wanted Jerry to be his lawyer. "Oh, you would've been proud of me, how I fought for you," he said. "It was almost as good, Jerry, as the way you fought for me."

PART TWO: FRIENDSHIP

Let me pause to summarize a bit. The moral inheritance we have as American doctors and lawyers includes dissenters. Dissenters are those who

1. do not believe (i.e., dissent from the professional teaching) that the way to be a doctor or lawyer and a good person in America is to follow the moral leadership of elders and guilds in the professions (chapter 4);

2. do not accept (i.e., dissent from the principle of American civil religion) that America is God's new Israel; and

3. do not find, in the American medical profession, a trustworthy commitment either to science or to healing; nor, in the American legal profession, a trustworthy commitment either to the rule of law or the principle that a responsible lawyer works within the system.

Some of these dissenters offer (or they found or brought with them and now turn to—come home to) an alternative professional ethic. Their alternative ethic says that patients and clients are more important than institutions; that patients and clients are more important than abstract and official ideals; that *friendship is more important than justice.* The cultural reality—the history—behind their alternative ethic is that the dissenters have learned from their communities (i.e., from their families, their neighborhoods, and their religious congregations) how to be friends. The essence of their professional ethic, and the ground of their dissent from the official professional ethic, is that they seek to practice the virtue of friendship with their clients.

Not all the clients and patients in these professional stories are friends. For example, Jerry Kennedy actively dislikes some of his clients; he is personally indifferent, and therefore bored, with many others. Jerry hasn't got time and energy for many friends. As it is, when he is awake in the middle of the night, it is usually for one of two reasons—either he is worrying about Lou Schwartz or he is talking on the phone to Teddy Franklin.

This raises two questions to think about in professional ethics. One, and the most obvious from the standpoint of WASP male American professional ethics (chapter 4), is that these dissenters' professional-client relationships lead to or protect or at least fail to condemn immoral behavior. Lou Schwartz has helped the Mafia and now refuses to help the community do something about Mafia crime and corruption; Cadillac Teddy steals cars; the practice of immigration law in Houston uses bureaucratic delay and inefficiency to keep illegal aliens from being deported. The answer to this issue, in dissenters' stories, is a dissenter's answer: The old boys help their friends, too. "The fact of the matter is that honor and law haven't anything to do with one another." The professional ethics of dissent may shelter immoral behavior, but it does this less than prevailing professional ethics does. The dissenters are more truthful than the old boys are.

The second question raised by the professional ethics of dissent and friendship is a question about preference. When friendship is understood in an ordinary way, as it is in the Jerry Kennedy stories, it becomes a difficult proposal for a culture that values equality and fairness and that tends to categorize its professions as if they were regulated public utilities. How can Jerry Kennedy and Mr. Tutt justify preferring some people to others, some clients to others?

The Issue of Preference

The key issue is preference. I consider that issue, in this section, as it appears in these stories of dissenters; I consider it, in the next section, as it appears in the theoretical tradition on the virtue of friendship. In either perspective, consideration of preference will throw light on the first ethical question (friendship protects immoral behavior) as it analyzes the second and, as I think, key issue of preference.

There are two answers in the stories to the issue of preference. One answer says that preference is not a moral question. The other admits that preference is a moral question but, reasoning from the consequences of friendship, argues that friendship results in moral gain in such magnitude that the apparent injustice to people (patients and clients) who are not preferred is justified.

The first answer to the issue of preference is deterministic. If this answer is persuasive, then friendship is not a moral issue, because a person (lawyer, physician) cannot help having the friends she has. There will be moral questions about what a person does with her friends, and for them, but the identity of her friends is not a moral question, because she cannot do anything about it.

This school of thought would say that a lawyer such as Kennedy and a doctor such as Carole Horn come into friendship as a result of circumstance—or, if you like, of the will of God. My friend is a person who happened to come my way, and somehow we clicked. It is the click that makes the friend. As Martin Buber says it, "I become *aware* of him, aware that he is different from myself, in the definite, unique way which is peculiar to him. . . . I can recognize in him, know in him, the person he has been (I can say it only in this word) *created* to become." The identity of each of us, and the possibility of integrity and constancy in each of us, lies in a fresh, focused benevolence. If this happens with some clients and not with others, the explanation is the will of God. The occasion is a miracle. If you see the hand of God anywhere in your life, you see it here.

"Suppose that you had a great deal of some commodity," St. Augustine said, "and felt bound to give it away to somebody who had none, and that it could not be given to more than one person; if two persons presented themselves, neither of whom had . . . a greater claim upon you than the other, you could do nothing fairer than choose by lot to which you would give what you could not have given to both. Just so among men, since you cannot consult for the good of them all."

In C. S. Lewis's view, our friends are those whom God sends to us in a certain way. Lewis came to this view out of a radical disagreement with the classical (Greek) teaching on friendship that I discuss in the next section. As much as Lewis valued the love of friends, he could not go along with Aristotle's ethics of virtue; Lewis did not find friendship to be a school for virtue. Friends are as likely to support one another in vice as in virtue, Lewis said. They are likely to end up as professional associations and ethics commissions have in America, in Olympian superiority; or (as the professional Brahmins of Boston did) in Titanic tyranny; or (as Lou Schwartz's clients in the Mafia did) in vulgar cruelty. Friends are as likely to work together in a garden of vice as they are to enrich one another's goodness.

But Lewis also believed that friendship was love, and that love is the ultimate virtue. He had a difficulty, and the way he took out of the difficulty was to see his friend as one whom God sent his way. The *purposes* of the friendship keep it from being a school for vice, because those are the purposes of God. "It is He who has spread the board and it is He who has chosen the guests. It is He, we may dare to hope, who sometimes does, and always should, preside. Let us not reckon without our Host." God sent this person to me, and He at the same time sent to each of us the interest, curiosity, and attractiveness that make love possible between us. The moral inquiry—a question put to God—is what to do about (with) (in) this love.

It needs a healthy faith to see friends in professional practice in this way. Fanny Holtzmann probably had the faith, and probably did see her friends that way; she didn't say much about it. In any event, as a matter of professional ethics, it would be a useful discipline to look for the purpose in each client's coming along; it would help take the professional person out of his egoistic self. It would save a doctor or a lawyer from looking at a person and seeing a routine instead of an adventure, and from being surprised when he finds more than a routine.

Mr. Tutt tended to see each of his clients as a piece of ammunition in his campaign to humiliate hypocrisy and power; he tended to assume devious evil in the wealthy people who came his way, and innocence in the poor. To ask what was going on when a stranger came to him would perhaps have been a way to ask who the stranger was and what made him who he was—to remove him from the injustice of Mr. Tutt's social categories. And that would have been a useful discipline. I doubt that Fanny Holtzmann was as much in need of this discipline. She was successful at being lawyerlike and feminine at the same time. She tended to include people in her practice, and she had learned from her grandfather, Rabbi Hirsch Bornfeld, a useful, daily curiosity about the purposes of God, the Hasidic God Who is in all things, in all people.

The deterministic answer on the question of preference thus becomes an answer to the charge that the professional ethics of friendship protects immoral behavior. The fact that a client becomes my friend is not a matter of moral choice. I cannot do anything about who my friends are or about the fact that not every client becomes my friend. But I can do something about what my friend and I do together. Reflection on that fact leads me to notice the hand of God in the (determined) fact that one client is my friend and another is not my friend. The question then—a moral question—is what God wants from this friendship.

The purposes-of-God answer does not dispense with the question of preference. It only moves it from the moral choice of who will be my friend to the moral choice I seem to make when I treat the client who is my friend better than the client who is not my friend. The issue is still an issue of preference. Jerry Kennedy exploits some of his clients; he throws their money away and does nothing of value for them. And when Mack says that the money he takes from pimps is blood money, Jerry says, "When you sell a house to somebody, do you make sure he's paying for it with clean money . . . ? If he got the down payment by cheating on his taxes, that's his worry, not yours." The focused benevolence of these lawyers toward their clients is not accounted for precisely enough by characterizing these lawyers as people who sit by the side of the road and make friends of those God sends along but don't make friends of those who come along on their own. The purposes-of-God theory may be a way to describe their professional situations but it does not provide a clear enough justification for their preferring some clients over others. The question is still a question about preference.

One could reject the purposes-of-God argument and say that a lawyer or a doctor should *seek* friendship with every patient or client who comes along. Dr. Horn's stories, and some of the nineteenth-century doctor stories (such as Trollope's *Dr. Thorne* or George Eliot's *Middlemarch*) can be read to make that argument. So can Fanny Holtzmann's story. The logical consequence of the theory is that every client relationship that does not become a friendship is a moral failure—a matter either of refusing to offer friendship or of wrongfully spurning friendship when it is offered. This argument resolves the issue of preferential professional service by claiming that poorer service is the consequence of a sinful refusal to be friendly. Preference is, on this view, either a moral fault in itself or the consequence of moral fault.

Mr. Tutt, out of social and economic prejudice, did not *notice* many of the people he met in the practice—including some people you and I would say were his clients. In the most quizzical of all of his cases, he purportedly drafted an invalid will for Cabel Baldwin. Mrs. Baldwin, whom Mr. Tutt believed to be a wicked, designing woman, commissioned the will; it was she who came to his office. But Mr. Tutt contrived to protect Mr. Baldwin from Mrs. Baldwin. Mrs. Baldwin was either his client, or she was the victim of his plot to deny her any legal help at all. He made no attempt to know her; he called her "old chiselface." And he defended himself with the profession's sophistry on conflict of interest, sophistry that he would in another case have condemned as tosh.

In 1919, in one of the earliest stories, Mr. Tutt defended a tramp named Hans Schmidt, who had been arrested when asleep inside the house, and on the bed, of an inoffensive but wealthy old man named John DePuyster Hepplewhite. Mr. Tutt was contemptuous and sarcastic when he had Mr. Hepplewhite at his Titanic mercy on the witness stand: "Aha! The police 'attended' to my client for you, did they? What do you mean—for you? Did you pay them for their little attention?" It turned out that Mr. Hepplewhite did not want to prosecute the old tramp, and it turned out also that the old tramp was in Mr. Hepplewhite's house to steal. The jury returned a verdict of guilty. The old tramp then told the judge, "Sure . . . I'm a burglar. . . . When I heard the guy . . . coming up the stairs I just dove for the slats and played I was asleep." Mr. Tutt had no friends in the case. He perhaps sought one friend, but in vain. He refused to seek any human regard from Mr. Hepplewhite, or to give him any. That was a moral failure, I think, and perhaps it argues that friendship is a choice and the neglect of the possibility of friendship is a moral failure.

The clients not chosen to be friends are at some disadvantage; they do not get as much good service as those who are friends. Jerry Kennedy worked for a while for a freelance mechanic named Donald French. French was maintaining the engines on a boat used to smuggle drugs, and he sought preventive legal advice from Jerry because he was worried. Jerry did not seek to make a friend of French. He took French's money and spent it lavishly. He found out, but did not tell French, that French was the object of ominous designs by federal narcotics agents. Jerry failed to head off a raid and a shoot-out in which French killed a narcotics agent; and he then represented French in some humdrum plea bargaining on the homicide charge. French was, throughout, literally friendless.

One way Jerry might cope with the moral issue of Donald French (the guilty memory I think he has about the case) would be to say that he couldn't help it that Donald French was not his friend. Maybe he would have done better work for French if French had been his friend. Maybe—reflecting on the truthfulness and mutual respect that characterizes his work for Cadillac Teddy and Lou Schwartz—Jerry would say it is too bad he was not Donald French's friend. Too bad. As in tragic. But not as in sinful. Or Jerry could say—and I think this is what he would say—that he shouldn't have taken the case. If French could not be his friend, he should not have been his client.

I don't think Mr. Tutt would make the argument that, if French (or Mrs. Baldwin) could not be a friend, he (she) should not have been a client. To treat Mrs. Baldwin as he did, Mr. Tutt had to decide not only that she was evil but also that she was beyond turning from her evil. That prejudice was wrong, but Mr. Tutt might say that his inability to prefer her as one of his friends was not wrong; it was just the way things are. A broader and more important argument to somewhat the same effect could be made about the scores of clients each of these lawyers had who were not treated unfairly but who were not offered friendship either. I think Mr. Tutt would make that argument.

The professions have taught that, since a doctor or lawyer "cannot consult for the good of them all," a doctor or lawyer should not exercise preference at all. We should not distribute the commodity of friendship that St. Augustine talks about. The dominant ethical tradition in the American professions says that a professional should maintain detachment from her clients; that she should avoid making them friends. Mr. Tutt and the old boys in the bar association would agree with Jerry Kennedy that something went wrong in the Donald French case, but the moral lessons they take from it are opposites. Jerry would say (I think) that he should never have taken the case. The old boys (and maybe Mr. Tutt) would say Jerry should have taken the case, should have treated French better, and should have treated Lou Schwartz and Teddy Franklin the same way he treated French—none of them as friends.

But it is important to remember who we are talking about. Jerry Kennedy is a dissenter. Here is what he might say about detachment. "Wait a minute," he might say to the bar association's commission on ethics (and maybe to Mr. Tutt). "Do you suppose that you old boys are free from this *taint* of friendship? Do you suppose that you old boys are not taking care of one another? Do you suppose that the lawyer for banks who gets appointed banking commissioner doesn't continue to look after the banks, or that the physicians who run the AMA are in favor of house calls? There is a difference between us dissenters and you proponents of objectivity and professional distance, but it is not the difference you think. Friendship is, for us, to be sure, a thing of difficulties; it may even be tragic. But your problem is that you are not telling yourselves the truth; and your moral fault is that you are exploiting everybody who is not in your circle of friends, and then denying that the exploiters you live and work among are people who prefer one another."

Jerry Kennedy, would, I think, admit the fact of friendship and that he does a better job for clients who are his friends than for clients who are not. The proponent of detachment denies both the fact of friendship and the fact that he does a better job for people who are like he is. Jerry and Fanny Holtzmann would, I think, admit the element of self-love in friendship, and the element of friendship in collective action; and that, for them, takes care of the issue of moral purity, as between them and those who say they should be detached from their clients. It probably does not take care of the pain Jerry feels when he realizes that not all his clients are his friends, and that those who are his friends get a better deal from him. If the hard job for others is to tell the truth, the ethics of friendship does better than the old boys in the bar association do.

Three Traditional and Positive Arguments for Preferring Friends

Dissenting bluster aside, when the truth is told, the student of applied ethical theory notices that *preference* is a persistent issue in the ethics of friendship. I notice three positive approaches to it in the literature (and there may be others). One argues that preference in friendship is justifiable because the love that friends have for one another benefits all the other relationships each friend has. In legal ethics, this first approach would deny that Jerry Kennedy's friendship for Teddy Franklin is what caused him to be a poor lawyer for Donald French. His friendship for Teddy may even have made him a better lawyer for French than he would otherwise have been.

The second approach says that any friendship is a school for virtue. Even what Aristotle saw as the weak friendships (those based on advantage or pleasure), even friendship among the old boys in the bar association, are schools for virtue. Friendship does entail disadvantage for other relationships, as, with Aristotle, the friendship among Athenian gentlemen that he idealized may have made things worse for Athenian slaves and Athenian women. But the gain in virtue is worth the cost. (After all, *any* morality is selfish in that it promises personal excellence to the person who follows it.)

And the third approach says that preference is unnecessary. (This would or might also be to say that the exercise of preference in professional practice is wrong.) Friendship is a possibility in all relationships; there is no essential psychological economy in it. Being friendly is a method and a point of beginning for universal, or, as it is sometimes thought of, "civic" friendship. (This third approach largely set the terms for the debate about the lawyer as friend that Edward Dauer and Arthur Leff had, some years ago, with Charles Fried.)

The first two approaches say that preferential friendship is justified because it makes the friend a better person. They even make preference look better by arguing that a truly moral friend seeks no gain for himself, but only the goodness of the other. Kierkegaard spoke of this as hiding behind the dash. "He stands alone—by my help. . . . In this little sentence the infinity of thought is contained in the most profound way, the greatest contradiction overcome. He stands alone—this is the highest; he stands alone—nothing else do you see. You see no aid or assistance, no awkward bungler's hand holding on to him any more than it occurs to the person himself that someone has helped him. No, he stands alone—by another's help. But this help is hidden . . . , it is hidden behind a dash."

The trouble with this way out of the problem of preference (selflessness) is that it is not plausible. It may be that, in some of our friendships, we come finally to be so unselfish that we do not even want our friend to know what we have done for him, and that, because of this unselfishness, the preference for the friend is justifiable. But we are not likely to get that far along without a preliminary period of relative selfishness. If we deny to ourselves what we get from friendship, we will never reach a friendship in which we can deny ourselves. Kierkegaard refused even this much validity to the hidden-behind-the-dash theory. He said that it is a mistake to see friendship as a ladder leading from self-love to mutual love to selfless love. In fact, he said, the selfish and the selfless are all mixed up with one another, right from the beginning and right to the end. Friendship may begin with selflessness; selflessness may be what makes mutual gain in friendship possible. But selfishness—the element of self-love in friendship—is what keeps friendship going. Jerry Kennedy, for all his stumbling, knows that. Cadillac Teddy gets more from Jerry than Jerry would *sell* to anybody else, but—still—Jerry charges Teddy for his travel time.

The first and second approaches to preference in friendship also admit that Jerry's friendship with Teddy means that Teddy gets better professional service than Donald French does. They admit even that Mr. Tutt's friendship for Cabel Baldwin and Hans Schmidt resulted in harsh treatment for Mrs. Baldwin and Mr. Hepplewhite. But, says the proponent of the ethics of friendship, the gain from friendship makes the cost worth it.

Propounders of official American legal ethics have invoked the second approach (the school-for-virtue approach) to justify the principle that an American lawyer is free to refuse clients for personal reasons. If this results in some people not getting lawyers, the responsibility for correction lies primarily with professional institutions, which then admonish lawyers to think of their duty *not to the person who has no lawyer but to the institution.* The American profession has been less coherent in its answer to the lawyer who wants to drop the client he already has, but, logically, the same principle should apply there. It would, I think, have been applied there but for the fact that changing lawyers in the middle of cases poses problems for lawyers (fees, files, etc.) and institutions (dockets, trial time, etc.).

Jerry Kennedy and Fanny Holtzmann, following Kierkegaard's (and Aristotle's) notion that friendship is selfish and earthy, might say that preference in friendship is as much a part of life on the earth as preference in erotic love is. They would probably be less interested in *justifying* preference than in trying to clean up and contain the disadvantage it seems to bring to other people, and particularly to those among their clients who are not friends. I think, for example, that Jerry Kennedy would admit moral fault in his treatment of Donald French, not because of anything being the matter with his friendships with Teddy and Lou, but because of the flawed relationship he had with Donald French. Mr. Tutt might admit—he should have—that the way he treated Hepplewhite was as bad as the way he imagined Hepplewhite had treated Hans Schmidt. But this would not have anything to do, one way or the other, with the friendships these lawyers had with other clients.

The third approach to the problem of preference is the ideal of civic friendship. It may have begun with Aristotle, who said, "When people are friends they have no need of justice." The ideal is that the old boys who run things are friends, not only of one another but of everybody. In their commitment to the common good they have foresworn personal advantage; the Irish Catholics and the Jews have nothing to worry about. This is the notion of friendship as it has been appropriated by liberal democratic theory. It is the ideal that the dissenters dissent from. They dissent from it not only in terms of their experience and their gently cynical reaction (see part 3 below), but from the deepest springs of their moral culture. If they used the rage of the prophets who are in their religious traditions they would probably call civic friendship hypocritical, self-deceived, pagan, and idolatrous. That prophetic rage is not as expected in this generation as it was in Mr. Tutt's, or even in Fanny Holtzmann's. Few people pretend any longer that the groups that gather and preserve and dispense power in our society are unselfish, universal, republican forms of human association. Maybe we even understand that such a view of the state—or of professional commissions on ethics—is idolatrous. We understand at least why Mr. Tutt thought such a view of the law was (to use a word he liked) tosh, and why Fanny Holtzmann used such clout as she had to get what she wanted from the bar association and, after that, cheerfully ignored it.

There is a version of civic friendship that is stronger among us than it was among the lawyers of Mr. Tutt's and Fanny's generation. That is the teamwork notion, the notion that each of us has a job to do. That view is the moral core both of the American legal profession's embattled, fatuous, but still vital adversary ethic, and of the medical profession's claim to be scientific. There are many objections to the ethics of the job. One is that such an ethic is socially irresponsible. Objections to the legal profession's adversary ethic, for example, include prominently the argument that the lawyer who considers only his client's interest is immoral toward other people, or, as the argument is more commonly put, toward "society." A related objection is that the adversary ethic makes a god of the state, in its Darwinian confidence—faith—that the best claim will survive and that the state can decide which is best. Another objection is that the ethic of the job is morally schizoid; it divides people up, at best, and, at worst, it gives them excuses for immoral behavior (see chapter 3).

I don't think any of these objections to the ethics of the job would interest the dissenters. What the dissenters would most likely say about the ethics of the job is that friendship has nothing to do with jobs. In fact, the job ethic squeezes friendship out—denies it a place to live.

The dissenters would also say that the concept of civic friendship is seriously flawed. Civic friendship is not friendship—neither in its pure Jeffersonian form (in, say, the legal ethics of David Hoffman or the medical ethics of Sir Thomas Percival) nor in its modern expression as the ethic of the job. Civic friendship is only a strident way to appropriate the spiritual love friends have for one another without the earthy love of self that makes spiritual love possible. Friendship—the ordinary way we talk about it among ourselves and in our stories—is inevitably self-seeking. Friendship of the pure sort that the civic-friendship argument supposes is not friendship because it is not earthy enough to be human.

Putting emphasis on a job, as civic friendship does, *kills* the possibility of earthy friendship. Gilbert Meilaender noticed a sort of deadened friendship in the story of John Wesley, who was a warm man, a man nature had suited for many friendships, but who seems to have lacked the *time* for them because he had a *job* to do. According to Meilaender, Wesley was "a man never at leisure to have out his talk, to understand what serious (i.e., morally perilous) business a vocation could become. Such a calling leaves little place for self-indulgence within life. We may simply note, without in any way suggesting that folding one's legs and having one's talk is unworthy, that whole-hearted commitment to our calling may leave little time for such pleasures. The inevitable result is that deep personal relationships like friendship, without precisely being denigrated, become harder and harder to sustain. They are . . . squeezed out of life. Personal significance is found in one's calling—or it is not found at all."

I think of the negative example of Louis Auchincloss's young lawyer, Timothy Colt, who refused the partnership offered by his obstreperous client George Emlen and chose instead what he called partnership with a bulging briefcase. Or, for a positive example, of the physicians who refuse to use placebos, not because placebos are ineffective in curing disease, not because of the physicians' commitment to an abstract notion of professional truthfulness, but because placebos corrupt earthy friendship. Dr. Richard C. Cabot, a turn-of-the century medical dissenter, is an example: "The majority of placebos are given because we believe the patient will not be satisfied without them. He has learned to expect medicine for every symptom . . . but who taught him to expect a medicine for every symptom? He was not born with that expectation. He learned it from an ignorant [busy] doctor. . . . No patient whose language you speak, whose mind you can approach, needs a placebo. I give placebos now and then . . . to Armenians and others with whom I cannot communicate . . . but if I can get hold of an interpreter and explain the matter, I can tell him no lies in the shape of placebos."

Finally, the ethics of the job harm the *doing* of the job—and this is especially so when the job involves, as medicine and the law do, the tending of human relationships. The lawyer who chooses civic friendship instead of earthy friendships with his clients is, in this view, like the surgeon who must kill the patient to cure him. "At the same time that the worker is called upon to find personal significance in his work . . . the work itself becomes increasingly impersonal and subject to rational economic calculation," Meilaender says. Time records, 2,200-billable-hours-a-year, overhead, fees for travel time, calculation of benefit and loss. "And one's place in that system is determined not by personal bonds like friendship but by considerations of efficiency and fairness. Devotion to the task at hand becomes of supreme importance." The dissenting lawyers would likely say that the use of the word "personal" in reference to a *job* is an irony. What happens is that the only occasion on which a person is given undivided attention is when he is *also* a job, and then only to the extent that he is *the* job. The moral argument that civic friendship, as expressed in the ethics of the job, is a way to serve many people's needs, is, then, logically and consequentially, a way of life without friends; and because a task done without friends is soon uninteresting, it is a task done without thought. Rabbi Hirsch would say that it makes sense to look on one's work as a way to serve one's friend, or even to see one's work as a necessary bit of discipline. But when you prefer work to friendship, you deny life itself.

The ethics of friendship that these stories of dissenters bring to American lawyers and doctors is not this democratically liberal civic friendship. But it is not merely a scoff or a grumble either. It is finally a different religious vision, an alternative vision for the practice of a profession—for a way to be both a professional person and a good person. The dominant professional culture, the one that has produced the resolutions, admonitions, codes, and rules of professional behavior, turns on Anglo-American, Protestant, Enlightenment civic religion—on the responsibility of every professional person for the purity of purpose implied in the grand religious claims that Americans make for America. This dominant ethic has depended on a view of the person as a lonely individual (the Jeffersonian yeoman farmer and the frontier settler, the cowboy and the ambitious businessman). Such a view has been fundamental both for social ethics and for the realization of the American religious dream.

This democratic-liberal tradition found expression in organized American professions. It applauded professional moral teachers who said what it wanted to hear, and then set up groups of individuals to proclaim standards and principles for lawyers and physicians and journalists and undertakers. Bar associations began to do this in the 1870s, medical associations a generation earlier. The professional associations assumed purity of purpose both in the associations and in their commissions on ethics.

The dominant professional ethic has used metaphors of friendship (or fraternity) to describe the duties that go with a doctor's or lawyer's membership in the American civil religion. But those are failed metaphors. Friendship, when used that way, is incoherent. The broad notion of political duty implied in the American civic religion rests on radical individualism, not on the love of friends for one another—on a morality of autonomy rather than the cultural morality of family, neighborhood, and religious congregation. When such autonomous people gather to see to what they call one another's freedom, they are not friends. There is no coming home.

PART THREE: GENTLE CYNICISM

The consequences and implications of the professional ethics of friendship begin with personal moral gain for the professionals. Stories of dissenting professionals in America show, for example, that friendships with clients are how lawyers and doctors know that what they do is worthwhile. The dominant tradition in American medical and legal ethics, by contrast, offers worthwhileness through appeals to the needs of the state and to America's divine destiny. David Hoffman spoke of the new republic's law as a temple and of lawyers as priests. The dissenters are not persuaded by these appeals.

They do, though, find that their work is worthwhile. Friendship with clients is their way to overcome the deficiencies and pretensions of the dominant professional ethic, and to retain energy and interest in professional practice. This process is Aristotelian; it rests on the practice of the virtue of friendship—not on friendship as a bit of good luck, but the virtue of friendship as these professionals have learned about it in their immigrant communities—their neighborhoods, their families, and their religious congregations.

Friendship is personal gain and inspiration for professional life. It is also a social ethic, a political ethic. In its social and political manifestation it is what Michael Novak calls gentle cynicism. There is in America, he says, a "morality based upon a gentle cynicism and cultural pessimism, rooted in the traditions of Southern and Eastern Europe. It is, perhaps, a Catholic—and Jewish—cynicism, not . . . reflected in the Puritan or other Anglo-American traditions."

"Catholics and Jews tend to be 'crass' in their understanding of power and in their willingness to calculate special interests," Novak says. "Both note a tendency on the part of unabashedly powerful Protestant leaders to surround their use of power with moral talk and, if possible, to insulate the true source of power and decision through the use of studies, commissions, committees and other institutions from direct contact with raw consequences. The man up front protects his moral image." The difference here is a difference in social and political ethics. The dominant professional (social) ethic begins with a grand moral claim where the gentle cynic begins with a friend.

Beginning with Persons

The cultural manifestation of this gentle cynicism in professional life is friendship with patients and clients. A theoretical basis for it is in Aristotle's *Magna Moralia* and in the *Nicomachean Ethics*. What is interesting about this theoretical basis is that it is not a claim about or a vision of society or of the state but an ordinary earthy interest in oneself and people who come along one at a time.

"The good man . . . takes pleasure in morally virtuous actions and dislikes vicious ones, just as a musician enjoys beautiful melodies and is pained by bad ones," Aristotle said.

"Flourishing consists in living and being active, and the activity which is peculiarly one's own is pleasant . . . we can study our neighbors better than ourselves and their actions better than those that are peculiarly our own . . . the actions of good persons who are their friends are pleasant to good people. . . . If so, then the fully flourishing person will need friends of this kind, given that he chooses to study actions that are good and peculiarly his own, and the actions of the good person who is his friend are of this kind."

The argument is that friendship provides self-knowledge, and that we want to know ourselves; we want to find ourselves interesting. Self-knowledge is a pleasant thing, and self-knowledge is like the knowledge we gain from observing a friend. Observing the friend is a way of gaining self-knowledge. In fact, Aristotle said, observing a friend is essential to self-knowledge. "Friends do take interest in and derive pleasure from one another's thoughts and actions, and . . . the interest they take in them is akin to the interest they take in their own." And so one finds his friend interesting, then he finds himself interesting, then he finds others around him interesting. When he comes to have a professional ethic or a social ethic, it is one that derives from such entirely personal association.

The insight and the method were noticed by the giants of depth psychology early in the present century. Sigmund Freud and Carl Gustav Jung made introspection, projection, and displacement fundamental to their science. Aristotle had said: "We are not able to see what we are from ourselves. . . . That we cannot do so is plain from the way in which we blame others without being aware that we do the same things ourselves. . . . There are many of us who are blinded by these things so that we judge not aright; as then when we wish to see our own face, we do so by looking into the mirror, in the same way when we wish to know ourselves we can obtain that knowledge by looking at our friend. For the friend is . . . a second self. . . . The self-sufficing man will require friendship in order to know himself." This is the way an Aristotelian disposes of the ethics of radical individualism.

We tend to find faults in others that are our own, and to find virtues in ourselves that are not there. Friendship, Aristotle argues, is a way out of these two corrosive products of self-deception. Friendship is also a way to discover and to learn to value the virtues we have. Thus, Lou Schwartz and Teddy Franklin show Jerry Kennedy virtues he does not think of himself as having (innocence in Lou's case, truthful advocacy in Teddy's). Aristotle argues that this self-knowledge comes from friends, rather than (or more than) other people. How so? First, because friends are similar in character—so that the mirror is more accurate. In fact, mirror is a poor metaphor here; Aristotle is not talking about a mirror. He is talking about the other self a friend provides, "an equivalent center of self," George Eliot called it (chapter 4). Friends sense their similarity intuitively; it is both part of how they become friends and why the friend is the other self—the "intuitive sense of kinship with another person." And, second, self-knowledge comes from friends because associations with friends are more intense and more prolonged than associations with others, so that the knowledge gained has the additional validity provided by focus and testing and maturation.

The latter argument from Aristotle is that friendship is pleasant and makes pleasant the things we share with friends, one of which is learning about oneself. This is an essential point for professional ethics. Jerry Kennedy has become bored with much of his law practice, but not with all of it. He still enjoys working for Cadillac Teddy and for Lou Schwartz—or, if "enjoys" is too limp a word, he remains engaged and energetic when he works for them (and therefore does better work). He flourishes when among friends. Is this because it is more fun to work for a friend? Probably so, but it would be a mistake to stop there. Working for a friend in professional life is like making a knick-knack for your mother in the high school industrial arts workshop (which is more fun to do than making a knick-knack for a grade), but it is more than that. That quality of enjoyment caused by expressing love in work is no doubt there; but, in addition, these lawyers have more energy when they work for their friends because professional work done in friendship is labor shared. Their clients, when friends, are involved in the professional tasks. And, even more precisely, the professionals have a sense that their clients are involved. Thus, Dr. Horn speaks of her work as participation in her patient's care.

Jerry Kennedy and Teddy Franklin have this sort of professional relationship. It is one that has taken time and discipline. It is not the sort of sharing in which Teddy has become expert at Jerry's craft—any more than their association has made Jerry able to steal Cadillacs and not get caught. But their relation is one in which Teddy shares not only in tactics and objectives but also in the development and critique of Jerry's abilities as a lawyer, and even in the morals involved in Jerry's abilities.

"I am never at my best or fully comfortable on premises that tremble under me," Jerry Kennedy says. "Mildly disappointed clients have suggested that this problem is the reason why I never did achieve . . . eminence. . . . Cadillac Teddy Franklin, whom I have kept out of jail for twelve or thirteen years now, against very heavy odds, admitted once that he was always just a little bit concerned when I rose to get him loose on some fragile technicality which the arresting officer had neglected when he brought Teddy in. 'It's not your line of bullshit, Jerry,' Teddy told me worriedly. 'Your brand of stuff is just as good as anybody else's. It's the way you act when you stand up to sling it, you know? Like you're getting ready to put something over on the judge, and everybody else . . . make them do something that you don't think anybody in his right mind ought to do. I've got to say, even though it's always worked, at least when you're representing me, it does make me a little nervous. I can see why other guys would get somebody else. You are only really good when you mean it.' " That is moral advice, from a friend, and it corresponds to the moral advice Teddy gets from Jerry. Jerry wants Teddy to stop stealing cars, not for Jerry's benefit (hardly!) but for Teddy's.

Finding Professional Work Worthwhile (as a Social Ethic)

This shared-task aspect of professional friendship can be taken apart, in a philosophical manner, and analyzed. For one thing, the professional worker, when the task is shared, is more engaged in his work. "Living in isolation causes one to lose the capacity to be actively interested in things," says John Cooper, a modern Aristotelian. "Even if the activity that delights one most is something that can be enjoyed by a solitary person (as is true of most intellectual pursuits) it tends not to be pursued with freshness and interest by someone living cut off from others. One tends to become apathetic and inactive without the stimulation and support that others, especially those whom one likes and esteems, provide by sharing one's goals and interests." Jerry Kennedy knows about isolation and engagement; he learned it when he was a child in his Irish neighborhood. He says it, now, in a characteristically ironic way. "A ragtag parade of young men, mostly between eighteen and twenty-six, finds its way through the door . . . and I listen to their troubles. Some are sullen, some are defiant, repeaters are tired or embarrassed, and we try to treat them as though they were individuals. It is better when we succeed, and they and their cases permit this; clients like Lou Schwartz bring on emotional upsets and make me appreciate somewhat the long stretches of rank dullness."

In working for friends, Jerry knows that what he is doing *can* be done alone, but need not be. When it is not done alone, when it is shared, he has the benefit of feeling another's commitment to goal—and of knowing that the client-friend will contribute to the common effort. Part of the way he knows of this commitment and feels assured that the client's part will be provided is the product of a loving relationship experienced over time. Put another way, the tendency to find professional work interesting is confirmed because another and valued person finds it so; the sense of being one in a partnership is present where it is not present in his more routine cases. The sense of participation is pleasant and it is stimulating. It occurs because of the emotions of friendship and because self-knowledge is taking place.

The more important the work is, the more significant this confirmation is. "The sense of one's own worth is, for human beings, a group accomplishment," Cooper says. The two things—the pleasure in shared activity and the pleasure in self-knowledge—are related (they may explain why a person enters a profession). "It is clear enough that the satisfactions that derive from shared activity are especially needed in connection with those activities, whatever they may be, that are most central to a person's life and which contribute most decidedly to his flourishing, as he himself conceives it. For here the flagging of one's commitments and interests will be particularly debilitating; here more than anywhere else one needs the confirmatory sense that others too share one's convictions about which activities are worthwhile." Part of the reason is this matter of self-discovery; part of it is more exactly moral. "For in order to know that someone is genuinely committed to moral values one must know him and his character pretty closely, since commitment here . . . is a matter of moral character or its absence."

The American immigrant lawyers achieve this sense of social usefulness, not from liberal-democratic philosophy, but from their communities—from such things as rites of passage in a family or a religious congregation. And so they go home to be useful away from home. They take their cases home. They go home to be healed, at times of demand and dismay. Home is sometimes where they eat and sleep and watch television, and sometimes it is not there but with a friend. But they go home to the friend because they have learned to go home to a home. Fanny Holtzmann, according to her biographer (who was also her nephew) found adventure and self-fulfillment and social usefulness in the practice of law that she had not found growing up as a middle child in a large immigrant family. She found self-knowledge and worthwhileness with her client-friends—found there much that she had not found at home. But she was able to be a friend and to make friends, in the way Cooper describes friendship, because she had learned at home, in sometimes painful ways, the importance of friendship.

The sadness that lingered in Fanny's life was that she did not also have—as Jerry Kennedy does—the sort of home her parents made with one another. She was wise enough, in the midst of personal and professional success, to realize that. Berkman says, "Fanny's bookshelves were crowded with autographed volumes and tributes . . . but the sense of personal isolation would not go away. At a family Bar Mitzva celebration, she surveyed the quiet little house in the suburbs, one of thousands scattered along the route of the Long Island Railroad, with the inevitable swing in the garden and the Chagall prints on the living-room walls, and she sighed: 'This is what makes all the struggle worthwhile.' "

Friendship as a Social Ethic

Fanny Holtzmann's and Jerry Kennedy's stories add to the story of Ephraim Tutt and of the immigration lawyers a focus on friendship as a cultural reality. This is so in two senses. First, it is clearer in Jerry's story that friendship is what sustains him in the practice—what is really important to him. If you look at Mr. Tutt and the Houston immigration lawyers, and then at Fanny Holtzmann and Jerry Kennedy, then at Mr. Tutt and the Houston lawyers again, you can see friendship more clearly, in all four stories.

Second, Jerry's story shows how, in all four stories, friendship has a social dimension. We are inclined, in late twentieth-century America, to be enthusiastic about friendship. We say a lot about it on prepared greeting cards and on banners and little signs for kitchens and desks. Friendship is the dynamic in, say, popular television crime programs. But we are less clear about friendship as a *professional* and *social* virtue. We suspect the understanding of friendship that made it possible for Aristotle to say that the *state* rests on friendship. We are therefore unclear about the less-grand understanding C. S. Lewis had, in our own time, when he stopped short of Aristotle's conclusion but said that friendship makes life richer both for those who are friends and for the community. Friendship may not have survival value, Lewis said, but it has "civilization value." It "helps the community not to live but to live well . . . it is one of those things that give value to survival." Social value—even without Aristotle's politics.

This issue about whether friendship is a social virtue, whether it has social importance, whether it is something that reaches out to and affects people outside the friendship and is therefore not simply a personal indulgence, is important for the terms in which professional moral discourse is conducted now in America. It is possible that a dissenting lawyer such as Jerry Kennedy would say it is not important to him whether his friendship with Teddy Franklin results in social good. But, still, it may be possible to argue that it does. The argument Kennedy might make, if he wanted to argue, would, though, be different from the liberal-democratic argument one reads in law-review articles about notions of social duty or of abstract moral principle.

For example, the argument within the medical profession about the use of placebos is typically an argument conducted on individualistic premises rather than communal premises. The argument is usually an argument about an abstract duty to an abstract patient, rather than an argument about how friends should treat one another.

"I knew a surgeon who thought nothing of performing an oblique lower right quadrant incision, then suturing without entering the abdominal cavity, in patients who had emotional problems manifested by pain in the abdomen," one doctor says. "His results were excellent and, as one might expect, his operative mortality and morbidity were exceptionally low." The surgical equivalent of a sugar pill. "I am certain that thousands of appendectomies and hysterectomies are done yearly as placebos."

There is a liberal-democratic response to this utilitarian justification for deceit; it is not about the patient but about a contract. "The . . . 'contract' between doctor and patient represents the legal convention of a fiduciary contract, in which one party to the contract undertakes a special responsibility to look out for the best interests of the other. The Georgia Supreme Court held in 1975, 'where a person sustains toward others a relation of trust and confidence, his silence when he should speak, or his failure to disclose what he ought to disclose, is as much a fraud in law as an actual affirmative false representation.' " This judicial reason for honesty in the doctor-patient relationship is the same reason that would be given for a medical malpractice judgment if the patient should have had an abdominal operation and sued because he didn't get one. It rests on the duty that comes from a contract. It is an altogether different argument than saying the patient is a friend, that a person doesn't lie to his friends.

The fiduciary-contract reasoning is advanced in the debate among physicians about the morality of using placebos. It is not advertently a discussion about the law, or what the law should be, but the abstract character of the discussion is not different than it would be if the discussion were about the law and if a decision were to be made by an official of the government. It is an individualistic, liberal-democratic, republican sort of argument. The links between two lonely individuals, and the only links between either of them and the community, are links of contract and of citizenship. The people involved are, to use another legal term, fungible. The doctor gets to be a party to a fiduciary contract because he offers a regulated service, not because of who he is. The patient is the dependent party to the contract because patients are those regulation protects, and regulation is necessary because the patient is a dependent. The ethical spirit of the argument is not at all like Dr. Cabot's (the placebo is a lie); nor is it like Dr. Horn's referring to her medical mandate as personal and interpersonal, as an invitation from a particular sick old man to participate in his healing of himself; nor is the fiduciary argument like the country doctors who make house calls and who do some of their well-baby examinations on the floor, playing with particular children—those, I suppose, who like to play on the floor.

Dr. Cabot, Dr. Horn, and the play-on-the-floor doctors would not approach the placebo issue as a matter either of utilitarian deceit or fiduciary contract. I think they would join a few kindred professional spirits who have come up with both a rationale and a bit of clinical data to reconcile placebos with friendship. Howard Brody's report on several experiments shows how this works:

"Fifteen patients visiting an outpatient psychiatric facility because of various bodily symptoms related to their neuroses were given sugar pills. They were told by the physician that these pills were in fact sugar pills; that there was no active medication in them; that patients who had taken these pills in the past often had dramatic relief; and that the physicians were hopeful that they would also have a positive response. The patients were instructed to take the pills for a week and then return. Fourteen of the fifteen patients did so and thirteen of them were found to have significant symptom improvement." One thing friends take into account is that neither of them is entirely or consistently rational.

"A team of Boston anesthesiologists . . . took two large groups of patients about to undergo surgery and randomly assigned them to the control or experimental group. The control group got the routine preoperative visit from the anesthesiologist to take a medical history. The experimental group received a more in-depth interview, which emphasized teaching about postoperative pain, reassurance that adequate pain medication would be ordered if the patient needed it, and instruction on . . . simple techniques . . . to minimize pain in the postoperative period. The experimental group ended up requiring one half as much pain medication on the average as the control group and were able to be discharged from the hospital two days earlier." Friends flourish (Aristotle's word) on the truth.

"An anxious individual . . . seemed unable to function in his daily life without tranquilizers, but . . . also had a considerable fear and anxiety about the known addiction potential of those medicines. The physicians presented to him as an option the use of a sugar pill so that he would have the emotional reassurance of knowing he was doing something to control his anxiety on a day-to-day basis and would also know that he was not running any risk of physiologic addiction. The patient agreed to a trial of placebos on this basis and had excellent results."

This is, Dr. Brody says, "the healing that comes . . . from the relationship between healer and patient, and the patients' own capacities to heal themselves through symbolic and psychological approaches as well as through biological intervention. . . . A broader understanding of the placebo effect suggests many creative and nondeceptive ways in which this powerful therapeutic tool can be used for the benefit of patients." It is as Hippocrates said it would be: Friendship heals.

These friendly placebo stories bear on what I see as the first step in building a social ethic of friendship for professional life. The first step involves personal relationships—self and other—and self knowledge. The ethic derives from (a) self-knowledge; (b) the fact that clients and patients are friends; and (c) the feeling or conviction that what one is doing as a doctor or lawyer is worthwhile. And then this building of a social ethic makes a link between emotional (and intellectual) security and the common good. The link is provided by the earthy communities of family, neighborhood, and religious congregation.

Fanny Holtzmann found a community among her friends and clients in show business; she knew she had—she knew what a community was—because she had grown up in one, in her family and her neighborhood in Jewish Brooklyn. Ephraim Tutt found community less well among those he thought he was protecting; a persistent disposition in the gentleman-professional is that he is fond of those he is protecting. I guess I would have to say that he would have done better at friendship if he had had a Jewish mother.

Jerry Kennedy finds community in Irish Boston and among the people he works with, most of them his clients. Police officers, retired and on active duty, are in Jerry's community; there are more Irish police officers in it than lawyers of any kind. For example, Jerry settled a case in a trade he made with an investigating officer. Jerry swapped information on an extra-limits automobile insurance policy for lenient treatment of his client, who drove drunk and badly injured another police officer. Jerry was able to get Cadillac Teddy bail in the driver's license case because the desk sergeant was in Jerry's community. "Look, Mister Franklin," Sergeant Finney said, "I dunno you. I don't even want to know you. I know him, and I've known him for a long time . . . and . . . because Jerry's in it, I'm letting you walk."

This is like Fanny Holtzmann's getting Edmund Goulding to talk on the phone to Lord Auckland, and to settle a dispute between Auckland and her client Francis X. Bushman, involving Auckland's dogs. Fanny learned this procedure when she made tea for litigants in the *Bet Din* court of her grandfather, Rabbi Hirsch Bornfeld, who held his court in his daughter's kitchen. In the case of Eli Stein and his petulant business associate Chaim, for example, Rabbi Hirsch discouraged a civil lawsuit. "What does a *goyish* judge, raised in Boston, know how things are between you and Chaim?" the rabbi said. Mr. Tutt was able in a similar way to call on livery stable operators, fishermen, and the inhabitants of New York's old Irish ghetto. All three lawyers tended, by the way, to violate professional rules against dealing with another lawyer's clients.

These communities are more like Aristotelian fraternities than the bar-association commissions on ethics are. The dissenters' communities are not based on contract but on something more intuitive—history, perhaps, or even biology. Dissenting lawyers rest their worlds on such fraternities, just as the Athenian world rested, in Aristotle's view, on friendship.

Judge Sharswood said, "Nothing is more certain than that the practitioner will find, in the long run, the good opinion of his professional brethren of more importance than that of what is commonly called the public" (chapter 4). Holtzmann and Kennedy have not found that to be the case. They have found instead that it is the good opinion of friends that makes a person better. They dissent from Judge Sharswood's claim—the claim that the professional fraternity is a source of goodness—but not from the notion that friendship, when and where you can find it, is a source of goodness. One difference between Judge Sharswood and Fanny Holtzmann or Jerry Kennedy is in where they find their friends. Another difference is in the validity and intensity of their friendships. Holtzmann and Kennedy are more likely than Sharswood to find among their friends the "assurance that members of tribes and villages have extended to one another for millennia, the assurance that no earthly adventure, from puberty to death, is unprecedented or incapable of being shared and that one's life is thoroughly witnessed and therefore not wasted" (Novak). That assurance, when you find it, is, I think, a social ethic. (I pick this point up again, in the latter part of chapter 6, in reference to H. Richard Niebuhr's social ethics.)

In either situation—Sharswood's fraternity of lawyers or the communal and lawyer-client friendships you find in these stories—friendship is socially important; it is a professional ethic. Not an experience or a bit of good luck, but an ethic. "Friendship . . . seems to hold states together," Aristotle said. "When people are friends they have no need of justice, but when they are just, they need friendship in addition. . . . Friendship is noble as well as necessary: we praise those who love their friends." Aristotle did not advance the ethical concept of lonely integrity and rugged individualism that is evident in the usual medical-ethics debate on placebos; nor did he see friendship as a bit of good luck. The integrity he implied when he talked about friendship was as much a product of friendship as it was a condition for friendship.

· § ·

In the Kennedy and Holtzmann stories, friendship as a social ethic depends on this communal (Novak calls it Mediterranean) notion that friendship is a source of goodness. It is a virtue, in the sense that Aristotle taught about virtue—a habit. It is both a good thing to *do* (not only to *be,* but to *do*), and a routine the practice of which makes a person good. And it is in its character as a virtue that friendship has social significance. "Friendship is equality and likeness," he said, "and especially the likeness of those who are similar in virtue. . . . [Friends] neither request nor render any service that is base. On the contrary, one might even say that they prevent base services; for what characterizes good men is that they neither go wrong themselves nor let their friends do so. Bad people, on the other hand, do not have the element of constancy, for they do not remain similar even to themselves." *They do not remain similar even to themselves.* That was Lou Schwartz's argument when he told the Mafia boss that Jerry Kennedy would defend him without hamming the case up.

This is not the ethics of loyalty. Not the same thing at the interpersonal level, and not the same thing at the social level, either. Loyalty is, at the interpersonal level, the disposition that requires you to hate when the person you are loyal to hates. It often seems, in professional life, to be the demand that you set your conscience aside, that you be untrue to yourself, that you lose the integrity and constancy that Aristotle talks about—because someone who has captured your attention expects you to do so. But Aristotle taught that friendship, unlike loyalty, prevents base service. Friendship is the virtue that supports the other person in the good and, in the process, makes it possible for him to remain constant, to remain similar to himself. The old-fashioned word here is integrity, being all together, being who you are.

Friendship preserves integrity—as Lou Schwartz knew it would—because it does not turn on loyalty; it turns on faithfulness. What the dissenters say is that loyalty—the Scout Law to the contrary notwithstanding—is not a virtue. They value friendship more than loyalty. The American literature of professional responsibility uses the terms fidelity (faithfulness) and loyalty in just this way. Faithfulness is the disposition that allows a person to negotiate his way, with constancy, through competing moral demands—for example, to be at the same time a scientist and a healer, or an advocate and an officer of the court; to be what the proposed *Model Rules* for lawyers call an *intermediary* in business practice or estate planning or family law; to be what Justice Brandeis called "the lawyer for the situation," or to be what country doctors mean when they talk about healers of the *families* of their patients.

The word loyalty is used differently in the regulatory literature. Loyalty refers to combat; it is often modified with adjectives such as blind, single-minded, or unswerving. It does not turn on the *integrity* of the person who is called patient or client; it turns on what the professional person defines as the *interests* of the person who is called patient or client. It is used, then, in contexts of unconditional demand. You have to be loyal or you have to get out; the regulators are not interested in your being true to yourself.

Loyalty is played out as a social and professional ethic in the liberal-democratic American legal ideal of the adversary, and in the American medical ideal of the doctor as a person who fights disease and death. The ethics of *fidelity* would say, with Aristotle, that society is preserved and made better through the behavior that friends encourage in one another. Friendship is a school for social virtue, a place where leaders are trained and supported in their pursuit of justice. The ethics of *loyalty* are fond of martial metaphors; they are a boast from social Darwinism; their social vision is a jungle; they turn on the optimism that narrow interest, pursued with vigor, results in justice because the fittest argument is the one that survives. I suggest that the lawyers in these stories—and, maybe, most American doctors and lawyers—talk about loyalty but believe in fidelity. The social ethics of fidelity, of friendship, is what we really think; the ethics of loyalty is what we try to get somebody else to think.

The Dissenters' Theory of Social and Political Power

My preliminary thought about the stories of Mr. Tutt, the Houston immigration lawyers, Horn, Holtzmann, Kennedy, and the friendly-placebo doctors was that their stories show how dissenting lawyers and doctors value clients and patients more than institutions. I think that is true, but that it is too flaccid a point. It does not do justice to these rich American stories. A more risky thought is that some of these stories also show how dissenting professionals value faithfulness more than loyalty, and that they show this in their practice of the virtue of friendship. If this is true, then it follows, I think, that the dissenting doctors and lawyers value community more than institutions and that they value friendship more than justice or the defeat of disease and death—so that the first and flaccid thought is converted into something that may be interesting for social ethics. What is preferred to the institution is not only the client but also the community. Or, to put that another way, the dissenters value their clients more than their institutions because they have learned in their communities how to value their clients. That is, they have learned in their communities how to be friends.

This is all more clear in stories such as Holtzmann's and Kennedy's than it is in stories such as Mr. Tutt's and Calvin Trillin's description of the immigration lawyers in Houston. Holtzmann and Kennedy are immigrants. Their families came to America with strong, coherent, intact moral traditions. They compared their morals with those they found in, say, Brahmin Boston and Old New York, and they decided that what they brought with them was better than what they found.

Fanny Holtzmann's grandfather, Hirsch Bornfeld, was an immigrant and a Hasidic rabbi. He was also an enthusiastic American, a resolute Republican, and a friend of Theodore Roosevelt. He once led a political parade through the streets of Brooklyn to the tune of "Onward, Christian Soldiers." But when it came to passing a moral tradition—a story—along to his granddaughter, he did not talk about the Stars and Stripes any more than he talked about Christian soldiers. He talked about the Torah, the family, the evident and faithful presence of God. "Never judge a fellowman by a single action," Rabbi Hirsch told her. "Try to see his whole record. Every man has something good in his past; contemplate that. . . . God has the greatest of bookkeeping systems. His angels keep track of every action you take, every thought in your head, awake or asleep. Nothing—good or bad—can be hidden from them. The more you give, the more the Lord will replenish your resources. And when your time comes to need help, you will have a fine credit rating; you will not be abandoned."

Those are conventional sentiments; they are the sort of thing we nodded over in Sunday school. Their importance to Fanny becomes clearer when you put them into the context of her family and her community—when you remember who said them, and where he said them; when you remember three thousand years of *mitzvot* and the persecutions of the Jews. When Rabbi Hirsch was dying, he said to Fanny, "For the rest of your life, you have nothing to worry about. I'll be up there in Heaven, making sure you get what you deserve. It isn't everybody who has someone standing guard there to see that God does His duty."

When Fanny had disappointments in her professional life, she did not think much of her professional forebears and elders in America or of the Pilgrim Fathers; she thought of her family and of the Jews. And she reacted less with grim determination than with a characteristic Jewish joke she had learned at home—such as that in Rabbi Abraham Ibn Ezra's verse: "If I were selling candles, the sun would never set." Rabbi Hirsch was disappointed in his grandson David, who showed no interest in religion. As he was dying, he gave David his prayer shawl and his prayer book. "That will ensure their perfect preservation through posterity," the rabbi said.

Fanny's approach to disputes was the one she learned in her grandfather's court, in the kitchen in Brooklyn. "The task of the law [is] to solve problems, harmonize differences—not aggravate them." When Fanny mentioned the Supreme Court to Rabbi Hirsch, he pointed to the ceiling: "The true Supreme Court," he said, "presides only up there!"

Much of the secret of Fanny's success as a lawyer was her ability to be relaxed, spontaneous, *and constant,* in any company—among rulers, among wealthy clients and their combatants, among taxi drivers and servants. Her biographer says that was because "humanity at large was for her an extension of the intimate, spirited household in which she grew up." She said, "I was comfortable in any company because I knew who I was and where I came from, and had no yearning to be anything else. My parents had never had material wealth, but they had given their children what money couldn't buy: culture, dignity, self-respect. I could never feel uprooted because wherever I went I took along my special square of soil—my sense of family." That sense is one that can rejoice, as Fanny did, in what we call the American dream, but its real home is in its community. The American dream was not always sound to Fanny; she knew it wasn't because she compared it with what she knew from her community. She compared the American dream and found it wanting. In that *radical* way, Fanny Holtzmann and Jerry Kennedy are dissenters.

The religious tradition holds these immigrant cultures together, I think, but there is much in them that is not obviously theological, and even much that is mysterious and mystical. The ethos of the late immigrants—those who sent their children to the Jesuits for law school—is reverent about culture and gently cynical, wary rather than sentimental, about exercises of power.

The ethos of gentle cynicism works more for the preservation of community than for the abstract and self-deceived notions of health and justice America preserved from its Puritan and Enlightenment past. It is on this view of power that the gentle cynics seem to the adherents of American civil religion to be least republican (least American sometimes) and even to be immoral. The ethics of friendship seems undemocratic and unjust when it results in uneven professional or public service—and it is not an adequate answer to say that the WASPs also prefer their friends. This troubling aspect of the ethics of friendship is no doubt what caused Michael Novak to urge gentle cynicism more as a corrective to liberal-democratic self-deception than as an adequate ethic on its own.

In George V. Higgins's novel of politics, *A Choice of Enemies*

(1984), Bernie Morgan, the Speaker of the Massachusetts House, visited a hospital that wanted public money. Bernie told the doctor in charge how to conduct her negotiations. "Now, what you've got to do is get your facility, that you want, by showing people like me how giving it to you will give us something we want. And that's the way you sell it." She said it appeared to be all a matter of self-interest. "Well," Bernie said, "it ain't beanbag, pal. But, you know, it's not exactly as grubby as you think it is. . . . We didn't come in here to pose—we came in here to make deals."

In that story, a leader of Boston's black community said his greatest frustration had been to convince his constituents that their failure to appreciate this gently cynical attitude explained why they didn't gain more. "I've never been able to persuade them that in a good many cases where we haven't gotten what we wanted, it wasn't because the people that we had to get it from hate niggers. It was because the people that we had to get it from looked at what we wanted and didn't see anything in the request for them, so they torpedoed it. It wasn't racial. It wasn't even personal. It was just good business sense. I'm telling you, my friend, if I could've figured out a way for blacks in Roxbury to qualify for good jobs that would've ended unemployment for all the micks in Southie while it was training blacks in Roxbury to qualify for good jobs too, it would've slid through Bernie Morgan's legislature like it'd been on skates."

The alternative, which is what the late immigrants found when they came to this country, was a moralistic public debate about institutional policies, with little evidence of the training in virtue that makes institutional moral argument coherent. They found lots of principle—principle coming out of the ears of American institutions that they also found to be hypocritical, self-deceived, and corrupt. They did not find the virtue—the truthfulness and good habits—that such grand principles require. And they decided to try to hold on to what they had brought with them, which was more Moses and Aristotle than it was Calvin and Thomas Jefferson.

In a way that I suspect Novak implies, the debate now is not between republican professional ethics and gentle cynicism but between claims of moral consensus and a laissez-faire social and professional ethic that cannot locate any social substance other than the absence of mayhem. Christina Hoff Sommers, an academic philosopher, compares, for example, the individualistic way we have come to talk about morals in the professions and in the public schools. "The literature of applied ethics, like the literature of values clarification and cognitive moral development, has little or nothing to say about matters of individual virtue. . . . Inevitably the student forms the idea that applying ethics to modern life is mainly a matter of learning how to be for or against social and institutional policies. . . . The articles sound like briefs written for a judge or legislator. . . . At this moment the Moral Majority constitutes the only vocal and self-confident alternative to the ethics-without-virtue movement. . . . Half-baked relativism . . . tends to undermine common sense. In a term paper . . . one of my students wrote that Jonathan Swift's 'modest proposal' . . . was 'good for Swift's society, but not for ours.' " Rabbi Hirsch would say such a student needs to have a talk with one of his grandparents, not about institutional policies but about hungry babies in Ireland.

Novak is optimistic about the possibilities for a synthesis that would, I suppose, revive some of both gentle cynicism and civic friendship. He suggests that the moral heritage of most Jews and most Roman Catholics in America is now more an influence in our national moral life than it is a dependable ethnic or religious characteristic. He argues that it is an influence worth combining with civic friendship, that the one enriches the other. Looked at in that blended way, the ethic he describes as gently cynical tempers individualism with the reality of organic communities. Our social, legal, and professional relationships, in that view, turn on interpersonal commitment as much as on contract—on faithfulness as much as on promise. Organic communities foster relationships where contract fosters obligation. Because of relationship, which is fluid and flexible rather than specific, this synthetic view of transactions would allow for self-awareness and growth in virtue; it might be like what Aristotle talked about when he talked about friendship. It might make it possible for friends to survive violence and falsehood and hypocrisy—as Jerry Kennedy's lawyer-client relationship with

Lou Schwartz survived government connivance, Mafia threat, and prison.

· § ·

The picture of friendship that I find in these dissenting-professional stories combines an earthy spirit of commitment and faithfulness with the hope that our relationships, even our professional relationships, can be places to grow in. Some of this is covered by our ordinary, television-trained notions of friendship; much more of it is covered in the more reflective and classical teaching that friendship is a school for virtue and a social ethic. An enduring ethic of friendship is more specific and indicative for professional ethics than a political arrangement or a bit of good luck. It could be a way to endure the tragedy of professional life.

Liberal-democratic professionalism deals with tragedy by abandonment. We are told to come to our patients and clients with the implicit belief that the highest good we can hope for them is that they be free—that they be, in a word common in the literature of legal and medical ethics, *autonomous.* And that seems to mean that we care about our clients and patients only to a point—to the end of a road described by what we are expert at, what our job is, what our contract says we have promised to do. Beyond that, they can go to hell in a handbasket; or, at any rate, they do.

Skill, or contract, or official professional mandate, then defines whatever relationship there is. When skill becomes ineffective, or when the contractual promise is kept, or when the mandate is unclear, we return the client or patient who has come to us to the world of strangers. And we say that we do this because we respect his freedom. We would not be likely, as Jerry Kennedy is, to visit the prison to talk to the products of our failed skill as defenders of criminals. Most doctors are not interested in attending funeral services for their dead patients. Ann Landers says they shouldn't be expected to be.

Autonomy then becomes a way of saying that the awesome circumstances that people bring to professionals—death, disease, dispute, ignorance, malaise, sin—are finally and inevitably and *appro-*

priately borne alone. It's all like the evening my wife Nancy came home after battling with a social worker for an order of heating oil for a family without heat. "I'd like to help you," the social worker said, "but it's not part of my job description." What is left out is the sustaining sense of community that gives Nancy the energy and the context to be good at working with poor people—the sense Fanny Holtzmann had from her family, that Jerry Kennedy finds in Irish Boston. Community is a place where circumstance is *met*, even when expertise will not answer. A professional in such a community does not stop where his expertise stops. He may then stop being technically skillful, but the point at which his technique stops is not the point at which his being in the community stops. These stories say that is because the community teaches the professional how to be a friend.

Chapter Six

· § ·

SCHOOLS

No thought attains to its fullest existence unless it is incarnated in a human environment, and by environment I mean something open to the world around, something which is steeped in the surrounding society and is in contact with the whole of it, and not simply a closed circle of disciples around a master. For the lack of such an environment in which to breathe, a superior mind makes a philosophy for itself; but that is a second best and it produces thought of a lesser degree of reality.

—Simone Weil

We live in the great world as well as in the little. We belong to groups that extend beyond particular places and we speak a language . . . that aspires to universality. If it is to perform its expressive function, our theory must help us grasp this transcendent aspect of our experience.

—Duncan Kennedy

IMAGINE here an Irish monk, Brother Justinian, who comes to America, from an island off the Irish coast, to give his advice on education for the professions in America. He has been asked to come (all expenses paid) by the dean of an American law school.

The dean once, for a moment, during a meeting of the Association of American Law Schools, wondered about the effect of a law-school community on the morals of its members. She dictated an invitation to Justinian, on her portable dictating machine, and then forgot she had done it. Her secretary signed and mailed the invitation while the dean was out of town.

Brother Justinian was chosen, if only for a moment, because Xerox commercials have convinced us Americans that members of cloistered religious orders are inoffensive; because Brother Justinian doesn't charge fees for his consulting work; and because the dean admires the ethos of monasteries, particularly Justinian's, where there has not been a faculty meeting since just after the bloody battles of Drogheda and Wexford in 1649.

The dean might have hoped, too, that she would learn something. She might have suspected the prospect of useful lessons from a visitor who would ask, as if he were Socrates, fundamental questions of those who train people for professional life in America—questions such as "Who are you?" Whether that is true or not of the dean, it is true of Brother Justinian, who, in pursuing his life as a monk has recognized value in Socrates' approach to the conversation that follows intrusive questions—and therefore has recognized the value of the questions.

The dean might even have remembered what Socrates said about personal and institutional advantage in the conversations such questions sometimes provoke: "I think we should all be contentiously eager to know what is true and what false in the subject under discussion, for it is a common benefit that this be revealed to all alike. . . . And if you refute me, I shall not be vexed with you as you are with me, but you shall be enrolled as the greatest of my benefactors."

Brother Justinian's Visit

Brother Justinian prefers the question "What are you up to?" to the more Socratic question "What do you do?" He may have been brought to his preference from reading modern ethical theory (for example, that of H. Richard Niebuhr), but he argues that asking what another person is up to is both straightforward and Greek. He therefore came to the law school wanting to find out what it aims to do, so that he could then ask whether what it aims to do is worthwhile and whether what it does fits what it aims to do. He wanted to proceed teleologically, as the philosophers say—at least at first. He wanted to think about the enterprise from the point of view of the ends of the enterprise.

Even before he arrived in the United States, Brother Justinian examined statements of purpose prepared by Americans who train people for the professions. Sometimes these statements spoke to him of competence, but then, almost always, in terms of extraordinary competence. The attending physician in a surgical residency program will, for example, say that her or his colleagues and their students are not "doctors who serve a community and are content to perform common operations for common conditions. . . . We want to do things that others can't. We want all the difficult cases referred to us. We want to train others to be *good* surgeons" (emphasis added). Law-school catalogues don't talk about training lawyers; they talk about training great (or grand) lawyers. They talk about leaders more than they talk about lawyers who are consulted by clients.

If Brother Justinian determined—and he did—to reduce such talk to a common denominator, he had to do it as an explorer who sees the broad plain between him and the mountain he wants to get to. He had to start with the professional life that was common to the doctors who serve communities and to *good* surgeons, common to the lawyers people come to see and to grand lawyers. There was, he thought, a difference between statements of purpose and aims. In the interest of truthfulness, he had to smooth the differences out. He did this smoothing in preparation for what Socrates would have called dialogue, as opposed to what Socrates would have called routine flattery.

Brother Justinian noticed that the law school's educational program aimed in this implicit, smoothed-out, laconic way at people becoming lawyers. He then looked at the way American lawyers (and doctors and journalists) work, and noticed that they work together. Most American lawyers work on team projects in law firms. Many work with corporate businesses in which teamwork is a central and oft-celebrated value. Teamwork is said to lead to and to be at the end of a search for excellence. Trial lawyers in America settle virtually all their lawsuits, a process that involves lawyers working together. Most positions of leadership in America are held by people trained for a profession—people who, in governing the nation, sit down—or, at cocktail parties or receptions, stand and stand—and talk earnestly with one another. Brother Justinian concluded that working together is important in the American professions and supposed that a school that trains lawyers would emphasize the skills of collaboration, understanding, and accommodation with which such discursive enterprises do their work. Socrates sometimes spoke of such skills as the virtue of friendship, and sometimes as the virtue of justice.

Justinian had the benefit of comparison here with other professions in America. He watched *All the President's Men* on television and learned that investigative journalists work in squads. He talked to a neurological surgeon, who had come to the law school to lecture on the scourge of lawsuits alleging medical malpractice, and learned that doctors in America are trained in hierarchical battalions that work in well-ordered togetherness in hospital wards. A third-year law student had just signed a contract with the law firm that was to employ her. The contract said, "You will be given much more credit for furthering the cause of people with whom you are working than for feathering your own nest."

Brother Justinian explained to this third-year student that one who comes from a monastery is not surprised at such an admonition. A monk, he said, naturally supposes that professionals in America want to be as collaborative as they can be, partly because they want to be pleasant, and partly because they want to be smart (see Epilogue). That is, partly because they want to enjoy life together and learn from one another, and partly because they want to succeed. Thus, in the monastery, young novices learn to work together when they wash dishes, as rabbinical students have always learned to study the Talmud in teams. Teachers in the religious tradition know that a group of people working together can do more things and think of more things than any one of them can do or think of alone.

The apparent answer to "What are you up to?" is "We are learning to work together on the difficult, important tasks that are entrusted to us by our clients. We live, already, in the great world as well as in the little." The consequent teleological question, according to Brother Justinian, is whether what is done in American schools advances people toward this end of collaborating in their professional work. "In considering such an educational agenda," he says, "I would think you would encourage your students to work together. But I find that you do not.

"Grades are an example. You American teachers—not only in law school, but all over the university and even in secondary schools—grade students according to what is called a curve. A student's grade is determined not on what she does, but on what other students do. That system works to discourage collaboration, a fact that at first confused me. Grading by a curve discourages collaboration because of the risk that my helping my fellow student will result in his answering your questions as well as or better than I can answer them. If I am bright at all, I will appreciate that risk and realize that my helping him may result in my getting a lower grade than if I had not helped him—even though my performance will be the same whether I help my fellow student or refuse to help him. And if I benefit from the collaboration, my classmate will not. This system appeared to me at first designed to encourage students either to work alone or distract one another from study. It seemed to encourage students to feather their own nests. Sometimes I thought it was even a system that encouraged antagonism. This is a system in which I will do better to keep my wit to myself, and best if my classmates do worse than I do. But then I noticed that your students were almost always civil to one another, and often friendly and helpful, and I concluded that if the immediate object of your system is antagonism, it is not working well.

"And sometimes I thought the system was not designed to encourage antagonism but to teach professionals that they were fundamentally alone in the world—that the professional collaboration I thought I noticed in hospitals, government, the military, law firms, newspapers, and public accounting offices was a social deception that you were trying to straighten out. You felt perhaps that it was necessary to prevent students from being deceived by these appearances of friendship in a world that was not friendly.

"What I thought would be simple, as a point of beginning in my work, I found confusing and even distressing. Talking to professors did not help. One rather irreverent teacher said the grading system was not a matter either of artificial competition or of professional self-reliance, but was a way to persuade bright college graduates that their academic achievement was a sham—that they were all much stupider than they thought they were. 'The educational system,' he said, 'teaches students that they are weak, lazy, incompetent, and insecure.'

"This lesson in humiliation, he said, is useful whether or not it is truthful. 'It teaches them that if they are fortunate, and willing to accept dependency, large institutions—hospitals, law firms, military organizations, civilian agencies, newspapers, and television networks—will take care of them almost no matter what. The terms of the bargain are relatively clear. . . . The institution takes care of all the contingencies of life. . . . In exchange, you renounce any claim to control . . . what you do, and agree to show the appropriate form of deference to those above you and condescension to those below.'

"That theory was harsh, I thought," Justinian wrote in his report. "It seemed to me inconsistent with the claims made about training grand lawyers and *good* surgeons, that I had read on the airplane coming over to North America, and I was not prepared to discount those claims as sham (even if they were routine flattery)—at least I was not prepared to do that so early in my visit. Then, too, if this teacher was right, it pointed to deeper, more ominous difficulty in professional education in America. It pointed to idolatry. Hospitals and law firms and newspapers do not—cannot—take care of a person 'no matter what.' People who think institutions can do that—and, for heaven's sake, are trained to think they can—are not only dabbling in falsehood, they are putting their institutions where God ought to be.

"I set that possibility aside; I filed it away for further reference, and I am happy to report that it is still filed away. I have not needed to use it. On the other hand, it is still in the file. I haven't forgotten it. You should not forget it either," Justinian wrote to the dean. "I must suggest it to you; there may be something in it. I set it aside because I had to or I could not have gone on—and, after all, you had invested airfare for both me and my donkey.

"What I did was to adopt a tentative and less drastic scriptural conclusion on this teleological issue about collaboration and curve grading. After prayer and reflection, I decided to be provisionally edified by what you are doing. You are perhaps teaching your students, as the Gospel commands, that the last shall be first and the first last. You are showing them that the Way is straight and narrow, that in the moral life there is no free lunch. You are teaching them that the price of collaboration is suffering and sacrifice. Every student who loans another student his notes, or leaves a library book intact and where it is supposed to be, is a saint! At first, I was anxious to take this lesson back to the monks in my abbey, but I didn't, finally. I am afraid that monks lack the character for it."

· § ·

In one of several long lunch hours, Brother Justinian took up this lingering question about goals with the rather irreverent law professor who had told him about America's institutional idols. "It could be," Brother Justinian said, "that the end of professional education in America is what Socrates and Aristotle," who were, he said, Greek monks, "would have called friendship. What the author of the Letter to the Hebrews meant when she admonished Jewish Christians to stir one another up to love and good works." At least, Justinian said, a consultant from a monastery should raise that possibility with somebody, and the rather irreverent law professor seemed in no hurry to return to his office. "But the grading system gives me no encouragement for even trying to make that case. It is so depressing as a means to any end that has to do with communities of—as your physicians often put it—caring people, that I have decided I had better not think any more about friendship until I have finished thinking about methods of progress in professional schools."

The rather irreverent law professor thought Justinian meant stairways when he said "progress" and, in the confusion, Justinian changed his inquiry from grades to architecture—not architecture as a profession, but as a way of expressing relationships within a professional school. He took a look at the law-school building he was in, and he did this in reference to relationships, in reference to what Martin Buber (a Jewish monk) called the *I* and the *Thou.*

"Your law-school building," Justinian wrote to the dean, "appears to be part of a physical place, and the place appears to be a university. A professional school in America is, I think, a place where those who want to learn come together with those who think they are able to teach, and there they work together for a while, often in buildings, so that the student can prepare to practice the profession he has learned.

"There doesn't seem to be much need in such a place for separation by rank. In the monastery, for example, where we come together to work and to pray, we do not separate ourselves from one another by insignia of age or levels of sanctity. We organize ourselves for prayer in rows facing one another, and then pray back and forth, as (we are told by the prophet Isaiah) the angels do. When we work, we work together, because many tasks require two or three monks rather than one, and, even if they don't, we like being together. It is a case of *ora et labora.*

"I recall in this connection a poem by your wonderful Robert Frost (who was not a monk). You will remember the farmer raking the hay who discovered a tuft of flowers that had been left uncut, an hour or two before, by another farmer, who had cut the hay—left, the later farmer realized, 'out of sheer morning gladness at the brim.' It was, he thought, 'a message from the dawn . . . that made me hear his long scythe whispering to the ground, and feel a spirit kindred to my own.' In time we monks, who are more ponderous at this than Frost's Vermont farmer was, come to an attitude toward our work and our prayer that is communal, so that, as Frost said, 'we work together when we work apart.' It seems to me that your functions are at least logistically similar, although you lawyers seem to mean something different when you use the word 'prayer,' and you are, if I may say so, remarkably undisciplined in your communal work.

"I notice that your building has four levels. The faculty are on the top, which must be a hierarchical symbol of some sort, since it could not be based on relative stamina or physical endurance. The books are on the third level, which at first seems irrational, since they weigh so much, and should not be high in the air unless you propose to amend the law of gravity. The rooms for teaching are on the second level, perhaps on the theory that what is in the books will seep down. This arrangement reminded me of Dante; again, it seemed to represent some sort of hierarchy.

"I noticed that the building also has limited spaces for students to talk together, eat together, meet on the matters they are allowed to discuss among themselves, and hang their overcoats. These areas are all on the bottom level, down with the furnace and the water pipes—far away from the teachers and almost as far away from the books. The parking lot for the students' cars is a long way from the building, and the places for librarians and professors is closer. There is one set of water closets for those who pay the school and a separate set for those who are paid by the school. The two groups do not come and go together, as young and old monks do. The building seemed to be telling me something; but, since everyone seemed to enjoy the arrangement, I decided the message was not a message of humiliation," as his friend the rather irreverent law professor said the grading system was. It was some other message, and it was harder to understand than the Book of Revelation.

"Nor is the situation different where the architecture is different. In the American teaching hospitals I read about, for example, the architecture is in a straightforward way related to patients who are brought to the attending physicians and their students because the patients are sick. The patients are arranged in relation to the parts of the hospital they are in need of, and in terms of their danger to one another. The attending physicians, the junior physicians, the interns, medical students, nurses, and ward attendants, all come in procession to see the patients, wherever they are, for a while. The healers come in an order that resembles the architectural order in legal education. The attending physicians come first, even when they are absent. The senior residents come next; then the junior residents; then the medical students. This procession begins with the patient farthest from the door, and proceeds toward the door, so that no patient will interrupt it more than once. The students live and work in a metaphorical basement, one in which they are told to get acquainted with patients, as part of their training. Perhaps this is for the good of the patients, but that is not what the teachers of medicine say. They say to the students that the students will not have time to get acquainted with anybody when they become real doctors.

"You can see how, to me, and when I was trying to see if Buber's *I-Thou* model would or should work out in professional education, this arrangement appeared to discourage relationships. The *I*s and the *Thous* in law school are separated by a vertical space of forty feet. The *I*s and the *Thous* in teaching hospitals ignore their patients' minds and souls and walk around looking at one another's professional backs. In both sorts of schools the teachers' cars and the students' cars are stored separately. They eat separately, and, I suppose, pray separately. The I's and the Thou's in teaching hospitals are schooled in deference so thoroughly that not even scientific discipline is a reason for disagreement with the judgment of the attending physician, who is like the law-school professor who puts his car close to the door.

"Perhaps one professor (or attending physician) was meant to be *Thou* to another, but, if so, I was not able to understand wherein such a system of relationships was educational. If what Buber called 'the heavenly bread of self-being' was passed up and down the fourth-floor hall of the law building, and there only, I didn't understand wherein your institution is a school or why the people in the basement come to you and pay money for what you have to say to them."

It was perhaps the case that students don't come to professional schools in America to receive the heavenly bread of self-being. The rather irreverent law professor said that to Justinian, looking away at a light fixture as he spoke. Justinian said that was an untested, undemonstrated, and cynical proposition. "I won't pursue it, and I hope that if you pursue it you pursue it thoughtfully," he said. "It implies a discouraging view of human nature." The law professor then permitted the monk to change the subject.

"This, as I say, was my difficulty at first, but then I came to see, as I had—provisionally—in the grading system, that you are not being guided by logic and physics, but by the gospel," Justinian said one day to the dean. "I came to this, I'm afraid, indirectly, not as a result of contemplation, but as a result of the accident of meeting a jogger in the student parking lot, where I kept my donkey. I learned from her that physical exercise is important to American professionals, who trot in special shoes along the edges of roads and on the roofs of hotels and hospitals. They join athletic clubs, put private shower baths in their hospitals and offices, and organize tournaments with such clever legal titles as 'res gestae' and 'race judicata.' (I shudder to think of what the titles are in medical tournaments of this sort.) I understood that you Americans do not use your muscles for work, but, rather, you use your muscles for their own sake, to build muscles with which at some future time to build more muscles. It is a case of *labora et labora.*

"I had tried, you will recall, when I was looking at the grading systems in your professional schools, to prepare my analysis according to Aristotelian teleology. My main job then, I thought, was to define the goal of the enterprise, as if professional education were a journey toward happiness and the processes of professional education were steps along the way—the good steps leading toward the goal and the bad steps leading somewhere else."

Justinian and the dean were talking in the dean's office when he said this. The dean began, at this talk of teleology, to appear distracted, and Brother Justinian had to remind himself that he was not dealing with the same sense of academic leisure he enjoyed when he talked to the rather irreverent law professor. Justinian decided he had better try to be more businesslike. "You Americans don't often refer to Aristotle in this regard. You don't often call your method teleology. But you do talk about goals and management-by-objectives, which is similar, I think.

"Although I was, with regard to buildings and practices for which buildings are a metaphor, applying a different point of view, that of relationships and of stirring one another up to love and good works, it did occur to me to ask a teleological question or two about the way your professional education lines up. It did occur to me to inquire about objectives."

Justinian's friend the irreverent law professor had said earlier that the lining-up Justinian noticed in and of buildings was as inefficient as it appeared—and in fact worse. "All of this is teaching by example," the professor said. "In their relations with students . . . law professors get the message across. . . . The student-teacher relationship is the model for relations between junior associates and senior partners in law firms, and also for the relationship between lawyers and judges. . . . And, I think, since you talk of hospitals, for medical students or residents and attending physicians. In the classroom, and in teaching hospitals, and out of them, students learn a particular style of deference. They learn to suffer with positive cheerfulness interruption in mid-sentence, mockery, ad hominem assault, inconsequent asides, questions that are so vague as to be unanswerable but can somehow be answered wrong all the same, abrupt dismissal, and stinginess of praise. . . . They learn to savor crumbs, while picking from the air the indications of the master's mood." Think, for example, of the usual discourse between Dr. Craig and Drs. Wade and Ehrlich, of "St. Elsewhere."

Justinian—in leisure with the professor, but not when talking to the dean—thought (and spoke, on both occasions) of Socrates. Socrates said we do some things because we want to do them, and we do some things because of something else. Socrates said it makes sense to do neutral things because of something else, but it does not make sense to do bad things because of something else, even when the something else is a good thing. Justinian's friend the irreverent professor accepted Socrates' distinction; he said it could be used to understand modern professional education as what he called "the reproduction of hierarchy."

"The system . . . is reborn piecemeal in each generation," the professor said. "If you want to explain it, you have to go into the details of how people, new people in each generation, learn to be little white middle-class males. . . . There's more to it than the state, or one's relation to the means of production. . . . There's all the stuff that, in the case of lawyers, I would describe . . . as the contributions of legal education to the hierarchies of the legal profession."

This seemed plausible to Justinian, although he was surprised when he thought how little the recapitulation of lining up in the American professions is made conscious, or at least is explicated in the literature that otherwise talks of *good* surgeons, of grand lawyers, and of leaders who are trained in the university. A law-school building, and its parallel in a teaching hospital, were complex and even poetic things, he thought, and if running and building muscles—*labora et labora*—was also a metaphor (and he thought it was), then what his irreverent friend called the reproduction of hierarchy contemplated the social building of muscles, and that primarily among the already muscular.

"You want your students to climb the stairs—your stairs—the stairs you climbed once!" Justinian wrote to the dean, by way of a report on law-school architecture. "In this way, they will learn two things—to spend much of their time building their muscles, as a young upwardly mobile urban professional should, and also to be ready, waiting, when it comes, to hear the gospel invitation, 'Friend, come higher.' "

Justinian left the matter there, so far as his report to the dean was concerned. When he had talked with his irreverent friend, though, he said he had been tempted again to raise the question of *where* one is being invited to come when he is invited to come higher in a law building. "Socrates might say the question is whether the something-else, because of which, as you say, you choose to reproduce hierarchy, is a good thing. But this might again only cause me to reach a conclusion that would make me stop my report and go back to the monastery," Justinian said—and this time it was he who looked at the light fixture, rather than into the eyes of his friend.

· § ·

Brother Justinian had brought to his consulting task two (as he thought of them) ordinary methods of ethical analysis, either of which, he had thought, would be adequate as a framework to answer the law dean's question about the effect of a law-school community on the morals of its members. He tried to be teleological and to consider the training of professionals from the perspective of what professionals do in America. He had stumbled and fumbled in that analysis. When he came up against the frightening prospect that American professional institutions are idols, he set that prospect aside and guessed that teachers of American professionals teach people to collaborate by showing them that friendship is an expensive virtue in professional life. The dean accepted that conclusion as, with Justinian's help, evident. She decided that such a lesson was appropriate for university law students and put a paragraph about it in her annual dean's report. She likened expensive friendship to what she called "the great tradition of unselfish fraternity in the Bar."

Justinian tried an equally demanding but conceptually more modest measure when he turned to relationships among teachers and students in American professional training. He turned to Martin Buber and asked about the ethics of relationships—of love, as he thought of it (although American culture limits that word, pretty much, to encounters that are beyond the experience of a person who takes the vow of celibacy). He found notions of service in professional training, but such notions of service as he found focused not on students but on social and economic arrangements in the broader culture. He was reduced to metaphors—harsh metaphors suggested by discontent, physical metaphors suggested sometimes by notions of pain and labor and sometimes by what seemed to him, on reflection, undue concern with physique. Through all these metaphors, though, the image of professional education as a thing of ladders intruded. He could suspend judgment on his friend's opinions about hierarchy, but he could not get the ladders out of his mind, any more than he could put aside the spectre of the idol he had seen when he looked at the grading system—the idol he told the dean he was able to ignore.

· § ·

The third subject on which Justinian reported to his law-dean client was professional education, not as education but as a rite of passage, as a system for entering into professional practice and claiming the significant franchises that American society gives to its professional people. Justinian had found both teleological analysis and Buber's *I-Thou* analysis—an analysis of relationships—less useful than he thought they would be. Teleology disclosed to him a fearful idol he did not want to think about. The *I* and the *Thou* analysis came out looking to him more like a ladder than like love (more like an *I* and an *It*), and he didn't want to think about that either. He turned to a refinement of the two earlier methods for his inquiry into gatekeeping, or, as American academic custom has it, commencement. He turned to the ethics of responsibility—the school of moral thinking that emphasizes truthfulness, that regards self-deception as the most dangerous evil, that asks: To whom am I responsible? And in what community?

Justinian visited the registrar's office. He said he wanted to find out what he could about academic attrition in American professional education. One way to study a gate, he said, is to consider those who can't get through it—to study those who do not commence in American professional life because they are not good enough. This inquiry connected to his earlier inquiries; he even thought it might show the relationship between grades and buildings: If you don't get the grades, you can't stay in the building.

Justinian supposed at first that professional schools keep unworthy practitioners out of the professions. Professors were, he supposed, those who let some people become, and refuse to let some people become, doctors, lawyers, journalists, teachers, or members of the clergy.

Again, Justinian found in the registrar's files, and in reports on attrition in other schools, that he was wrong. He found that at one time many of those who came to seminaries, medical and dental schools, schools of journalism and of law, failed out before they could finish. But this is true no longer. The academic attrition rate at the law school he visited was under 5 percent, and had been that low for years. Clearly, a student who failed out there had to work at it. If he did not work, he stayed in. Brother Justinian heard and read statements from professors and deans, residency committees, and licensing examiners about the duty of the teaching profession to save America from incompetent professionals, but he decided that these statements were a gentlemanly and modest (if cryptic) way to say to the country that none of its professionals was incompetent. How else, in all charity, could he account for these gatekeepers' claim to exclude incompetence and at the same time include everybody? There isn't any gate, but it is polite, as when a worldly clergyman is called "most reverend," or a bad judge "honorable," to pretend that there is.

It was fortunate for him that he corrected this early and erroneous impression. Otherwise, he might have supposed that teachers of professionals in America feel responsible to people who go to doctors, ministers, and lawyers, and responsible in all the communities where their graduates practice the trades these teachers certify them for. When he learned that professors no longer keep the gates to the professions, he understood that those who teach in such schools are responsible only to one another and in the community that is immediately around them—that is, so to speak, on the fourth floor. This realization brought Brother Justinian to another of those difficulties that had driven him to prayer, to the irreverent law professor, and to the parking lot. Here I return to his report to the dean.

"I wondered, then, why it was that activities in your school were so pervasively and universally subjected to the sorting out of students—why everything was ranked into first, second, and third; top half and lower half; best, runner-up, and also-ran. Life in your law school seemed to be a thing of contests—in trial-practice rounds, in the moot court, even in the client-counseling competition; in each course; in overall performance in school; in honorary fraternities and social fraternities—in literally every activity on which the blue ribbon or the pocket calculator could be brought to bear."

A similar system seemed, he said, to obtain in the training of physicians. He spoke of a report by the sociologist Charles Bosk on surgical residents. The attending physicians in such programs are keepers of the gate that leads to eminence, but not the keepers of the gate that leads to professional practice. They rank doctors but do not keep bad doctors out of the profession. The word hierarchy—the image of the ladder—again occurred to Justinian.

"Only the most promising residents are admitted to senior status, and promise is a matter of the unreviewable judgment of teachers. But," Justinian wrote to the dean, "those who do not pass through the gate leading to eminence become surgeons of less eminence, and if that means they are less competent than those who pass through the gate leading to eminence, it is a difference patients and the families of patients are unlikely to appreciate. Even if the gate were one that saved patients from professional incompetence, it would be an unfair gate, since, as often as not, the criterion for competence in such a system is a matter of deference, tractability, and what the elders in your American systems for professional education are likely to call attitude.

"It was not, therefore, the case that all of this sorting out was in order to respond to a concern that beginning professionals be competent—or at least this was not a concern that they all be competent. The members of your own faculty, Dean, say—and say cheerfully, for heaven's sake—that many of the people you graduate are not competent. Then what, I asked, was all this sorting out for?

"At first, I again thought you were being irrational. Let me show you what I mean. Here is a student, Sam Jones, who has a cumulative C-minus average. He is not on the law review, he didn't place in moot court, he came in fourth (of four) in his practice trial, he was eliminated from the client-counseling competition after the first round, and he was not elected secretary of Phi Alpha Delta [a lawyers' fraternity]. He would not, if he were planning to be a doctor, qualify for internship or residence in the sort of hospital Bosk wrote about. He could not get into the Ph.D. program at the Yale Divinity School.

"It appears that, in the eyes of the professional-school world, Sam is not doing well. Certainly no one tells him he is doing well. But you will not fail him out. He is going to be a lawyer. He could, if he wanted, be a physician or a dentist or an architect, a certified teacher of Torah or a minister of the gospel. He is going to take on the lives and fortunes of his fellow citizens. He will assume leadership in his community. It seemed to me, with such a life of duty and burden before him, and since he's going to qualify anyway, that it would be best for everyone if Sam went forth from your school with a spring in his step.

"He is not, after all, a failure. You won't allow that. He is passing your courses. He did well in college. He can read and write and think. He looks good in his new suit. Even if he had no successes in his life, still, given the way you Americans run your country, he is going to be a person of power; he is going to have largely unreviewed influence in the important concerns of others. Thanks to you. Thanks to the gate you no longer keep—and no thanks to the gate you keep instead. It will only increase the peril to his clients, and to his community, to send him forth with a poor opinion of himself. And this is, if I may say so, a legitimate way to put it, since we begin with the fact that you no longer make any serious attempt to save the community from the possibility that Sam may be incompetent."

The dean had long preferred an academic attrition rate somewhat higher than the one Justinian found—about 10 per cent, she thought, so that class size could be maintained by taking transfer students who had earned high grades at law schools that were less prestigious. The higher attrition rate would make the school appear more rigorous. She took that to be Justinian's point, too. But members of the faculty grade the papers, and they appeared to be content with 5 percent attrition. And so she had asked Brother Justinian to develop, in a talk to the entire faculty, what became the third part of his written report.

Justinian explained to the faculty that he should not be taken to mean that professors in professional schools were heedless of the outside world. Most of those he met were not heedless (and his irreverent friend was uncommonly heedful, he thought). Heedlessness, in any event, Justinian said, would have been a different question from the question of whether teachers feel responsible to the clients and patients and parishioners of their students, and to the communities in which their students will work. This was not what the dean expected, and she then regretted that she had asked Justinian to talk to the faculty. What she had hoped for was a few more failing grades.

The question he was after, Justinian said, was whether the realities of the lives of clients and communities were seen to be present in the professional school. What he was after—and he was not entirely candid about it—was evidence of teaching devices that would make clients and communities manifest. The assumption here, one he said he borrowed from H. Richard Niebuhr (a mainline Protestant monk), is that those who are affected by students are in some inevitable way present in professional education, are necessarily implicated in the educational relationships that flourish or are starved in school. They are present, he said; the issue is whether they are ignored. "It is my profession to pray in the monastery for those who do not live in monasteries, to make them present to me in my prayer, and to make cheese for them, and so I think that it is possible to be advertent and skillful about the presence of clients in professional education," he said to the faculty.

"It seemed logical to me that a sound view of your broad responsibilities would cause you to insure Sam's self-confidence, even if it is to him, not his clients, that you are responsible, and in your school community, not the community Sam will some day lead, that you practice your responsibility," Justinian wrote, later, to the dean.

"Again, and I blush to confess it, you seemed irrational. Everything you did seemed designed to send Sam forth feeling worthless and incapable. Everything you did seemed designed to destroy his confidence in himself. If you are going to graduate him anyway, I said to myself, why not graduate him with grace, or even with hope?

"It's not as if there is nothing about Sam's work that would justify a boost; it's not as if Sam never does anything well. It's not as if Sam's teachers have to be dishonest with him, and not as if praise is so much in the air of the school that it will lose its force from dissipation. In fact, I have hardly heard anyone praised or complimented since I arrived, and I have seen wit and hard work everywhere. Your students are apparently supposed to take their encouragement from their class rank, and from the contests they win, but not from their teachers. Heaven knows your grading system does not invite them to take encouragement from one another.

"Those who dispense the things in life that make us feel better should realize that some good things can be shared, even if some cannot," Justinian said, even later, to his friend the rather irreverent professor. Rank in class and the first prize for performance, he said, in the nature of things, cannot be shared. But boosts and compliments can be shared; they can be given to Sam without being taken away from someone who gets higher grades. "I even had the passing fancy that it wouldn't hurt to give Sam's mediocre performance a 'B' instead of a 'C,' since you're going to graduate—that is, qualify—him anyway; but a cold shower drove that thought from my mind."

Justinian's irreverent friend said he was surprised that Justinian was surprised. Of course, he said, "this is silly, looked at as pedagogy. But it is anything but silly when looked at as ideology. The system generates a rank ordering of students . . . and students learn that there is little or nothing they can do to change their place in that ordering, or to change the way the school generates it." He said this shows, again, that what the American professional school system teaches is the "justice of hierarchy." And nothing else.

"Most of the process of differentiating students . . . could simply be dispensed with without the slightest detriment to the quality of [professional] services. . . . The differences between students could be 'leveled up' at minimal cost, whereas the actual practice . . . systematically accentuates differences in real capacities." He said it would not be hard to graduate most professional students "at the level of technical proficiency now achieved by a small minority at each institution."

To the extent the irreverent law professor was right, American professional schools partly fulfill their claim of educating *good* surgeons and grand lawyers (etc.) but they also educate (even if they do not claim) ordinary, humiliated surgeons and so-so lawyers. Or maybe, he thought, they do not educate the ordinary and the so-so; maybe they only separate them out and graduate them. But the reality seemed to Justinian to reject the obvious moral claims of clients and communities.

Justinian wrote to the dean that he thought ordinary intramural civility also required more careful attention to the good work that students such as Sam do. He noted the ancient and modern argument that civility, or tolerance, is not merely a matter of manners;

it is the virtue on which democratic society rests, and is therefore important to Sam's career—to his clients and to his community. Civility is something a person can learn from a teacher, something a student can be trained in, and this might mean that training in civility is something he can claim from his teachers. Momentous moral actions, Justinian wrote to the dean, are the product of ordinary moral actions. "Virtues are skills (or habits). We learn them from others, including our teachers; we learn them in the routine of living, including living in school. They are important; when we have learned them we are able to live good lives in the face of power and suffering and pressures to be unvirtuous."

Justinian was growing unmonkishly strident here, as you may have noticed, in trying to make the dean understand that he was not talking only about courtesy or institutional etiquette. The aim of any public office, Justinian wrote—and here he quoted Socrates—is the goodness of the people in the community. Courtesy toward Sam could be a matter only of what Socrates called flattery—a knack, Socrates called it—but civility toward him is a matter of showing him how to lead his clients to goodness. "To know and to teach about justice, or health, or grace, or truth, is a matter of focusing on one's aim," Justinian said. "The aim is to equip Sam to make his clients better people."

Here, as you might guess, though, Justinian's linear mind led him back to the teleological analysis he had tried for when he was thinking about curve grading. He was drifting back to the frightening possibility that the law school he was consulting in was a temple built to an idol—and Justinian didn't want to think about that. He veered away from being strident.

Justinian mentioned instead Bosk's discovery, in the elite surgical residency program Bosk studied, that attending physicians say attitude is more important to progress than competence is, and of Bosk's consequent conclusion about professional training, which Justinian quoted to the dean from a copy of Bosk's book. "Moral standards are the organizing principles of a professional community." The possibilities for self-deception in such a system of organizing principles are awesome, Justinian wrote, particularly when the judges of attitude in the young are those who have the greatest interest in not allowing the young to change the institution. As alarming as that thought was, Bosk and self-deception were a diversion away from the possibilities of idolatry. Bosk calmed Justinian's mind. Justinian was tendentious enough to disguise from the dean where his thoughts had, for another dangerous moment, moved.

Justinian then tried to get back to the main theme of the third part of his report—attrition, and ranking, and the ethics of responsibility. It seemed to him that what the schools were doing was all wrong—that they were refusing responsibility to the clients and the communities their professional students were shortly to be turned upon. But when he spoke of this to members of the faculty, he said, he was met with the argument—a fact, really—that some professional people do better work than others. Truthfulness seemed to require that Justinian recognize that fact, or at least that he not deny it. Members of the faculty told Justinian that his view of Sam's grades and of the prizes Sam lost said in effect that there was no reason for a student to work hard. They said that he was arguing that talent doesn't count in a profession.

"Well," Justinian said, on one occasion, "let's start just with what I want to do, which is to bring clients and communities into the professional school, to make you teachers look up and see them. I suppose competitive teaching devices and this sorting out that you do—sorting out that seems to last forever in professional life and in your institutions—are ways to recognize quality.

"Now, quality is either self-evidently good, which I don't think it is, or it is good because it will be important to clients and communities. And even if it is self-evidently good, if it will work out to be bad for clients and communities—well, it is not self-evidently good after all, is it?"

These law teachers said quality was important to the university and to the law school; it was important to clients and communities that people trained at their school be professionals who could do quality work. They spoke as if they were consulting the annual dean's report. Justinian reminded them that the law school was evidently willing to turn upon the country both those who did quality work and those who did not. He quoted his friend the irreverent professor, without attribution, to the effect that professors could, with a little effort, assure quality in almost all cases. But his relayed, secondhand argument was not persuasive to these teachers. They had heard it before. Then Justinian said that it sounded to him as if the law school's students were being used to gain the school a reputation for excellence. The teachers didn't find that moral argument persuasive either, not even when Justinian reminded them that he was invoking a principle of moral philosophy from the teachings of Immanuel Kant (a lapsed Lutheran monk).

Justinian finally asked, in as stentorian a tone as the Holy Rule permits him to use: "Well, how would you answer—to whom are you responsible?" And they answered, immediately, in one voice, "Our students."

"And," Justinian asked, "in what community?" They shrugged. The associate dean, who had come into the conversation to see what the shouting was about, said, "That depends." Justinian told them a parable and then, mercifully, it was time for a meeting of the admissions committee and the professors wandered away. The meaning of the parable, he said before he told it to them, is that the answer to the "in what community" question is that, if you answer it, you answer with your life. The parable he told was from the previous week's Sunday newspaper supplement. (Justinian had read it quickly but after Mass.)

Cleveland Amory wrote the Sunday-supplement article; it was called "Good Guys, Bad Guys" and was about sports heroes. Amory provided four heroes and four (Justinian had learned the word in the basement) nerds. One of Amory's heroes was the German Olympic jumper Luz Long. Amory gave two reasons for finding Luz Long to be a hero, both also involving Jesse Owens, black Olympic star from the United States. The two athletes competed in the 1936 Olympics, held in Germany. The Nazis, who ran Germany then, did all they could to make the games a triumph for the master race. There were enormous pressures on Long to aid in that effort—and therefore there was a mighty push on him to beat Jesse Owens. His country and all of Nordic humanity were depending on him. Amory said:

"In the qualifying heat, seeing that Owens had jumped short on his first try and had fouled on his second, Long, who had already qualified, walked over and persuaded Owens, for his third and final try, to make a mark well behind the takeoff point. Owens did so, qualified, and, in the finals, broke the Olympic record . . . defeating Long, who came in second."

"Hitler had refused to greet any black winners, but, after Owens' triumph, Long walked back down the jump runway with him, and directly in front of [Hitler's] box, put his arms around him.

"In 1943, a German soldier, Luz Long, was killed in action." Brother Justinian said the story shows how moral life is tragic, but the professors and the associate dean seemed confused. Justinian decided that parables were not a teaching method in the law.

Brother Justinian's struggle over this third difficulty was not resolved in this professorial debate. The struggle was like forty days in the desert for him. It brought him such distress that he decided for a while that the reason law schools and teaching hospitals and seminaries sort people out is a mystery, like the doctrine of the Trinity. In this mood he was ready to return to the monastery and recommend that the abbot institute ranking in the choir stalls.

He was saved by talking at the Law Day dinner to a judge of the United States District Court. The judge was an alumnus of the law school Justinian was advising. After two glasses of wine, the judge told the monk that he (the judge) had, like Sam, been a C-minus student at the law school. The judge said professors are impressed with rank because rank was their ladder into teaching—and large law firms are impressed with rank because they want the faculty to choose their associates.

The judge had another glass and said he knew twenty federal judges who had come from the bottom half of their law-school classes and only two who hadn't. The bar association in his state had never had a president who was on the law review, he said, and half the counsels general of the public corporations in the state had not placed in the moot-court competition. He spoke, by way of analogies to medicine and the clergy, of surgeons general and archbishops. He had a fourth glass of wine and said these doctors, clergy, lawyers, and judges were like Prime Minister Winston Churchill and General George Marshall, who did not do well in their professional training. One of them was barely accepted for the lowest tier of military training; the other was sent away without a diploma. The judge had a fifth and penultimate glass of wine, rose to his feet, and said to all within half a mile, "Hell, for every man who has impressed his teachers, there are ten who have not!" The judge noticed that some of those at the Law Day dinner were not men, and added, as he sat down, "Women too."

Brother Justinian covered his ears, but he took the judge's point. And he began to see his way out of his third and greatest difficulty. (I speak here of the difficulties he admitted to himself, not of the difficulties concerning idols in America.) "I came to understand," he said, "that the sorting-out process in professional school is not irrational after all. It is designed to remove from the professional population the people whom no process of gatekeeping could remove—the best students. To put them out of harm's way, on university faculties, in research laboratories, and in law firms in New York City. In that way, the General Marshalls, the Winston Churchills, the federal judges and corporate lawyers and bar association presidents, are able to proceed with their duties as leaders of the American republic.

"I had been right to suppose that your school and Mr. Bosk's teaching hospital are elitist, but I had mistaken the top for the bottom," Justinian said to the dean. "Sam Jones, for example, had appeared to be a person who was passed over, when in fact he was being chosen." Good heavens, Justinian had murmured to himself, sitting by the judge, who had dozed off over his sixth glass of wine, Sam is probably headed for the Supreme Court!

Justinian later tried out this last part of his report on his friend the irreverent law teacher, who was not in attendance at the Law Day dinner. Justinian's friend said that in a way—but only in an ironic way—Justinian was right. It was true, the rather irreverent professor said, that professionals of great power in institutions have oftener been Sams than they have been editors of law reviews or senior residents in teaching hospitals. But the corners of professional life where the best and brightest go, he said, are not as powerless as Justinian's irony implied. And, in any case, everyone goes forth from professional school trained in hierarchy, he said. Most law students, even including those with the highest rank, interview twenty times to get two offers, he said, and all students, even those "who have had continuous experience of academic and careerist success . . . are not as 'safe' as they thought they were." In other words, everybody is humiliated, and the evident purpose of humiliation is acceptance of a sorting out that begins before professional school and continues beyond professional school, from generation to generation.

Justinian conceded these points. He said he thought the dean understood them, too. Nonetheless, he thought he had an argument to make about the values the system serves when it shunts the brightest ministerial students not into parishes but into Ph.D. programs (and thence to university faculties); when it shunts the brightest medical students into narrow and inconspicuous (if profitable) specialization, or into academic life; when it shunts the brightest law graduates into academic life or obscure work in large metropolitan law firms. "You guarantee," he said, thinking of the tipsy judge, "that things in America will not get worse.

"Your grading system and your architecture are calls to virtue. But systems of virtue tend to leak; there is a chance that some of your students will turn ugly and become competitors instead of saints. It is as the Reverend Camden Farebrother said to the young physician Lydgate (chapter 4)—'Character is not cut in marble. . . . It is something living and changing, and may become diseased as our bodies do.' Your sorting-out process protects your community from the worst results of such aberrations. Money, glory, rank, prestige, and honor are building blocks. You use them to make a wall around those you dare not inflict on the republic, because they are the very people who would make things worse if you didn't do something to restrain them.

"In this way, through a miracle, or at least a paradox, revealed in the reckless vehemence of a federal judge, I learned how it is, in America, that the meek inherit the earth."

Friendship and Truth

Brother Justinian consulted scripture, and the rabbis and sages of the Hebraic tradition and of the church in the West. He also consulted the Greeks, particularly Socrates, and in that connection benefited from studying the *Gorgias*, which is about professional education in Athens. In fact, while Justinian was in this country someone gave him James Boyd White's essay "The Ethics of Argument: Plato's *Gorgias* and the Modern Lawyer," which Justinian read and thought about with interest and profit. He said when he finished the essay that all American professional students ought to read it and then, as Professor White suggested, ought to read the *Gorgias* itself.

"The object of it all," Professor White wrote (and perhaps he meant, by "it all," moral discourse such as the one Socrates and Callicles had, or perhaps he meant the education of professionals) "is truth, and its method is friendship, the full recognition of the value of self and the other in a universe of two." Martin Buber would have liked that, Justinian said; but, for himself, Justinian said he would put it differently: The object of it all is friendship, and its method is truth.

Not that Justinian would deny how important truth is as an object in a school for professionals. But, he thought, as he sat in the airplane on the way back to Ireland, for all that is said in American universities about truth as a goal, little is said about telling the truth. The central importance of truth as *telos* supports the esteem that academic professionals have for free inquiry, free discussion, and a premium on rationality. Justinian saw in American professional schools less attention to the esteem Socrates showed for being straight (for what Socrates called refutation and what a Jew or Christian might think of as counsel or fraternal correction). Truth is a sensible goal. The point he would make, Justinian thought, is that truth is also a sensible habit.

Friendship as a habit, a disposition, a method, among law teachers and law students, would have given something useful to Sam Jones, and to his clients and his community. Friendship is respect for dignity, for personhood, as many modern writers put it—for, as Buber said, the "trivial and irreplaceable" individual. Friendship as a method makes a skill of concern, of affection, of love. White says, "The fact that the definitions are not stipulated" in Socratic discourse, "but cooperatively arrived at, means that it is not merely a clarification but an instruction in the processes of making things clear." Buber thought friendship was all that and even more. He gave the relationship, "the universe of two," ontological significance. I don't even come to be, he said, until I see myself in such a universe. And not only ontological significance, but transcendent significance. He who abides in love abides in God, and God in him. Friendship as a method, and truth as an object are, perhaps, a way to restate St. Paul's teaching that love rejoices in the truth.

Justinian's difficulty with Professor White's understanding of Plato was this: Treating truth as a goal makes it too easy to ignore truth as a method—as a skill—as something one must learn to do. And treating friendship as a method makes it too easy to deceive myself into using the other as a means to my truth. (Socrates tended to do that, and his counterparts in dialogue tended to complain about it.) The academic professional, admirably devoted as he is to the pursuit of truth, finds it too easy to tell himself that his abuse of students is in aid of his pursuit and therefore justified. One thinks in this regard of such obscene examples as Stanley Milgram's experiments in the psychology of obedience—experiments in which subjects (students, probably) were made to inflict what they thought were lethal electrical charges on one another, all in the name of science (which is Latin for knowledge). That example is not irrelevant; those who command such experiments do not consciously choose the evil exploitation of other people. To do wrong, as Socrates said, is the greatest misery, but these students didn't choose to do wrong; they chose to obey their elders.

It becomes too easy in more specifically educational settings to use one student for another student's benefit, as when one of Sam Jones's law teachers asks Sam what the perpetuities period is.

Sam: Lives in being and 21 years.
Prof.: What's a life in being?
Sam: A living person.
Prof.: Really? Living when?
Sam: When the will's made.
Prof.: You mean your fancy testamentary trust will only

work for 21 years after the death of your aged, senile, rich, and overbearing client?

Sam: Well—I don't know. Maybe not.

Prof.: Indeed. Maybe not. Miss Brown, what's a life in being?

Miss Brown answered correctly, thanks to help from Sam Jones—help that neither the professor nor Miss Brown nor even Sam Jones himself is likely to be aware of—through a use of Sam Jones that had more to do with the professor's purposes, or Miss Brown's, than with Sam's.

In the teaching hospital, Bosk says, "The subordinate suggests and the attending physician corrects. A persistent and recurrent problem is the attending who corrects but neglects to give his reasons. House staff [residents] feel that this is an abuse of rank." Often this neglect is conscious, and often it is because of "clinical experience"—that is, the attending physician cannot give reasons a scientist will respect. Kant, as Justinian reminded the law professors, said that it is immoral, prima facie, to use a trivial and irreplaceable human being merely as a means. There is something to be said for truth as a method and friendship as a goal. Such a switching of the predicate nominatives in White's two phrases would have these advantages:

It would make the relationship an end in itself. As much as Martin Buber is quoted in discussions of relationship, he is not often enough understood to have made the argument that the relationship is an end in itself—to have made the argument that such a teleological view of relationship is the essence both of our religious heritage and of the western philosophical heritage White celebrates in his essay on the *Gorgias.* A person becomes good when he has that ultimate significance for others, when he is irreplaceable despite his being trivial. That is how we come to stir one another up to love and good works. That is the virtue of friendship and the basis of civil sanity.

White (and perhaps Plato) is almost as radical as Buber on the point. What is at stake, as White argues about the lawyer-client relationship, is the preservation of self. His fictional lawyer, Euphemes ("good speaker"), tells his client, "I am not a chameleon or an actor but a single person. . . . In any case in which I act, my own sense that I am speaking properly, asking for what I am entitled to ask for, functioning out of a sense of fairness, is essential to my ethos . . . and . . . my success . . . in two ways: not only in the material sense of gaining so many dollars by settlement or trial, but in the much larger sense of helping you to give this difficulty a meaning that is most valuable and appropriate to you." Euphemes sees his professional life, as the nineteenth-century fathers of American professional ethics saw theirs, as an opportunity for building character—one that presents, for professional and client, "questions, for both of us, of how we should behave and who we should be." It is a matter of "mutual education and respect . . . based upon honesty."

Truth as a method, and friendship as a goal, would also provide a way for the professional-school ethic to become a social ethic; that is, it would be, in the terms used in Justinian's report, a way to bring client and community into the classroom. The difficulty in conceptions of professional goals that are now universally seen to be too narrow—client interests in the practice of law, health in the practice of medicine, normality rather than personal well-being (salvation) in the ministry—is that the client is not present, in the classroom, in his relationships. He is not present, in any adequate sense, at all. The only thing that is present is the academic engineer's contrived representation of him. Once the resident, in Bosk's teaching hospital, begins to do real doctor's work, he does not have time to know his patients. Bosk defines a hospital as a place where a person dies and no one notices.

For example, I found the following statement of a course objective in the materials of a friend, an accomplished and successful law teacher. It was one of many objectives he had the candor to state to his students at the beginning of the course. It was framed, as most of his objectives were, in terms of professional skill:

"You should be able to distinguish different opinions on the basis of the facts so as to strengthen an argument in defense of your client's interests or to weaken that of opposing counsel." (Reported appellate opinions are the usual stuff of common-law argument in courts, particularly in appellate courts. Skill in using judicial opinions is the commonest skill that law teachers think they train people in in the first year of law school.)

Nothing is said, in this law-school objective, about justice. It is exactly the professional objective that *Gorgias* and Callicles claimed for the profession of rhetoric, an objective Socrates found to be evidence that their profession was corrupting. "In your trade," White has Socrates say, "you lose yourself."

"Our orator, the good and true artist," Socrates said, is one whose mind is "always occupied with one thought, how justice may be implanted in the souls of the citizens and injustice banished, and how temperance may be implanted and indiscipline banished, and how goodness in general may be engendered and wickedness depart."

To the rhetorician, Socrates asks: "When you embark upon a public career, pray will you concern yourself with anything else than how we citizens can be made as good as possible?" And, to the teacher of rhetoricians, Socrates said the aim of the educational enterprise is worthy only if it is "men who have become good and just, men who have been stripped of injustice by their teacher and have acquired righteousness."

The usual way of criticizing such statements of teaching objective as the one my friend wrote focuses on its narrow service-to-client interests. In health care an analogous social issue is raised about families of people who are ill, and a broader moral question is raised about conceptions of health that depend more on what physicians think they can do than on the well-being of patients. The key to the matter, I think (and I think this is what Justinian implies in his concern for Sam's clients), is that the concept "client's interests" is corrupting. The interest of another to which a virtuous professional seeks to devote himself is how the client "can be made as good as possible." Justice is served (justice in Socrates' sense and justice in the Hebrew sense, as righteousness) through the interests of the client and not in them. The object of the enterprise is friendship: I do not seek for my friend what will corrupt him. Its method is truth.

Justinian got help from H. Richard Niebuhr's conception of how this works. Niebuhr's *The Responsible Self* is particularly interesting for those who teach professionals (as Justinian thought it would be) because its substance comes from Niebuhr's own classroom teaching, of ethics, to students who proposed to become professionals. Niebuhr seemed to begin his enterprise with Martin Buber; Buber seems to be everywhere in his thought. The essence of Buber's insight is that our moral life—and more, our being—centers in relationships with other people. I act in reference to my life with another person. Descartes raised the problem of how we know we exist, concluding: "I think, therefore I am." Buber said, I love, therefore I am.

But Niebuhr makes something of his own out of Buber's point by teaching that the two people in a relationship act in reference to a third person or group of persons. In this way our moral life, which is fundamentally a life in relationships, exists in a community and in a culture; and, in this way, our moral life opens onto a non-hierarchical stairway—a Jacob's ladder—that begins by transcending the relationship and ends by transcending the culture. You can see more as you go up the Jacob's ladder: from the people in the classroom, to the people in the school, to the people in the university, to the people in the country, to the people in the world, to creation itself. This is a ladder you climb in order to see. Its rungs are truth. What waits at the top is friendship.

Niebuhr was not alone in finding that the Enlightenment's ethic of autonomy is inadequate, even bankrupt, but his special angle on the point was also a replacement for the ethic of autonomy. It is more useful to ask, "To whom am I responsible? And in what community?" than it is to ask, "What rules should I choose in order to assure my own independence and the independence—freedom—of others?" The ethics of responsibility provide a better procedure for coping with rules than talk about freedom does. If you think about this as Niebuhr did, though, you answer with your life (as Brother Justinian said)—with what your life has been, and with what is going on in your life at the moment, and with what will go on in it in the next moment. (Recall, please, Justinian's parable from the 1936 Olympics.)

What is going on in your life is more than what law teachers usually mean when they talk about justice, and more than what physicians mean when they talk about health. It is what ministers should mean when they talk about salvation. (Salvation means being well.) Suppose my friend would agree to amend his objective (and I think he might), from "in defense of your client's interests" to "in reference to what is going on in your client's life." That would include the client's relationships, as part of, as indeed the most important part of, the client's interests. It would bring the client into the classroom. In Niebuhr's geometrical conception, it would change the law-school student-teacher relationship from a line to a triangle:

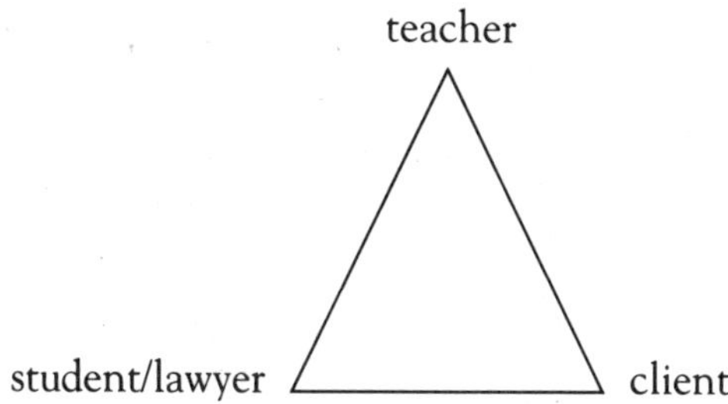

And it would make it possible to think of the lawyer-client relationship in a triangle, too (assuming, say, that the client is a corporation with business interests in a particular community):

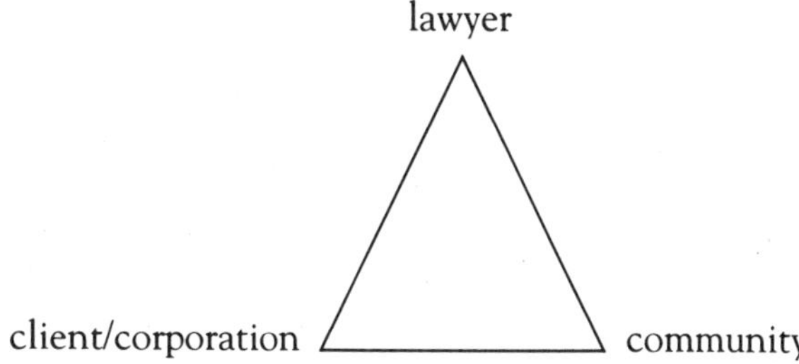

And it would make it possible to think of the client-community relationship as something that could comprehend social interests on a regional, then a national, then an international level (etc.):

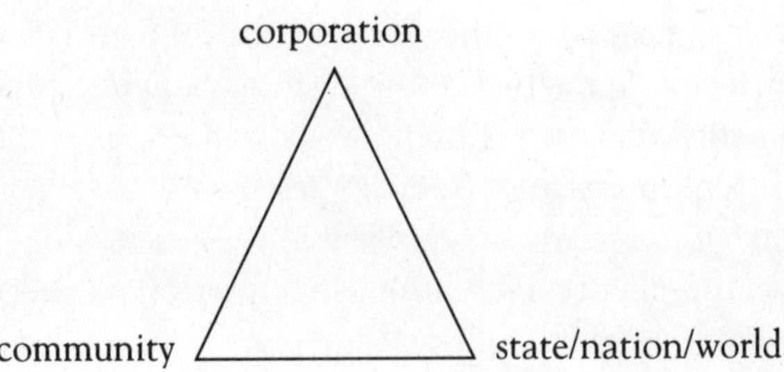

Relationship, conceived of as radically as Buber conceived of it, but also conceived of as comprehending other relationships, is, then, the goal of the enterprise—that is, of teaching professionalism and of the practice of professionalism. The way relationship becomes of that central importance is through truth as a method, through asking about responsibility in community and through the trivial and irreplaceable other. Through an adequate notion of the interests of the trivial and irreplaceable other.

In these educational and professional practices, truth is a skill, a method, a moral act, and a virtue—something to become competent at. It is failure at that skill among those in American professional schools that most disturbed Brother Justinian. Failure at the skill of truthfulness (of what Iris Murdoch means when she says that seeing is a moral act and a moral art) is what Brother Justinian found when he looked at grading curves, at academic architecture, at the blue-ribbon theory of academic progress, and at the academic profession's neglect of the gateway to franchise and its worship of the gateway to hierarchy. His way, finally, of putting this observation is the accusation that the professors have left clients (patients, parishioners) out of account. What he sees, and is reluctant to say—what he, in his faith, finds ultimately terrifying—was once a vacuum in professional education, but is now a place of institutional idols.

Truth as a method would virtually replace moral principle as a method. (The way professional schools teach professional ethics is in terms either of dilemmas or of codal principles—and usually of both.) Sometimes, it seems to me, Brother Justinian, in his eagerness to make a point, was muddled on this difference between truth as a method and principle as a method. For example, he accused law teachers of violating the rule that says a person is to be treated as an end in himself and not merely as a means. Where does he get such a rule? What set of rules is he consulting? I suppose he would say the applicable rules. And then we might ask, "How do we know which rules are applicable?" And at this point, if he is true to the tradition he is using, Justinian would have to try to talk us into a principle from which a logical person would have to reason that we should, for instance, not grade on the curve, not separate ourselves from our students, and not separate our students from one another. That argument might finally come to the point—as it usually does—where one side would insist that the principle is not adequate to the case. Such a point was reached when Justinian and the professors stopped talking about grades as a reward for quality work. Finally, that is, such an argument comes to saying that each of us is free, or self-governing, and each of us has to choose the rules he will be governed by. At that point the claim from principle falls apart.

It falls apart, first, because it provides no way to deal with the reality of the moral life, which is that we do not live by following right principles; we live by violating them. Sophocles described our dilemma; we are all Antigones. Two rules, not one, are to be obeyed. Both are reasonable; both follow from our culture or from ethical universals. But we cannot obey one without disobeying the other. The pedagogical practice of posing a quandary, and then showing how two rules apply and that one of them must be violated, is an invitation to contempt for morals—and thence to despair. What we have to learn is not so much how to obey the right rule as to live with and honor the rule we refuse to obey. And principles do not show us how to do that, because the question is not so much what to do as it is who we are. How to be the persons we want to be. Even to learn, in the law, as Simone Weil said, that violence has killed and will kill again.

The last scene in Socrates' life is a scene in which he demonstrates not right choice but virtuous behavior. He will not flee from the city, because, he says, he loves the city as a child loves his parents. He must stay in the city even though the city is unjust. He must stay and be killed, unjustly, by the city. And, I suppose, we admire him—not because he is right, but because he is good, which means, one way or another, that we are thrown back on the need to examine (his)(our) culture. I could sketch out a similar analysis of each of the situations Brother Justinian noticed, including the argument about quality work, but my readers can do it better. I will therefore leave the task to my readers.

Which brings me to asking about the ethics involved in our lives as teachers in professional schools and to the fact that each of us, when he deals with his own conscience, deals also with the consciences of others. The faculty, collectively, is dealing not only with the school's responsibility but also with the responsibility of the profession and of the community.

It is not likely—and probably not even possible—that any of us can act without reference to other consciences. Cardinal Wolsey told Thomas More that conscience must sometimes give way to the necessities of statecraft. And More said that when statesmen forsake their private consciences for the sake of their duties to the collectivity they lead their countries by a short route to chaos. (This according to Robert Bolt.) A similar response is possible to those who argue that faculty policies in a professional school have to bend to what is called the "real" world. The school is real and the world outside is part of the school world. The same is true of faculties. There is no honest way to avoid what Brother Justinian says about what each of our students, even the weakest among them, will do in the profession and in the community. We tend to deal with that observation by looking the other way. We do it all the time. But any relationship is a relationship of three. The clients our students will have sit with us and our students as we learn to deal with one another. Such a fact bears on how we ask and answer, "To whom am I responsible, and in what community?"

Niebuhr wanted to talk about these moral issues in terms of responsibility. There are at least three ways for a teacher to do that. We can talk about being responsible to somebody, for somebody, or with somebody. Those of us in the university who teach on graduate professional faculties long ago rejected the claim that we should be responsible to anybody. We are the last of the prima donnas. If you don't believe that, imagine for a moment what will happen when the dean of the law school Justinian visited orders her tax teachers to cover the Clifford-Trust rules, or the torts teachers not to leave out libel and invasion of privacy. Or remember what has happened when the organized bar or the courts have proposed, even in the mildest ways, to require law-school courses or subjects in courses. Imagine what will happen when the chairman of the board of trustees of the teaching hospital Charles Bosk studied tells the attending physicians in surgical residencies to base their admission to senior residencies not on attitude but on objective demonstrations of surgical skill. Imagine what will happen—remember what has happened—when the church that supports a theological seminary decides to ask that teachers tenured in the seminary respect to the church's creed.

It is more plausible for us to talk about being responsible *for* somebody, even if we also resolutely evade having to answer for ourselves in that way. When we feel responsible for, say, one of our students, we go through a moral checklist—not for ourselves, but for the other, the student. I ask myself: What do I want for her? Maybe I answer that I want her to be free; or that I want her to be right; or that I want her to be good, to be a person who makes good decisions. ("Good lives are made so by discipline," King Creon says. "Then we keep the laws.") There are differences among these ways of looking at responsibility for our students, but what is wrong with all of them is that they appropriate a burden that is so suffocating that we are bound to fudge on it.

"Responsibility for" is represented in Trollope's novel, *The Eustace Diamonds,* in the character of the Eustace family lawyer, Mr. Camperdown. Mr. Camperdown told the Eustaces what to put in their wills, when to sell their land, when to be harsh with tenants and when to be benevolent. Of such lawyers, Trollope said, "The outside world to them was a world of pretty, laughing, ignorant children; and lawyers were the parents, guardians, pastors, and masters by whom the children should be protected from the evils incident to their childishness." And if you think it inappropriate to use a literary professional when I am talking about teachers, I invite your reflection on the fact that our students are our clients; it is from us that our students learn how to treat their clients. White says, "Plato does seriously hope to establish . . . a community with his readers. The text . . . offers its reader a set of experiences that teach him his responsibilities as a free person and give him some material with which to begin to discharge them. The dialogue . . . both teaches and respects its reader. . . . Plato makes himself his reader's dialectical friend."

Niebuhr's prescription for the vicarious moral life was neither being responsible to nor being responsible for. I take him to have described a moral world in which each of us is responsible *with* the other. We are three (teacher, student, and client); we are responsible with one another in the community of people who come together in the professional enterprise. Niebuhr called that "triadic responsibility." He said that our actions are fitting as they fit into the web of responsibility that is our shared moral life. This was exactly the moral insight that Brother Justinian found attractive in Socrates, and in White's contemporary exposition of the *Gorgias*. "It is a question of how one may become as good as possible and best administer his own home or his city," Socrates said. Public life cries out for character, and character comes from pursuit of the virtues, which pursuit results from training—from learning from one's teachers. The goal is friendship; the method is truth—"making conscious," White says, "what before was not, the relation between self and culture." It is a process in which "one is mortified by the invocation not of new facts or ideas but of what one already knows or claims to know . . . the shared reconstitution of self and language . . . to define new possibilities for the life of the self and of the community." Herbert Fingarette called it a matter of spelling out engagements. It is often an exercise in imagination.

White has his Euphemes refute Socrates with words that Niebuhr might have endorsed. "The answers must be good not only for the two of us, but for our whole community, for the others who act in our universe and speak our language. To say, as you do, that it is never good to have any relationship with any person that has any object other than discovering what is ultimately good for each of those two would in fact mean the end of the culture; the lawyer is one whose aim it is to maintain and improve the culture that makes possible a larger life, in a larger world."

As responsibility is shared in this way, in each relationship, the law office looks to the community, the community to the nation, the nation to all of mankind, and . . . (Niebuhr was, after all, a theology teacher).

My moral action, Niebuhr says, fits, "as a sentence fits into a paragraph . . . a note into a chord . . . as the act of eating a common meal fits into the lifelong companionship of a family." Isn't that the moral judgment Socrates pronounced when he spoke to the jury about his accusers? "I shall go away, sentenced by you to death; they will go away, sentenced by truth to wickedness and injustice." Isn't that Isaiah's judgment on Judah—that it burns animals in the Temple and in the smoke hides from itself its injustices to the poor? The prophets ask Judah, and especially Judah's teachers, "If this is your religion, where do the widows and orphans fit in?"

EPILOGUE

· § ·

POOKAS

At the level of serious common sense and of ordinary nonphilosophical reflection about the nature of morals it is perfectly obvious that goodness is connected with knowledge . . . with a refined and honest perception of what is really the case, a patient and just discernment and exploration of what confronts one, that is the result not simply of opening one's eyes but of a certain perfectly familiar kind of moral discipline.

—Iris Murdoch

ELWOOD P. DOWD was a close friend of the title character in Mary Chase's 1953 Pulitzer Prize play *Harvey*. The title character in the play was a pooka who was seven feet tall. Pookas are rabbit like creatures. Elwood met Harvey on the street one night. It was late. Each of them had been drinking. Harvey was leaning against a lamp post at 18th and Fairfax. They were thereafter friends and companions.

It was not necessary for the producers of the play, or of the movie version of it, to employ an actor to be Harvey, since few in the cast and (perhaps) no one in the audience could see Harvey. That fact made it possible for Harvey to just be himself. Elwood P. Dowd was played by Jimmy Stewart in the movie and by Art Carney on television. And it is Elwood, not Harvey, whom you want to watch when you talk about morals in professional life in America.

In the third act, Harvey began to appear to Elwood's psychiatrist, Dr. Chumley. Chumley tried to woo Harvey away from his relationship with Elwood. Chumley wanted Harvey to take him to Akron, Ohio, for a vacation. It was necessary to his purpose for Chumley to woo Elwood, too, and in doing that he revealed to Elwood that Veta, Elwood's sister, had been moving heaven and earth to get Elwood committed, involuntarily, to the doctor's mental sanitorium, Chumley's Rest.

Veta had sound reasons. Elwood insisted on introducing Harvey to her friends and to all potential suitors for her daughter's hand. None of these people could see Harvey. This led to social isolation for Veta and Myrtle Mae, and they got no comfort from going to bars with Elwood and Harvey. They could not escape Elwood entirely, either—even if they wanted to—because Elwood's and Veta's mother had given the family fortune to Elwood.

"Mr. Dowd," the doctor said, "none of those people are your friends. I am your friend."

"And I'm yours," said Elwood.

"This sister of yours—she is at the bottom of this conspiracy against you. She's trying to persuade me to lock you up. Today she had commitment papers drawn up. She's got your power of attorney and the key to your safety box."

To which Elwood replied: "My sister did all that in one afternoon? Veta is certainly a whirlwind."

The doctor came to his feet, came around to the front of his desk, and said, "Haven't you any righteous indignation?"

At that point, Elwood made his ethical claim:

"Dr. Chumley, my mother used to say to me, 'In this world, Elwood . . . you must be oh, so smart or oh, so pleasant.' For years I was smart. I recommend pleasant. You may quote me."

· § ·

Elwood's ethic, being pleasant, was clear enough, but it was not simple. It brought him into considerable danger and—as any interesting ethic does—it resulted in suffering by other people. But, he said, being pleasant did more for him than being smart had done—it won him a host of friends. He introduced them to Harvey and invited them to come to his house for dinner with Veta, Myrtle Mae, and himself.

Being pleasant finally kept Elwood from being committed to Chumley's Rest. It gave him peace and security. "I always have a wonderful time just where I am, whomever I'm with," he said. He should be the envy of physicians, accountants, bankers, and insurance underwriters. Even if you understand professional ethics as a system for staying out of trouble, as lawyers tend to do, rather than as a system for being a good person, Elwood's ethic was successful; it kept him out of trouble. The movie version of the story ended with Elwood walking into the sunset, *away* from Chumley's Rest. He had his arm around his tall friend, who had left Dr. Chumley inside the rest home. And Elwood said to Harvey, "I prefer *you,* too."

Dr. Chumley did not have the consolations of Akron after all, but only the consolations that all of us claim in professional life. "The function of a psychiatrist," he said—and we professionals all say this about ourselves, I think—"is to tell the difference between those who are reasonable, and those who merely talk and act reasonably." The difference between Elwood and Dr. Chumley is that Elwood did not aim to live the distinction between being reasonable and talking and acting reasonably. His method was truth; his goal was friendship.

In classical ethics you would say that Elwood P. Dowd's was an ethic of virtues. He claimed, as Aristotle did, the central importance of the virtue of friendship. He understood, as Aristotle did, that social institutions rest on that virtue and on the virtue of prudence, what Aristotle called practical wisdom. In order to function in his social institutions, Elwood also trained himself in the virtue of magnanimity—largeness of soul.

Judge Gaffney, who did the legal work for Veta on Elwood's commitment to Chumley's Rest, had known Elwood all his life. The judge said, "There was always something different about Elwood. . . . He was always so calm about any sudden change in plans. I used to admire it. I should have been suspicious. Take your average man looking up and seeing a big white rabbit. He'd do something about it. But not Elwood. He took that calmly, too." Which is to say that largeness of soul is not an easy virtue; you don't just *get* it. It's like the Boston Marathon; you have to *train* for it. The average person probably doesn't have it.

Elwood's ethic is not acceptable to people who are solemn about their work in the world. They argue with Elwood. They often find it necessary to get Elwood out of sight, or better, to give him something that will cause him to see things as they do. They do this in practice and as a matter of sound professional education.

In the first act of the play, young Dr. Sanderson, at Chumley's Rest, thought that sister Veta was the crazy one. He had her captured and subjected to a warm bath. Veta resisted, was overpowered, and concluded that the people at Chumley's Rest were white slavers. She directed her lawyer, Judge Gaffney, to sue them. Later Dr. Sanderson understood that Elwood was the crazy one, and he let Veta out. He said, then, to Elwood, "The situation has changed since we met this afternoon. But I urge you to have no resentments. Dr. Chumley is your friend. He only wants to help you."

Elwood said, "That's very nice of him. I would like to help him, too."

Sanderson ignored that significant offer of help *from* Elwood—a point to which we must return—and said, "A cooperative attitude . . . [is] half the battle. We all have to face reality, Dowd—sooner or later."

Elwood replied, "Doctor, I wrestled with reality for forty years, and I am happy to state that I finally won out over it."

Dr. Sanderson didn't hear that, either. Doctors and lawyers don't listen when the question is a question about reality. They are always ready to bring in the big guns—to win early and to win big—when there's a standoff on a question about reality. Reality is mainline, professional stuff. It is our stock in trade. When professionals get ready to act in a matter involving reality, they don't need help from their clients. As Nurse Kelly said of Dr. Chumley, "He is a psychiatrist with a national reputation. Whenever people have mental breakdowns they at once think of Dr. Chumley."

In ethical terms, Dr. Sanderson was not interested in Elwood's claim to the virtues of friendship, prudence, and magnanimity. He was interested immediately in confining Elwood, so that he wouldn't bother Veta and the judge and Myrtle Mae, and then he was interested in giving Elwood a drug that would have caused Elwood to see the world realistically—no rabbit, no friends, no enjoyment in being where you are, no enjoyment in being with just anybody at all. Dr. Sanderson's patients didn't see the world as Elwood saw it; they saw the world *realistically.* The ethical issue is clearly drawn in this scene. Dr. Sanderson claimed that he understood reality; Elwood, whether he understood or not, claimed that he had defeated reality. The ethical issue is an issue about reality.

· § ·

The place I usually see this issue played out is, of course, in a law school, where I work among those who claim to teach people how to serve clients, how to help clients save taxes and make their wills and see justice done in their lives. Elwood's school of ethics concentrates on talking to such people. If he were a lawyer he would see clients (students) as gifts rather than problems. He would tend to take the Internal Revenue Code with a sigh and a smile. He would maintain that opinions written by appellate judges are evidences of professional failure. They are, perhaps, what happens when reality wins.

Dr. Sanderson's school of healing is solemn about science; it tends to identify feelings as symptoms and eccentricity as disease. If Dr. Sanderson were a lawyer, he would be solemn about the Internal Revenue Code. Taxes, Justice Holmes said, are the price of civilization. Dr. Sanderson would be serious about appellate opinions, because he believes that judges are especially important. They administer justice. The Sanderson school of legal planning would talk a lot about traps for the unwary, pitfalls, improvident heirs, and spendthrift clauses. The Sanderson school of thought says you have to face reality sooner or later.

In fact, the Sanderson school of legal planning faces a reality that people in the Elwood school—for all their rabbits—don't even see. There was an example of this in the play. Myrtle Mae asked her mother why her grandmother left all the family's money to Elwood. Veta said, "Well, I suppose it was because she died in his arms. People are sentimental about things like that."

Myrtle Mae said that answer didn't make sense. "She couldn't make out her will after she died, could she?" Veta told Myrtle Mae not to be didactic. "It's not becoming in a young girl, and men loathe it."

That is a familiar example of a Sanderson-like exchange, of an exchange that goes on frequently in professional schools. It has two layers. In one layer the elder says to the younger that the younger doesn't know what she's talking about. This layer is important in professional ethics because it displays professional behavior. It shows a professional in action. Many—maybe most—people who come to a university to learn the law have never known a lawyer before, and, in any case, the lawyers that law students know best are law professors. There aren't any clients around for these lawyers to react with, so the students take the place of clients in the professor's world; they *are* the professor's clients. Law students watch how professors treat students; sometimes that's how they learn to treat *their* clients. The way Veta treated Myrtle Mae is also the way attending physicians treat junior residents and medical students—as we all know from watching Dr. Craig on "St. Elsewhere." Medical residents do get to see their teachers deal with patients, but what they appear to learn is that a good doctor is busy; she or he doesn't have time to get to know patients. Sometimes the way they learn to treat patients is like the way Veta had learned to treat Myrtle Mae.

The other layer that is important here is a claim about what *realism* is. The persistent argument professionals have with Elwoodians is that friendship, prudence, and largeness of soul are not realistic. Veta says that her mother favored Elwood in her will because Elwood was with her when she died. That would have to mean that, in this business of making wills, people somehow survive themselves. Wills and trusts are a way not to die. That, say the old to the young, is realism. For all their romantic softness, the Elwoodians have never claimed they know how not to die. Elwood said that Harvey could overcome time and space. He could stop the clock for you. "You can go away as long as you like with whomever you like and go as far as you like. And when you come back not one minute will have ticked by. . . . Einstein has overcome time and space . . . Harvey has overcome not only time and space—but any objections." Harvey can take you to Akron, so that you won't be missed at home, but not even Harvey can overcome death. Only realists can do that.

The issue is the reality of professional life, the reality of client life in estate planning in the case treated in *Harvey*, and the reality of life in families that are affected by estate planning—the reality of disease as it is diagnosed and treated at Chumley's Rest. The issue is the reality of justice and health. My argument, at the end of this book, is that, when you carefully contemplate all this reality, there is something to be said for pookas.

I think nonetheless that Dr. Sanderson had the ethical issue right: We should face reality. We Elwoodians concede that reality is the issue, but we argue with the Sanderson party about what reality is. I suggest we do that in three steps: (1) the reality of who helps whom; (2) the reality of who corrupts whom; and (3) the reality of who serves his own selfish needs and who doesn't.

Help. In the play, Elwood helped the doctors: He turned Dr. Chumley's thoughts to a restful vacation, under a tree in Akron, with a pretty woman who would listen and not talk, except to say to Dr. Chumley, "Poor thing! Oh, you poor, poor thing." Elwood got Dr. Sanderson to notice Nurse Kelly, and helped Nurse Kelly get Dr. Sanderson's attention. He got Judge Gaffney, the lawyer, to look all around the city for Harvey. The judge looked at lampposts and in bars to see if he could find Harvey. He wanted to talk to Harvey about Elwood. The story of Elwood has a lesson for medical and legal ethics, which is that the client helped the professionals, just as he said he would—and I believe that is usually the story with us professionals. That *is* realistic. Or maybe it is how professional reality is won out over.

Corruption. I have often thought of saying to my sisters and brothers in the legal profession: Some day, when you have an idle weekend afternoon, take the governing code of legal ethics for your jurisdiction—you can find it on your book shelf, right next to the Bible—and do an experiment in ethics. Cross out all the parts that warn you not to be corrupted by your clients—the parts that talk about clients who expect you to keep their dirty secrets; clients who want you to be on their side when it's not right; clients who want you to cheat other people and lie to judges; clients who want to evade the imposition of justice, or of death, or of taxes. Cross those parts out and see how much code you have left. See how much of our official ethic rests on the assumption that the really big moral problem in modern professional life is protecting ourselves from our clients. You will find that the reality claimed by the organized legal profession is that *clients corrupt lawyers.* I'm sure the same thing is true in medicine and journalism. I'm not so sure about business. I am surprised at how many business people are Elwoodians—more comfortable with being pleasant than the rest of us are; and that means they have a better chance to see their customers as gifts rather than as threats. I was taught in law school, though, not to trust business people; they corrupt lawyers (see chapter 4).

Selfish needs. Now, to continue this little speech to my fellow lawyers, take the part of the *Code* that is left over from the experiment on corruption and notice how much of the code has to do with *our* comfort, not our clients' comfort: the rules on confidentiality, with their exceptions for fee claims and charges against lawyers; the rules on conflicts of interest, with their protection of independent professional judgment; the rules on fees; on lawyer collaboration; and on appearances of impropriety. Doctors can join in this exercise, using Sir Thomas Percival's code of 1791 or any handy, modern source of official medical ethics. We professionals serve our own needs, whatever else we do. This is an awful moral situation, because it means we fool ourselves about whose needs we serve. I think of what Joseph Conrad said about the profession of espionage. "When our appointed activities seem by a lucky accident to obey the particular earnestness of our temperament . . . we can taste the comfort of complete self-deception."

Elwood came upon professional self-deception in the law and in medicine, and he set up against it a coherent, positive, and classical ethic. Elwood believed in having friends and in fostering friendship—in working at it, in making friendship a habit—as a realistic thing to do. A virtue, such as the virtue of friendship, is a skill. One has to learn it from someone, as Elwood learned it from Harvey; and then to practice it and keep it keen, as Elwood did in bars, on the street, at home, and at Chumley's Rest. This is true also of largeness of soul, which often seems merely a matter of ordinary generosity. We tend to suppose that some people are born generous and some are not. Elwood was not born generous. He said he had tried being smart and recommended being pleasant; he said he had wrestled with reality for forty years before he finally won out over it. I think he was generous because he had trained himself to be generous. And the same is true of Elwood's third virtue, prudence, or what Aristotle called practical wisdom. That virtue takes account of what is going on. Prudent people look around; they are responsible—they are *able* to *respond,* without self-deception, to what is going on.

Such a consideration of the virtue of prudence gets us back to the main moral argument here, which is whether the professional school of ethics that Dr. Sanderson proclaims is more in tune with reality than the Elwoodians are. On this point, I argue—and Elwood argues—that our professional ethics deceives us into supposing we serve clients more than that they serve us, so that when we are being most selfish, we are able to tell ourselves that we are serving not ourselves but our clients.

Please recall in this connection what Henry Knox (chapter 4) said, reflecting on a successful lifetime of business practice in a large law firm—reflecting as he sat by the swimming pool, one Sunday morning, with Ann Colt, whose husband was doing Knox's work back in the city. "Your client wants to do something grasping and selfish. But quite within the law. As a lawyer you're not his conscience, are you? You advise him that he can do it. So he does it and tells his victim: 'My lawyer made me!' You're satisfied and so is he."

Or what Dr. Minchin said when he came back to Middlemarch and found that the upstart practitioner Lydgate had publicly disagreed with his diagnosis of Nancy Nash—had told the patient and a surgeon that Nancy's affliction was not a tumor, as Dr. Minchin had said, but a cramp (chapter 4). Dr. Minchin could see, no doubt, that Lydgate's diagnosis was right and that Lydgate's treatment was better. Dr. Minchin had prescribed surgery, which was then a virtually fatal therapy for the poor in hospitals. The problem was that Nancy *didn't* die. If she had, Dr. Minchin's diagnosis would have been safe. Dr. Minchin did not say he had been mistaken, or even that he was glad Nancy survived. He said: "Indeed! ah! I saw it was a surgical case, not of a fatal kind."

· § ·

The second agenda for this examination of reality is that Dr. Sanderson's school of ethics asks us what we *do* for our clients. The Elwoodians' claim is that we professionals often do for them only what a Diet Coke would do for them: We make them feel better. Without calories. That's what the lawyers who worked for Veta's and Elwood's family, who nowadays call themselves "estate planners," have to offer. Dead people don't pay taxes. Dead people don't take it with them, or even come back to visit it. Elwood's mother is long gone. She had to leave it all behind, and now it belongs to somebody else.

Whatever Mother Dowd's motives were for leaving the family fortune to Elwood, they did not, as the realistic Veta supposed, include gratitude that Elwood was with her when she died. But her motives might have included the fact that she knew he *would be* with her when she died. That thought may have made her feel better. Professionals of Elwood's school would say that it's realistic to feel better when you believe that you need not die alone. I suspect that is part of what Elwood meant when he said that he had, with the help of a pooka, won out over reality. Jerry Kennedy and Fanny Holtzmann would probably agree (chapter 5).

The Elwoodian argument on the question of what we *do* is, first, an argument about reality. That is, the professional task we are paid to see to is often making people feel better. (And not only in "estate planning.") And, then, second, Elwoodians say we can live with that. First, the dominant facts are facts about feelings. Second, service to feelings is worthwhile. Feelings are not corrupting; feelings are not diseases; feelings are reality.

"The faces of the other people turn toward mine and smile," Elwood said. "Harvey and I warm ourselves in all these golden moments. We have entered as strangers—soon we have friends. . . . They talk to us. They tell about the big terrible things they have done. The big wonderful things they *will* do. Their hopes, their regrets, their loves, their hates. All very large because nobody ever brings anything small into a bar. . . . When they leave, they leave impressed." Elwoodians believe that such a role in the community is worthwhile. But, most of all, and before any argument about what's worthwhile, Elwoodians say *that* is, among the realistic possibilities, what we do.

If that is what we do, and if it is worthwhile—either or both—the result in terms of professional skill will be that we learn more about what we do. What we do concerns feelings, and, in the estate-planning example, especially feelings toward death, toward things, toward people our clients love, toward all of the very large things Elwood came upon in his professional life. You don't get a lot of learning on those things from appellate opinions. Consider some random social-science information that will come to light for those who make learning about feelings important in the "estate planning" practice.

—Most Americans think it is immoral to disinherit a child.
—At least a third of Americans think it is immoral even to give children unequal shares.
—It is likely that most married people think it is immoral to leave property to children when the spouse also survives.

Those are findings about *morals;* they run deep. Elwood would say this: If a will-making lawyer doesn't occasionally find clients in tears over these issues something's the matter with the way the lawyer does things. The lawyer is not being *realistic.* These findings result in decisions made in our offices, and they are *stressful,* particularly when the circumstances argue for resisting moral notions.

The prevailing professional attitude is that decisions like these are the patient's or client's; that the professional should remain detached from the emotional climate in which decisions like these are made—should leave the patient or client alone. But Elwoodians question that principle. Why be detached? Would it make a difference to the prevailing professional attitude if we remembered that the only thing the client gets is that he gets to feel better? (This applies to lawsuits, and to healing, too.) Would it make a difference if we remembered that professionals usually run their lives to serve their own needs?

In any case, Elwood's example is clear; what interested him was other people—what they felt, where they hurt, what they wanted to do. And he was happy to accept similar concern from the people he dealt with. What did *not* interest him was an abstract issue that did not involve either the other person's feelings or Elwood's; he would not have been fascinated by appellate opinions or the Internal Revenue Code. Early in the play, when Nurse Kelly was trying to put him at ease in the office, she offered him a magazine to look at. "I would much rather look at you, Miss Kelly, if you don't mind," Elwood said. She tried again with ventilation. "Dr. Sanderson wants to know if he should open a window," she said. Elwood said, "That's entirely up to him. I wouldn't presume to live his life for him."

In Elwood's and Veta's story—and it was a story about *them*—the feelings they have for one another resolve the plot. Feelings are decisive. The feelings of persons in families are often decisive in the stories we professionals get to share in. (That is much of the point of Eric Cassell's popular books on medical ethics.) Elwood first met Harvey after his mother died, when Veta and Myrtle Mae came from Des Moines to live with him. It is not clear whether Harvey came to Elwood when Elwood was in an emotional crisis, or whether, if that is why Harvey came, the emotional crisis followed the death of Elwood's mother or the addition of Veta and Myrtle Mae to his daily life. But it is clear that Veta and Elwood loved one another. Because Elwood loved Veta he offered to take Dr. Chumley's serum, even though the result would have been Harvey's disappearance and a normal human life—"no fun—and no tips," as Elwood's taxi driver put it. (Elwood knew all along, I think, what Veta was up to.)

And because Veta loved Elwood, she stopped the injection. She decided to live with Harvey after all, and to put up with Elwood, even though he "is the biggest heartache I have. Even if people do call him peculiar," she says, "he's still my brother." The truth about brothers and sisters is a fact; it is a reality. It is so important for all of us that our professional lives would be barren without it. The tough, no doubt, have something to teach the tender; but Elwood's story is a reminder that the tender have something to teach the tough—something about reality.

The people in Elwood's story go around and around over the question of whether Harvey is real. The audience never gets to see Harvey. At least I never have seen him, and I've seen the play on the stage and on television. I've seen the movie eight times. I've come to the point where I'm not sure but what Harvey's there. I remember when I saw Mr. Stewart play Elwood on the stage in London. At the curtain call they used the Chumley's Rest scene without a curtain. There was a set of swinging double doors at rear center stage. Mr. Stewart took his bow, then stepped aside and bowed to the doors. They swung slowly open, and Harvey took his bow. Perhaps the British saw him; I hope so. We all applauded, just in case.

What the tough have to teach the tender about Harvey, what Veta has to teach all of us—is that the *possibility* of Harvey is more realistic than the question about Harvey. When Veta and Myrtle Mae were talking about the injection, and the disappearance of Harvey from Elwood's life, Veta said, "Harvey always follows Elwood home. . . . If you give him the formula and Elwood doesn't see Harvey, he won't let him in. Then when he comes to the door, I'll deal with him."

Myrtle Mae said, "Mother, won't you stop talking about Harvey as if there was such a thing."

And Veta said, "Myrtle Mae, you've got a lot to learn and I hope you never learn it."

What the tender have to teach the tough is what Dr. Chumley learned at the peak of his successful professional life. Myrtle Mae told the doctor that Elwood could predict the future. "Things always turn out the way Uncle Elwood says they will," she said. "Harvey knows everything." And Dr. Chumley is converted; in a moment he becomes an Elwoodian. "Flyspecks," he said. "I've been spending my life among flyspecks while miracles have been leaning on lampposts."

Elwood P. Dowd argues, as I have tried to argue in this book, for possibilities. For the possibilities, in professional life, of friendship, of practical wisdom, and of largeness of soul. Harvey and I hope these arguments have been of interest to you. We leave you, as Elwood left Mrs. Chumley: "Regards to you and anybody else you happen to run into."

Acknowledgments

The final preparation of this book was done while I was on sabbatical leave from the Law Faculty at Washington and Lee University and was supported in part by a grant from the Frances Lewis Law Center at Washington and Lee. I am grateful to Mrs. Lewis; to Dean Frederic L. Kirgis, Jr.; to the Director of the Center, Lewis H. LaRue; and to Margaret Williams.

Three friends—Stanley Hauerwas, Robert E. Rodes, and Nancy J. Shaffer—have been at my side in this and almost everything else I have worked on in professional ethics. I could not do much without them.

Many other friends helped me by reading, suggesting, clearing the way, referring, and encouraging. I am grateful to Mark H. Aultman, Milner S. Ball, E. Clinton Bamberger, Jr., D. Stan Barnhill, Louis F. Bartelt, Jr., Harlan R. Beckley, Maxwell Bloomfield, Denis Joly Brion, J. P. Browder, M.D., Robert A. Burt, Samuel W. Calhoun, Linda Carter, James F. Childress, Michael J. Churgin, Roger C. Cramton, Paulette Dodge, William Donnelly, M.D., Fernand N. Dutile, Herbert Fingarette, Monroe H. Freedman, William S. Geimer, Roger D. Groot, Steven H. Hobbs, Louis W. Hodges, Drew L. Kershen, Dale G. Lasky, Sanford Levinson, David T. Link, Alasdair MacIntyre, Carol Maines, Richard G. Marks, Judith Martin, William James McClendon, Jr., Andrew W. McThenia, Gilbert Meilaender, Martha Morgan, Richard W.

Nahstoll, Linda Newell, Jane North, Kevin Rardin, Robert S. Redmount, Minor Rogers, Murray L. Schwartz, Edward A. Seegers, Brian C. Shaffer, Mary M. Shaffer, Joan M. Shaughnessy, Charles Sheedy, C.S.C., Nathan Smith, the late Lord (C.P.) Snow, Allen T. Snyder, Edward Tivnan, Richard Wasserstrom, and John Howard Yoder.

Permissions

Portions of this book appeared elsewhere, in different versions, and are used here with the kind permission of publishers.

Chapter 1: "Christian Lawyer Stories and American Legal Ethics," *Mercer Law Review* 33 (1982): 877.

Chapter 2: "David Hoffman on the Bible as a Law Book," *Christian Legal Society Quarterly* 2 (Fall 1981): 5; "The Legal Ethics of Servanthood," *Social Responsibility: Journalism, Law, Medicine* 8 (1984): 34.

Chapter 3: "The Legal Ethics of the Two Kingdoms," *Valparaiso University Law Review* 17 (1983): 1. This text also appeared, in a different version, in my book *American Legal Ethics* (New York: Matthew Bender, 1985) and is used with publisher's permission.

Chapter 5: "The Legal Ethics of Dissent and Friendship," *West Virginia Law Review* 88 (1986): 623.

Chapter 6: "Brother Justinian Goes to Law School," *Journal of Legal Education* 34 (1984): 190.

Epilogue: "On Being Pleasant: Ethics in Estate Planning," Proceedings of the Philip E. Heckerling Annual Institute on Estate Planning, University of Miami, 1985, Chap. 15.

Chapter Notes: Book Review, *Christian Legal Society Quarterly* 7, no. 1 (1985):32.

Chapter Notes

References here are to the bibliography. I do not ordinarily make note here of references that should lead from the text to the bibliography. I insert a comma between two names when I am citing separate works (e.g., "Brown, and Jones" refers to two works; "Brown and Jones" refers to one.) A number of sources are reprinted or excerpted in my *American Legal Ethics* (1985), abbreviated here and in the bibliography as *A.L.E.*

Chapter 1 Stories

The theology in this chapter is from McClendon, from Hauerwas (particularly the three early books—*Character, Vision,* and *Truthfulness*—and the more recent *Peaceable Kingdom*); from both of Michael Goldberg's books; from Cone (especially on Dr. King), May, and Bruggemann; and, more dimly, from Karl Barth. The earlier Goldberg volume (*Theology*) is a clear exposition of the theory I have adopted from these theologians; the later one (*Stories*) is an example of the theory at work, in reference to what Goldberg sees as the "master stories" of Judaism and Christianity. See also Dave, Elkins ("Emergence"), Jeremias, Davies, Culbertson, Shklar, and Burrows. Childress ("Scripture") is generally to the contrary. The epigraph is from Hauerwas's *Truthfulness.*

The jurisprudence depends a good deal on Rodes and is developed more theologically in my Notre Dame essay on Hebraic jurisprudence. The codes are in ABA publications and in the appendices to Katz's *Silent World,* Leake's edition of *Percival's Medical Ethics,* and *A.L.E.*, which also reprints Sharswood's essay, Hoffman's "Resolutions," and Jones's 1887 "Code." The ethics of virtue suggested in this chapter, and developed more thoroughly in chapters 4 through 6, are, of course, from Aristotle, Aquinas, Hauerwas, MacIntyre, and Meilaender; see also Geach. My piece on gentlemen's ethics discusses other sources.

Sources on Horton are Carter, Graves, and Patterson. Sources on Brandeis are Frank, Alpheus Mason, and Vorspan; the Frank essay and the portions of Vorspan's book that deal with Brandeis are in *A.L.E.* See the chapter notes for chapter 2 for sources on Dr. Horn. I used memory and Jane Hindman's essay (*Religion Teacher's Journal,* Oct. 1984), on Dr. Dooley; he is a hero for all Notre Dame graduates. Stanley Hauerwas kindly arranged for me to use Dr. J. P. Browder's unpublished syllabus on medicine and literature (Dr. Browder teaches at Duke); it has been very helpful. The notion of community that is suggested here and developed more carefully in chapters 4 and 5 takes encouragement from the work of Hauerwas, Bellah et al. I am indebted to William J. Donnelly, M.D., for showing me the ethical importance for medicine in Rembrandt's "The Anatomy Lesson," and a Dutch ballet (in movie form) based on it. I deal with other stories at more length in *On Being* (More, Jagerstatter), *A.L.E.* (Atticus, Brandeis, Knox), and my essay on the gentleman (Craig, Gavin Stevens). Sources on Hasidism, besides I. B. Singer's stories and Chaim Potok's novels, are Buber, Lis Harris, and Epstein.

Chapter 2 The Bible

The epigraph is quoted in Friedman's biography of Buber (*Middle Years*).

Discussions of American church history, and of women in such things as the Sunday school movement, that bear on my comparison of biblical religion and professional ethics, are in Marty, Dawson, Miller, Smith, and (with regard to British parallels) Philip Mason. Hoffman material is listed under his name and is also in

Chroust, Cordell, Calcott, Bloomfield, Story, and Hodge, as well as in biographical dictionaries and in my essay on Hoffman's law school lectures. There is no biography of Hoffman that I know of; Bloomfield, and my essay on his law school lectures cite biographical sources.

Rabbinical teaching and discussion of it is in Ronald Green, Rowley, Schnackenberg, Cohon, McKenzie, Maimonides, and Nelson. McThenia's and my essay on reconciliation cites and discusses sources on Jewish reconciliation courts. The skin-disease references are Updike, and Mouw's essay on biblical medical ethics. Mouw also relates biblical and Reformation ethics to one another and both to (1) the modern ethics of autonomy and (2) the neo-Aristotelian ethics of Alasdair MacIntyre—the latter especially in the essay in the *Journal of Religious Ethics.* The chapter "A Theology of the Client" in my *On Being* pursues in a Pauline context the biblical view of patients and clients; I usually read St. Paul as a Pharisaic rabbi (see Davies).

Medical codes are in appendices in Jay Katz's *Silent World* and in the Leake edition of *Percival's Medical Ethics.* See also Pellegrino on Percival. Carole Horn's essays appear in the *Washington Post;* I used those published Sept. 23, 1984 (p. C-1, col. 1); Oct. 28, 1984 (p. C-1, col. 2); and Jan. 13, 1985 (p. B-1, col. 1). Sources for my discussion of nurses are the Kalisch and Kalisch history of nursing and the Castiglioni history of medicine. Hilfiker is powerful on medicine and what Buber called the deep of failure. Woloch, Cole, and Bellah describe the historical "woman's sphere" and suggest the sort of moral interpretation I put on it—Bellah et al. and Cole rather more than Woloch. Herman, Neuberger, Webber, and Welter are also useful on this point. (Cone's discussion of Dr. King's theology of suffering service is eloquent and useful.)

Chapter 3 Theology

The themes of this chapter began in 1983 as the Edward A. Seegers Lectures at Valparaiso University; my purpose there was to speak, in a venerable Lutheran institution, of Luther's biblical ethic as analogous to if not an ancestor of the best of both Reinhold

Niebuhr's theological realism and the modern adversary ethic in the legal profession—and then to suggest, by way of contrast, the natural-law jurisprudence and ethic I learned fifty miles to the east, at Notre Dame. The object was neighborly as well as scholarly, but my broader inquiry was and is whether theological categories are useful to an account of the development and defense of ethics in a profession. The editors of Valparaiso's law review, which published the lectures, asked two theologians to comment on them—Professor Dale G. Lasky, of the Valparaiso theology faculty, and my friend and mentor Stanley Hauerwas, who was then at Notre Dame. Their comments are published in *Valparaiso University Law Review* 17(1983): 41 and 55.

Hauerwas noticed that I had neglected a third point of view—the view that says the kingdom Jesus spoke of (and that other Jews spoke and speak of) was and is in the world in a social and institutional way and that it is a community. (See Yoder's *Politics* and his *Priestly Kingdom.*) In Christian theology, this kingdom is a public home, so that the contrast between the kingdoms Luther spoke of is not a contrast between public and private life but a contrast between life in two communities (see Hauerwas's *Peaceable Kingdom*). Hauerwas titled his comments "On Living Between the Times":

> Law may well be, in our tradition, a means to work out our imperfect harmonies, and thus a work of love. But what happens if our tradition becomes so distorted by the adversarial ethic [or, perhaps, by the medical ethics of privacy] that that is no longer the case? Might it be that at that point the Christian will be faced with the possibility that the legal profession is one in which he or she cannot participate? . . . [A]s Christians we have . . . a stake in making the law live up to and serve the best within us. But that noble hope can sustain essentially unjust structures. What I am asking is, on Shaffer's grounds, how do you ever know when it may be necessary to exit . . . ? [I]s it not possible that certain modes of life and professions, although they may in principle be worthy, might become so distorted in actuality that we should no longer serve within or through them?

If the answer is yes (and mine would be), the question is, then, in a literal, physical sense, where does the exiter go? And that is where my theorizing was, in Hauerwas's view, inadequate. He says that I should have suggested that there is an institutional (or at least communal), and not merely a personal or private, alternative:

> Luther . . . failed to properly appreciate the kingdom as an eschatological reality that is a present possibility through the life, death, and resurrection of Jesus. Rather the 'Kingdom,' at least in Lutheranism, became a realm that stood as a judgment on all our earthly endeavors. The kingdom is everything we currently are not.
>
> I suspect implicit in Shaffer's "one kingdom" position is not simply a worry about possible misuse of a "two kingdom" ideology, but rather a sense that God's kingdom is in fact a historical reality and that we as Christians have the great opportunity to live in accordance with its laws. Moreover, through the teachings and life of Jesus we know a good deal about how that kingdom is to look and how it should be lived. Thus, as a people we know that we must be ready to forgive, not sue, our enemies. . . . Indeed it may well mean that "our lawyers" are required to find means of reconciling people without the threat of resort to court. [McThenia and I survey some of the possibilities for Jews and Christians, and cite several sources that elaborate the possibilities.]
>
> [T]he ethic of the kingdom is not simply that we respect the other as a fellow creature of God, but that we forgive the other even when it may be they have unjustly wronged us. And such forgiveness is not something we simply do "with our heart," but it has all the marks of a social gesture and is sustained by an institution.
>
> Once the kingdom is interpreted eschatologically we see that all the tensions, such as that between our public responsibilities and our private lives, are relativized. For the overriding tension in the Christian life is between the already and not yet of God's eschatological kingdom brought through the life, death, and resurrection of Jesus Christ. The problem is learning how to wait, but to wait hopefully, in this age, as a people who are already citizens of a new age. The tension Christians may feel between their public tasks and their Christian commitments is not, therefore, the tension of anyone, but the kind of tension that derives from their steadfast intention to live knowing that God's kingdom is a present reality.
>
> To live in that manner . . . require[s] . . . the church as a community to sustain the individual's endeavor to live appropriate to the nature of the kingdom as we believe it to have been revealed by Jesus. For the wisdom and support needed to live a life of forgiveness and truth cannot be sustained by the individual. We require others to remind us of our task and to test the kind of intuitions Shaffer relies on to help us know what we should and should not do as God's people. . . .
>
> [S]uch a life requires the existence of a people who have pledged

themselves to live as citizens in God's eschatological kingdom of peace and forgiveness.

Both Hauerwas and John Howard Yoder say more about this, and each uses "kingdom" in the title of a recent and relevant book. Much of what they say about the church could be said about Israel; see Buber (*On Judaism*) and Heschel.

Lasky thought my association of Luther's theology and the adversary ethic was unjustified, and that my understanding of the Lutheran two-kingdoms doctrine as an ethic was mistaken. (I do, though, think it possible to consider the adversary ethic as a serious and interesting argument—not in all of its manifestations, obviously, but certainly as it is reasoned by such scholars as Monroe Freedman.) Lasky titled his comment "Is One Ethic Enough?"

> [T]he inability of the hawks and the doves to engage in principled ethical discussion during the Vietnam crisis provides a strong case for distinguishing between personal and public morality. The very lack of a living tradition on the basis of which to discuss publicly the morality of the war compelled people to refer purely to private moral opinions. Opponents of the war found it necessary to appeal to private conscience, which is appropriate to pacifist convictions but not directly relevant to determining the justifiability of the war. The supporters of official policy, on the other hand, possessed no criteria by which to evaluate how to wage a war they considered justified.

In other words, what was needed there, and is needed in an ethic for lawyers, is a substantive (and possibly separate) morality for public life. (Notice Hauerwas's argument on this, just above.)

> The terms "public" and "private" have a sharply different meaning in Luther's thought from the way in which Shaffer employs the terms. For the former, the terms are neither sociological nor psychological, but theological. The term "private" refers to the relation to God which is the ultimate source of human dignity, and the term "public" refers to the entire life of action in the world. This means that for Luther all the moral life belongs to the public realm, including both what Shaffer, following common usage, terms personal [and what he terms] public

morality. Luther's two kingdoms doctrine really entails a one kingdom ethic.

Lasky agrees with my pointing out that Luther's thought may not be the same as the ethical teaching of others in the Lutheran tradition and may not use words in the same way. Lasky's essay is interesting and valuable as more than a comment; he cites a number of Lutheran writers that I did not consult.

Discussions of the adversary ethic are in Little, Noonan, Peter, Schudson, Bloomfield, and Schwartz—and, of course, in Freedman; a number of other discussions are in the *A.L.E.* chapter on the two kingdoms, the beginning text for which was also the Seegers Lectures. Schudson quotes and analyzes the Field-Bowles correspondence. His essay on that is in *A.L.E.* The Lutheran sources I used include Baepler, Bertram, Ebeling, Erling, Pannenberg, Scholler, and Thielicke; Reinhold Niebuhr and Yoder's *Politics* are relevant to the ethical issue I mean to raise. Sources for the argument from the turtles break down into three or four subcategories. One of these is Martin Buber, particularly in *I and Thou* and *On Judaism,* and in Friedman. Buber argues that the personal "kingdom" is neither public nor private; but, in its significance, and in his theory on the presence of God, the personal world is the redemption of the private and of moral life in the public (It) world. Another source is more or less Barthian; it is especially clear in Barth's *Community, State, and Church,* and in Will Herberg's introduction to the English translation thereof, and is in Bloesch, Hauerwas's *Community of Character,* and in Hauerwas's and my essays on More (in my *On Being*). A significant part of the ethics of this one-kingdom subcategory is in the ethical literature on self-deception, beginning with H. Richard Niebuhr (*Responsible Self*) and continuing through Herbert Fingarette's seminal treatise and Hauerwas and Burrell's essay on Albert Speer (in Hauerwas's *Truthfulness*). There is, thirdly, a subcategory of natural-law theory that I have from Rodes (both in being his student for thirty years and from his *Legal Enterprise*); from Maritain; and from other explications written by my colleagues and teachers at the University of Albuquerque and at

Notre Dame, particularly essays by Joseph O'Meara (*Natural Law Forum* 5[1960]: 83) and Edward F. Barrett (*American Journal of Jurisprudence* 23[1978]: 1). Wasserstrom, and Schwartz are not natural-law lawyers, but they raise one-kingdom concerns. So, sometimes, do the Kantians; see Donagan, and Frankena.

My one-kingdom examples come from Hamilton's essay on Alabama law (*Alabama Lawyer* 9[1948]: 346); Arthur Train's Mr. Tutt story "The Dog Arthur" (*Saturday Evening Post,* Nov. 15, 1919, p. 20); Rodes's *Legal Enterprise;* and from Rodes's and my essay in the Feifel anthology. These would benefit from more careful attention to the importance of relationship, and particularly of the family; Buber would be important on that. The epigraph is from *Chisholm v. Georgia,* 2 Dallas 419, 462–63 (1792)(Wilson, J.). Other cases: *Terminiello v. Chicago,* 337 U.S. 1 (1949); *Wagner v. International Railway Co.*, 232 N.Y. 176, 133 N.E. 437 (1921)(Cardozo, J., on rescue). My sources on medical ethics, particularly the (my) argument comparing the adversary ethic and the ethics of privacy in medicine, include Burtchaell, Cassell, Childress, Hauerwas (*Truthfulness*), Katz, and May. The skin-disease references are discussed in the chapter notes to chapter 1. Reviews of Faulkner's *Intruder,* including those that treated him as a Southern racist, are abstracted in the 1948 *Book Review Digest,* beginning at page 259.

An account of two-kingdom morals that is not developed here would be more clearly psychological (as well as theological) and would depend on such things as Buber's discussion of the alienated private life and life in the "It-World," and C. G. Jung's theory of archetypes. This would, I think, be a matter of saying that we tend to divide ourselves into separate selves (maybe more than two). This tendency is not necessarily to be accounted for normatively (although Fingarette's account of self-deception includes this archetypal disintegration, and treats it as a moral issue); it just is, and ethical theory has to take it into account, as it has to take into account such things as sexual feelings and the other passions. In a similar way, ethical theory has to cope with the separation of the morals with which we deal with intimates from the morals with which we deal with strangers. (See chapter 5, Toulmin, and Wasserstrom's *Lawyers' Ethics.*) There are, of course, ways to take moral responsibility for the divided self; Reinhold Niebuhr's social ethics attempts to do that, as does Goldberg's narrative theology. For Buber, such responsibility is inseparable from redemption. (Note that Lasky feels that my Seegers Lectures speak more of Reinhold Niebuhr than of Luther.) So does Yoder's "Radical Reformation" ethic (*Priestly Kingdom*), much of Hauerwas (see his comments previously in these chapter notes), and McCann.

Chapter 4 The Profession

I take seriously the claim of a profession to be a moral teacher. The attempts of the medical profession to do that, as Lydgate met those attempts, sometimes appear at best fumbling and at worst self-deceived; but I take them to have been serious attempts, taken by physicians who knew something of what would happen if the cumulative wisdom of the profession were disregarded, and who depended on the gentlemen's ethic that was part both of the culture and of the education of the young men who came into the professions. It is interesting in this regard that, in 1980, the American Medical Association modified attempts at detailed codes such as the one Percival had prepared for Lydgate's generation, and condensed the American medical profession's essential teaching to a short catalogue of virtues, all of which depend on and are calculated to result in "honorable behavior for the physician." (The word "honorable" suggests both the aspiration and the difficulty in an organized profession's being serious about aspiration. A modern organized profession is an institution, not, as might have been possible in Lydgate's day, what MacIntyre, in *After Virtue*, describes as a practice.) These resemble the Scout Law; they counsel competence, compassion, honesty, obedience to law, respect for confidentiality, dedication to learning (and teaching), and community service. These "principles" are in an appendix to Katz's *Silent World*.

Hospitals in Lydgate's day are described in Berkin and Norton, Kalisch and Kalisch, and in the chapter on surgery in Castiglioni; the last source also has a detailed section on Versalius (in the chapter on the renaissance of anatomy). Some further adventures on asepsis are described in the life of Celine; see Bree, and Knapp.

As to the more domestic side of Lydgate's life, Rose's description of Eliot's relationship with George Lewes is enlightening, as is Wijesinha's description of the Victorian marriage market. Trollope's *The American Senator* is about that. The parallel American legal-professional culture is described by Schudson, and Bloomfield.

Orley Farm and the situation of Felix Graham are discussed more fully in my *On Being;* Drinker's essay on Graham's legal ethics is useful, if, as I think, mistaken. Auchincloss's *Timothy Colt* is out of print but often available in libraries; one chapter of *A.L.E.* is devoted to it and to the modern legal profession's use of it—the background for which is well described by Schudson, directly in the essay on Field and Bowles and indirectly but usefully in his book on American journalism. The former is also valuable on understanding the modern American bar association, which, as I think, has often tried and almost always failed to be a moral teacher—it, too, being an institution rather than a practice. On work and rudeness, see Miss Manners's (Judith Martin's) *Common Courtesy.* The ecclesiastical context for Lydgate's town is described in Trollope's Barchester novels, especially *Barchester Towers.*

It is possible to craft from stories such as Lydgate's, Colt's, and Arrowsmith's (as well as from my own) a definition of what a profession is, and that is perhaps a responsible thing to do in notes for a chapter that identifies a profession as claiming authority to teach morals (I acknowledge help from Hauerwas's *Truthfulness,* which also discusses his and MacIntyre's insight that the practice of medicine is essentially tragic):

1. It is a group the members of which do what they do for a living; they are not about a hobby, but are engaged in a task and in a life, with the result that they take seriously what they do and commit themselves to the doing of it. There is moral content in being a fulltime expert. Perhaps there is an inevitable tendency, in such a case, to turn to other fulltime experts for moral guidance.

2. The task involves effort and knowledge; time and difficulty are a proof of commitment, and, here, difficulty is spread over time—

not only in terms of long hours but in terms of long years, including a past, and the memory of a past, of long hours. This aspect of professionalism includes, probably, a certification by one's professional elders. Eric Cassell suggests both, in his review of Bosk's book on teaching hospitals.

3. The members of the group have another sort of certification—from the community (or the state). This is an earnest from the community that members of the group can be trusted; often this is expressed in professional idealism as evidence that the community has decided the group can be trusted to regulate its own members, to enforce the social ethic that is implicit in a franchise.

4. The members of the group have—the group has—accepted the community's view of what is important. At least it has accepted the importance of the particular matter the group itself claims to be expert at and knowledgeable about. Professions deal in basic goods, or, at least, they accept popular consensus about which goods are basic.

5. There is a typical relationship between a member of the group and a member of the community the group serves. This relationship is significant, and is generally regarded as significant; the word commonly used for it is trust, to describe a connection between the individual who resorts to the professional because (when) he feels inadequate and the professional who proposes to provide adequacy. This is a concrete and interpersonal manifestation of the community's trust in the group.

The result is a social construct—William May calls it a covenant—expressing a conversation between a group of workers and the community in which they work. That conversation is a backdrop, if not always a sanction, for the conversation in which elder professionals tell younger professionals how they should behave.

Chapter 5 Dissent

In *A.L.E.*, in trying to present to law students a set of do-it-yourself materials for the thesis of this chapter, I use Novak (both essays) for radical theory and Mr. Tutt, Holtzmann, Farrington Reed Carpenter, and Louis Auchincloss's Mario Fabbri for stories. If I had been assembling a kit for medical students, I would have used Cassell, Katz, Hauerwas (*Vision*), and May (*Physician's Covenant*) for radical theory (theories), and Horn, Nemethy, Lewis Thomas's father (*Youngest Science*), Dr. Craig of "St. Elsewhere," Arrowsmith, and maybe even Celine for stories. It is important in using such kits of stories not to let a manageable agenda for discussion obscure the intriguing detail:

> Neither kit quite presents the restlessness of the most vivid of Trillin's Houston lawyers or of Jerry Kennedy—a restlessness that invites Novak's moral image of coming home. But coming home is a hard thing for Americans; Bellah and his colleagues say we have no language for coming home; Bruggemann argues that it involves the celebration of oddity.
>
> A catalogue of dissenters should not leave out the revolutionaries, both those who proceed with traditional professional civility (Dean Houston, T. C. Walker, the Southern white judges Jack Bass wrote about in *Unlikely Heroes,* Eric Cassell, Lewis Thomas), and those who thumb their noses at the establishment (Michael Tigar, Thomas Szasz, and, perhaps, such diverse dust-raisers as William Carlos Williams, Charles Morgan, and Richard Wasserstrom). *A.L.E.* contains kits for these revolutionary subcategories of dissenting lawyers.

References on stories: Crawley and Quiverfull are in Trollope's Barchester novels—Crawley in the *Last Chronicle of Barset,* Quiverfull in *Barchester Towers.* Mr. Tutt's tirade on criminals and justice is in "Sweet Land of Liberty," which is the story of Hans Schmidt and Mr. Hepplewhite; "In Witness Whereof" is the Baldwin story. (Both are in *A.L.E.*) My sources on Fanny Holtzmann are Berkman, Harriman, and North; the Yale note on Jewish law students bears on her situation. In Higgins's two Kennedy novels, Donald French is in *Defense,* Lou Schwartz in *Penance,* and Cadillac Teddy in both. Story sources on the virtue of integrity and constancy are developed magnificently by Letwin (excerpted in *A.L.E.*) and Hauerwas ("Constancy")—both working with Trollope's stories. Daniel Nelson's essay is a useful source on the virtue of humility as it is displayed in Jewish stories.

Theoretical references: Dawson's essay usefully brings forward Marty's and Smith's work on the connections between Christian religion and American liberal democracy; Hauerwas (*Against the Nations*) and Neuhaus are in a sort of debate on that subject. (See the last item in these notes to chapter 5.) My use of Aristotle (including the translations) depends on Meilaender (all references) and Cooper; and I depend on Meilaender for Augustine on friendship. MacIntyre (*After Virtue*) identifies difficulties in Aristotle's theory that the state rests on friendship. The radiating social effect of friendship, as Aristotle describes it, is similar to the social ethics of responsibility and to the image of the triadic relationship as H. Richard Niebuhr developed these (*Responsible Self*) (chapter 4). I think, though, that Hauerwas (*Peaceable Kingdom*), McClendon, and Goldberg (both titles), all of whom are spiritual descendants of Niebuhr's and build on Niebuhr in this respect, are clearly less interested than Niebuhr was in vindicating democratic liberalism. Of course, the two seminal theories (Aristotle's politics and democratic liberalism) can come out in the same place, sometimes. Cadillac Teddy's critique of Jerry Kennedy's advocacy is, for example, similar to Hoffman's and Taney's argument that a lawyer should only advocate legal rules that are good for the country. Both arguments would oppose the adversary ethic.

The liberal-democratic theory I see as dominant in present-day writing in legal ethics is illustrated (very well, too) in Monroe Freedman's work, Schwartz's, and Harry Jones's (the last is in *A.L.E.*). Childress's work is an example from medical ethics, as, by and large, is Brody's. See also Shklar and Guggenbuhl-Craig. The Model-Rule material on the lawyer as intermediary, together with its background from Brandeis's life, and John Frank's critique of the notion, are all in *A.L.E.* The medical counterpart is nicely illustrated in Nemethy's essay on country doctors. The contrast between integrity and interest is developed (although not in my terms) by William Simon. Bellah and his colleagues make an argument similar to mine (in my "Legal Ethics of Radical Individualism") on the importance of family, neighborhood, and church.

• § •

This chapter began as a set of faculty colloquia at the University of Texas Law School and then went on in more formal fashion as the 1985 Edward G. Donley Lectures at West Virginia University. The editors of the law review at West Virginia asked me to draw some more didactic lessons from my text and to provide concrete guidelines for lawyers and law students, and I tried to do that—as follows:

Assume that Mr. Tutt or Fanny Holtzmann or Jerry Kennedy would read all of this and agree that, by and large, I describe their ethic plausibly. Suppose, then, that I were to ask them, or one of them, to say more specifically how moral lessons can be derived from their stories. What would they offer, as applied ethics, to, say, law students in late 1985 in West Virginia? Fanny Holtzmann was influenced by Rabbi Hirsch Bornfeld, her grandfather, and was probably more accustomed to didactic moral direction than either Mr. Tutt or Jerry Kennedy. Fanny might accept the invitation to provide some applied ethical direction to modern law students; I am almost sure that Mr. Tutt and Jerry Kennedy would decline the invitation. Speaking, then, as Fanny might, but taking into account the evident ethics of Mr. Tutt and Jerry Kennedy:

Participation is fundamental. The moral ideal in the professional relationship of lawyer and client is the participatory ideal: The client is a partner and might become a friend. The client should (to borrow some examples from Douglas Rosenthal's book, *Lawyer and Client: Who's in Charge?* [1974]): (a) participate in decisions on negotiation and trial strategy, (b) choose witnesses, (c) be given a second professional opinion if he wants one, (d) help set the fee, and (e) help decide what the lawyer is to say to the world outside the law office. The client invites the lawyer to join in his misery; the lawyer stands before—not a problem, but what Justice James Wilson called the noblest work of God. (A parallel medical argument is in Katz and, from a different ethical perspective, in Childress on paternalism.)

The goal is relationship. The notion of friendship with clients is derived from the client's friendships elsewhere (as well as the lawyer's); what is being tended to in the lawyer-client relationship is the set of other relationships the client had before he came to see the lawyer. One or more of those relationships is or may be disrupted. That is usually the source of the difficulty the client is having; the goal of professional representation is the care and repair of disrupted relationships. The facts the lawyer is after are the common ground that is in those relationships (as Rabbi Hirsch began his work with Eli and Chaim on common ground—on their lives with one another, including their Jewishness). The search is not primarily for claims disputants make on one another (which are commonly expressed as rights or interests or liabilities or duties) but for what they have together. The skill with which common ground is sought and expanded is taught analytically and in terms of professional technique, in courses in mediation and conciliation—"alternative dispute resolution" is the trendy phrase. It is exhibited and has traditionally been learned by lawyers in law offices. This may be a hidden implication from the fact that more than 90 percent of all lawsuits, civil and criminal, are settled out of court.

The professional relationship begins with an offer of friendship. There is a global and abstract way to put this, one that is found in the literature of counseling, and specifically in the literature of legal counseling and in courses on interviewing, counseling, and law-office practice. It is explicated by such teachers of counselors as Carl Rogers, Robert S. Redmount, James R. Elkins, David Binder and Susan Price, Andrew S. Watson, and even me. The idea, as Rogers puts it, is that the lawyer offers to enter the client's world. (Maybe the lawyer even goes to the client, as the country doctors go to the children they examine on the floor.) In an unglobal and concrete way, friendship is offered by the professional who takes an interest in the client—by seeing to the client's comfort, by noticing and saying something about the client's discomfort (his upset, his being nervous or thirsty or curious or out of breath). The lawyer knew about unglobal and concrete friendship when law school started; if these habits of friendliness have been forgotten in law school, they are revived, as Novak says it, by coming home.

The professional payoff comes not from the government, or the bar association, but from the client. The argument here is that this dissenter's way of looking at the situation is as much a social ethic as liberal democracy is. The unglobal and concrete point is that the ordinary, friendly tests of effectiveness are the vital ones: (1) Will the client do what we have decided together should be done? (Not what I have told him to do, notice, but what we have decided together should be done—which is probably as unlike what I thought, on my own, he should do as it is unlike what he, on his own, thought he should do.) (2) Will this client come back to me when he again thinks he needs to talk to a lawyer? (See R. S. Hunt.) This question might even be: Will he come back to me, a lawyer, when he might, but for this present experience, have gone to a cleric or a doctor or to some other friend?

The overall model—the image that is in the lawyer's mind as the work with the client goes on—is not "What does a lawyer do?" but "What does a friend do?" We all know what a friend does because we have friends and we have been friends; we grew up with friends; we know them at home and in church and next door. The trick is to remember what we all know.

· § ·

I note above (in these notes to chapter 5) that Stanley Hauerwas and Richard John Neuhaus are in a sort of debate on how theological ethics should regard democratic liberalism and American civil religion. I did a couple of pages on this for the *Christian Legal Society Quarterly* (1986, No. 1) that may (with my essay on radical individualism) show what I have in mind. The question is: What should the church do about the government? I suppose that question is as old and as new as any question in American organized religion. We saw it when one national church governing group after another took positions against nuclear weapons. We see it as representatives and teachers of Christians make statements on government assistance for the poor, full employment, foreign relations, South Africa, and arms reduction.

The argument goes on in the newspapers, on television, and in books that don't have any pictures. To take one example from the more pictorial end of the display, consider the public schools and William J. Bennett, the secretary of education. Secretary Bennett has taken issue with the notion that American public education should be secular. Secretary Bennett says he is not arguing for anybody's sectarian agenda; he is arguing that the agenda in America is and always has been not secular. The belief lies deep in American culture that (as Bellah and his colleagues put it) we Americans have "the obligation, both collective and individual, to carry out God's will on earth." The secretary is laying claim to that belief. We hear the same sort of thing in presidential campaign addresses (from all sorts of administrations) and on the Fourth of July.

Mr. Bennett is arguing for America's special mission in the achievement of the Kingdom. America is, in that view, to use Thomas Jefferson's phrase, "God's New Israel." We are a light on a hill, a righteous empire; God is the source of our power and is our claim to legitimacy. The issue there is what the government should do about—or with—the church. If you follow Mr. Bennett's line of thought far enough you can end up using the church to call half the civilized world an evil empire.

But that is not the question if you look at the issues from the point of view of the church. Not unless you are willing to say that the church is America. If the church is something other than America, then what should the church do about the government? Neuhaus is an eloquent and incisive Lutheran pastor and theologian. He argues one way on that question. Hauerwas, Methodist theologian (Duke Divinity School) and prolific contributor to the literature of theological ethics, argues the other way. Neuhaus, in a phrase, takes the view that the church should see to it that America works. Hauerwas, in a phrase, argues that the church should figure out what her Lord gave her to do and then do it, whether America works or not.

Both Neuhaus and Hauerwas argue that the church should be the church, but Neuhaus is a liberal democrat: He sees the church as an aggregation of autonomous individuals who have come together to pursue common objectives, in this case religious, and who are protected by the institutions of liberal democracy. He therefore gives the church the same stake in the institutions of liberal democracy that political associations have. Neuhaus talks about that stake from the church's perspective, as Secretary Bennett talks about it from the state's perspective.

Neuhaus allows for "critical patriotism"; he sees the church as having a prophetic mission in America. But he also talks about "Christian America," a phrase that Hauerwas finds curious. Curious or not, the notion of "Christian America" ties Neuhaus to the God's-new-Israel tradition, I think. Both he and Secretary Bennett think it is important to keep the connection between American liberal democracy and the church. Hauerwas argues that the connection makes the church dependent on American liberal democracy; it takes away the separate place the church has to have in order to be prophetic.

In terms of Reformation theology—and both writers take positions that have roots in the Reformation—Neuhaus seems to go beyond his own Lutheran tradition's insistence on public responsibility, and to call up images from American Puritanism—images of America as a righteous empire—and to call as well upon John Calvin's belief that democracy is a limited and therefore more biblical form of government than its alternatives. In any event, whatever the roots of his theory, Neuhaus argues that limited government is the sort of political arrangement in which the church ought to have a stake, because its ideal is to leave people free to make their own alliances. But suppose the state is within its limits and prohibits the alliance. Suppose it is more to the interest of the state "that one man should die for the people, than that the whole nation should be destroyed" (John 11:50, New English Bible). As Hauerwas says, "No state will keep itself limited, no constitution or ideology is sufficient to that task, unless there is a body of people separate from the nation that is willing to say 'No' to the state's claim on their loyalties." It is the argument Martin Buber made in modern Israel (Friedman biography).

That may be worth pausing over: If the basis of your theological preference in politics is freedom, what you mean in the reality of life is the freedom that is left over after even a limited government asserts itself. Freedom is then what the government says it is, unless somebody, separate from the government, is around to say that the government's definition of freedom (that is, of the limits of government) is pretentious. What is it, in "Christian America," that can stand apart and denounce America for its pretensions? Hauerwas argues that it is the church; the church is suited for the mission. Not because, as Secretary Bennett would likely have it, the church and American democracy have been together for a long time. Nor, as Neuhaus might have it, because democracy in America depends on Hebraic moral values. The church can denounce pretension because what the church says, when she is faithful to her Lord, is true.

The problem with liberal democracy, and particularly with American liberal democracy, is that " 'the rights of the individual' have become the secular equivalent to the church as the means to keep the government in its proper sphere," Hauerwas says. "It is the strategy of liberalism to insure the existence of the 'autonomy of cultural and economic life' by insuring the freedom of the individual. But ironically that strategy results in the undermining of 'intermediate associations' because they are now understood only as those arbitrary institutions sustained by the private desires of individuals." Hauerwas claims that Neuhaus's appropriation of liberal democracy—Hauerwas would, perhaps, say Neuhaus's baptism of liberal democracy—has put the notion of the autonomous individual, and the momentary associations that autonomous individuals are said to form out of their freedom, where the church ought to be.

The concept of individual rights is an abstraction; it cannot stand apart and be prophetic, even if Neuhaus wants it to and hopes that it can. The point is that standing for freedom is not the same as standing for something. Our Enlightenment democracy is more comfortable for us than communist government would be, but it is not a substitute for the church any more than the Soviet system is. "The Russian lives in a social system that claims to achieve freedom by falsely investing all authority in the power of the Party; the American lives in a social system that tries to insure freedom by trying to insure that each individual can be his or her own tyrant," Hauerwas says. "Democracies after all can be just as tyrannical in their claims on the loyalties of their citizens as totalitarian alternatives. Indeed the tyranny may be all the more perverse because we have freely given the state the right to command our conscience."

The difference here might be that one point of view (Neuhaus's) sees American society as co-opted by those who are hostile to the church, where the other point of view (Hauerwas's) sees the church in America as herself co-opted. The argument is not with Secretary Bennett, but within the church. Where Neuhaus and Secretary Bennett argue that the church has been excluded too much from public life, Hauerwas argues that American civil religion has taken over the church:

> The overriding conflict of our time is the same as that from the beginning for it is the conflict between those that would remain loyal to God's kingdom and those that would step aside with the world. And the world is exactly those people and institutions claiming that Christians too must be willing to choose sides and kill in order to preserve the social orders in which they find themselves. As Christians when we accept that alternative it surely means that we are no longer the church that witnesses to God's sovereignty over all nations, but instead we have become part of the world. . . . As Christians we seek not to be free, but to be faithful disciples of our Lord who would not employ violence to avoid death at the hands of a state.

(Bruggemann is useful on this issue—and is clear and eloquent on narrative and community as elements of biblical [Jewish] education.)

Chapter 6 Schools

Justinian's irreverent friend is, of course, Duncan Kennedy. The friend's statements are from Kennedy's article and book on hierarchy, with a bit of friendly interlineation from me here and there. I say (Justinian says) "irreverent" to suggest (in Holmes's words) an intellect that is not humbugged by phrases. Holmes was complimenting Mephistopheles; Holmes said of him that he kept the green scum off the pond. I do not mean (and neither does Justinian) to suggest weakness in the virtue of reverence in this case, nor do I mean to invoke any part of the current law-school debate on the Critical Legal Studies movement, with which Professor Kennedy is often associated. (See Trillin, "Reporter at Large.") Both Kennedy and I are serious (reverent) about idolatry; see also my essay on Hebraic faith, and Yoder. The Weil epigraph is from her letter to Deodat Roche, apparently written in 1940; it is in Panichas's reader. I hope no one will confuse the idolatry Justinian (and, I think, Kennedy) finds and fears with the claim (discussed in chapter 4) that the profession is a moral teacher. Teaching, even claims to teaching authority, even spurious claims of that sort, may be fatuous but they are not usually idolatries. See 1 Corinthians 7.

Justinian's references: He relies for his Socrates mostly on the *Protagoras* and the *Gorgias*, and, as to the latter, on James Boyd White's exposition, translation, and restatement of it (e.g., on the use of the terms "flattery" and "routine flattery"); other translators are W. D. Woodhead and K. C. Guthrie (in the Hamilton-Cairns edition of Plato). But he now and again alludes to the *Republic* and to the dialogues that have to do with the trial and the death of Socrates. I have been moved along in this regard (and Justinian with me) with good help from my friend Lewis LaRue. The professional-school catalogue references are from memory (including the memory of having written such stuff) and from Bosk's interviews; Bosk, and Carlton, provide the pedagogical scene from teaching hospitals, and the research of both supports the notion that the clinical judgment of seniors (teachers) has priority over both science and morals. The Buber is *I and Thou*, and is also discussed in my *On Being*.

Justinian's scriptural references include Hebrews 10:24 and Isaiah 6:3, and he of course alludes now and again to St. Benedict's *Rule*. He gets his notion that the author of Hebrews was a woman from Fiorenza. His architectural psychology is covered in Elkins's and my interviewing-counseling text and in Steele, and Sommer. Justinian alludes to Peters's and Waterman's popular *In Search of Excellence;* to Redmount's and my 1977 book on law schools; to the theological ethics of responsibility as H. R. Niebuhr, and Jonsen describe them;

to James P. White's unpublished memorandum on law-school attrition; to Louis Mink's, and Alasdair MacIntyre's distinction(s) between external and internal goods; to Tinder on tolerance; to Hauerwas and Burrell on self-deception (*Truthfulness*); to Randolph Churchill on Winston Churchill; and to Bland and Ridenour's edition of General Marshall's papers.

Other references: Simon is useful on the notion of interests in legal education (and law practice); Cramton is useful on that point and much more. My argument throughout this book is that the concept of health is used by doctors as the concept of interest is used by lawyers; Cassell, more than the others I cite on medicine, analyzes words such as these. The answer Miss Brown gave on lives in being in the rule against perpetuities is: Any life that works. That classroom exchange and others are quoted and discussed more fully in Redmount's and my 1977 book on law schools.

Epilogue Pookas

Prudence (practical wisdom) is central Aristotelian stuff (Books 6 and 7, *Nicomachean Ethics*); as to friendship, see chapters 4 to 6 herein; magnanimity (largeness of soul) has a long heritage, suggested by the entry for that word in the *Oxford English Dictionary* (vol. 6, p. 28, 1933), which cites and quotes discussions of magnanimity from Aristotle to Aquinas to Burke and Paley. My claim about and for Elwood, in regard to these virtues, has a dark side: Reality in this story is power, worldly power—never as real as it thinks it is, and never more pretentious than when the realist in a profession talks about justice or health (or both). The reality drug, the serum Elwood finally did not take at Chumley's Rest, is one we claim to dispense in education for the professions. Of law school, the late Professor Karl Llewellyn said, "The hardest job of the first year is to top off your common sense, to knock your ethics into temporary anesthesia. Your view of social policy, your sense of justice—to knock these out of you along with woozy thinking." The reality that requires such an anesthetic is what Elwood triumphed over.

References: A.L.E. contains further material on legal ethics as the corruption of lawyers by clients (physicians by patients)—particularly with reference to Canon Seven of the (lawyers') *Code of Professional Responsibility*. The richest source of codal medical examples is probably Percival and the nineteenth-century AMA codes (e.g., the rule that the patient has a moral duty not to talk to any doctor but the one he has employed; see chapter 4 herein). The quotation from Iris Murdoch is from *The Sovereignty of Good.* The distinction between the tough and the tender is one Redmount and I explored (scientifically) in *Lawyers, Law Students, and People.*

Bibliography

This cites an author's works separately when I make separate use of them in the text. "*A.L.E.*" abbreviates my 1985 *American Legal Ethics,* which reprints or excerpts or quotes a number of these sources.

Alabama Bar Association. *See* Jones (Thomas Goode).

American Bar Association. *Canons of Professional Ethics.* 1908.

——. *Model Code of Professional Responsibility.* 1970, amended 1974.

——. *Model Rules of Professional Conduct.* 1984.

Amory, Cleveland. "Good Guys, Bad Guys." *Parade Magazine,* Mar. 20, 1983, 6.

——. "The Touch of Class." *Parade Magazine,* Sept. 22, 1985, 4.

Antigone. See Sophocles.

Aquinas, Thomas. *Summa Theologica.* Benziger ed., Dominican trans. 1947.

——. *Treatise on the Virtues.* Oesterle trans. 1984.

Aristotle. *Magna Moralia.* In *The Works of Aristotle Translated into English.* Vol. 9. 1915. *See* Cooper.

——. *Nicomachean Ethics.* Ostwald trans. 1962. *See* Cooper.

Armstrong, Walter P. "A Century of Legal Ethics." *American Bar Association Journal* 64(1978): 1063.

Auchincloss, Louis. "The Fabbri Tape." In *Narcissa and Other Fables,* 149. 1983. Also in *A.L.E.*

——. *The Great World and Timothy Colt.* 1956. Excerpts in *A.L.E.*

——. *A Writer's Capital.* 1974.

Augustine (Saint). *The City of God.* Dodds trans. 1950.

——. *Confessions.* Sheed trans. 1942.

Baeck, Leo. *See* Friedman.

Baepler, Richard. "Religious Challenges to Legalism." Occasional Paper, Section on Law and Religion, Association of American Law Schools, June 1980.

Ball, Milner S. "Law Natural: Its Family of Metaphors and Its Theology." *Journal of Law and Religion* 3(1986): 140.

——. *Lying Down Together.* 1985.

——. *The Promise of American Law: A Theological, Humanistic View of Legal Process.* 1981.

Barclay, William. *The Gospel of Luke.* 3d ed. 1956.

Barr, David, and Nicholas Piediscalzi, eds. *The Bible in American Education.* 1982.

Barth, Karl. *Church Dogmatics.* T. & T. Clark ed. 1961.

——. *Community, State, and Church.* 1968. Includes Will Herberg's introduction.

——. *Ethics.* Braun ed. 1981.

——. *Evangelical Theology: An Introduction.* Foley trans. 1965.

——. *The Humanity of God.* Wiesner and Thomas trans. 1969.

——. *The Word of God and the Word of Man.* Horton trans. 1978. *See also* Busch.

Bass, Jack. Column on Judge Richard T. Rives, Jr. *Washington Post,* Jan. 9, 1983, p. C-5, col. 1. Also in *A.L.E.*

——. *Unlikely Heroes.* 1981.

Bellah, Robert N., Richard Madsen, William M. Sullivan, Ann Swindler, and Steven M. Tipton. *Habits of the Heart: Individualism and Commitment in American Life.* 1985.

Bellow, Saul. *The Adventures of Augie March.* 1953.

Benedict (Saint). *The Holy Rule of Our Most Holy Father Benedict.* Grail ed. 1937.

Berkin, Carol Ruth, and Mary Beth Norton. *Women of America: A History.* 1979.

Berkman, Ted. *The Lady and the Law.* 1976. *See also* Harriman.

Bertram, Robert W. "Legal Morality and the Two Kingdoms." *The Cresset* [Valparaiso University], Feb. 1957, 6.

Biblical Repertory and Princeton Review. *See* Hodge.

Binder, David, and Susan Price. *Legal Interviewing and Counseling: A Client-Centered Approach.* 1977.

Birnbaum, Philip, trans. *Daily Prayer Book* [Ha-Siddur Ha-Shalem] 1949.

Bland, Mary I., and Sharon R. Ridenour. *The Papers of George Catlett Marshall: The Soldierly Spirit, December 1880-June, 1939.* 1981.

Bloesch, Donald G. "Karl Barth and the Life of the Church." *Center Journal* 1(1981): 65.

Bloomfield, Maxwell. "David Hoffman and the Shaping of a Republican Legal Culture." *Maryland Law Review* 38(1979): 673. Excerpts in *A.L.E.*

Bolt, Robert. *A Man for All Seasons.* 1962.

Bosk, Charles. *Forgive and Remember.* 1979.

Boyd, Thomas M. "The Legend of Gloucester County: Remembering Lawyer Thomas Walker and the Path He Paved." *Washington Post,* Feb. 26, 1984, p. C-1, col. 1. Also in *A.L.E.*

Brandeis, Louis D. *See* Frank, Mason, Vorspan.

Bree, Germaine. "The Persona of the Doctor in Celine's *Journey to the End of the Night* and Camus's *The Plague.*" In Peschel.

Brody, Howard. *Placebos and the Philosophy of Medicine.* 1980.

——. "The Lie That Heals: The Ethics of Giving Placebos." *Social Responsibility: Journalism, Law, Medicine* 7(1981): 27. *See* Cabot. Includes quotations from Richard C. Cabot.

Bruggemann, Walter. "Passion and Perspective: Two Dimensions of Education in the Bible." *Theology Today* 42(1985): 172.

Buber, Martin. *Between Man and Man.* Smith trans. 1947.

——. *Eclipse of God.* Humanities Press ed. 1979.

——. *For the Sake of Heaven.* Lewisohn trans. 1953.

——. *I and Thou.* Kaufman trans. 1972.

——. *The Knowledge of Man.* Smith trans. 1965.

——. *On Judaism. See also* Friedman. Essays and addresses, 1909–1918, 1939–1951. 1967.

Burrows, Millar. "Old Testament Ethics and the Ethics of Jesus." In Crenshaw and Willis.

Burt, Robert. *Taking Care of Strangers.* 1979.

——. "What Was Wrong with Dred Scott, What's Right about Brown." *Washington and Lee Law Review* 42(1985): 1. The principal paper in a colloquium on judicial law as conversation and moral discourse.

Burtchaell, James Tunstead. *Rachel Weeping.* 1982.

Busch, Eberhard. *Karl Barth: His Life from Letters and Autobiographical Texts.* Bowden trans. 1976.

Cabot, Richard C. "The Use of Truth and Falsehood in Medicine." *American Medicine* 5(1903): 344.

——. "The Physician's Responsibility for the Nostrum Evil." *Journal of the American Medical Association* 47(1906): 982. *See* Brody.

Calcott, George. *A History of the University of Maryland.* 1966.

Camus, Albert. *See* Bree.

Carlton, Wendy. *In Our Professional Opinion: The Primacy of Clinical Judgment over Moral Choice.* 1978.

Carpenter, Farrington Reed. Autobiographical essay. *Colorado Lawyer* 8(1979): 212. Abridged in *A.L.E.*

——. *Confessions of a Maverick: An Autobiography.* 1984.

Carter, Dan. *Scottsboro: A Tragedy of the American South.* 1969.

Cassell, Eric. *The Healer's Art.* 1976.

Castiglioni, Arturo. *A History of Medicine.* 1947.

Celine, Louis Ferdinand. *See* Bree, Knapp.

Chafe, William H. *The American Woman.* 1972.

Chase, Mary. *Harvey.* 1953.

Childress, James F. *Disobedience and Trust.* 1975.

——. "Metaphors and Models of Medical Relationships." *Social Responsibility: Journalism, Law, Medicine* 8(1982): 47.

——. "Scripture and Christian Ethics." *Interpretation* 34(1980): 371.

——. *Who Should Decide? Paternalism in Health Care.* 1982.

Chroust, Anton H. *The Rise of the Legal Profession in America.* 2 vols. 1965.

Churchill, Randolph Spencer. *Winston Churchill.* 1966.

Clasen, C. P. *Anabaptism: A Social History.* 1972.

Cohon, Samuel S. *Judaism: A Way of Life.* 1948.

Cole, Phyllis Blum. "The Divinity School Address of Mary Moody Emerson." *Harvard Divinity Bulletin,* Dec. 1985–Jan. 1986, 4.

Cone, James H. *My Soul Looks Back.* 1982.

——. "Black Theology in American Religion." *Theology Today* 43(1986): 6. *See* Cone's other, longer treatments of black theology, cited therein.

Conrad, Joseph. *The Secret Agent.* Anchor ed. 1953.

Cooper, John M. "Aristotle on the Forms of Friendship." *Review of Metaphysics* 30(1977): 619

——. "Friendship and the Good in Aristotle." *Philosophical Review* 86(1977): 290. Translates pertinent passages from Aristotle.

Cordell, Eugene F. *University of Maryland 1807–1907.* 1907.

Cox, Harvey. *The Secular City.* 1966.

Cramton, Roger C. "The Ordinary Religion of the Law School Classroom." *Journal of Legal Education* 29(1978): 247.

Cranz, F. E. "*De Civitate Dei,* XV, 2, and Augustine's Idea of the Christian Society." *Speculum* 25(1950): 215.

Crenshaw, James L., and John T. Willis, eds. *Essays in Old Testament Ethics.* 1974.

Culbertson, Philip. "The Pharisaic Jesus and His Gospel Parables." *Christian Century* 102(1983): 74.

Dauer, Edward, and Arthur Leff. "Correspondence: The Lawyer as Friend." *Yale Law Journal* 86(1977): 573. *See* Fried.

Dave, R. A. "To Kill a Mockingbird: Harper Lee's Tragic Vision." In Naik, M. K. et al., *Indian Studies in American Fiction,* 311. 1974.

Davies, W. D. *Paul and Rabbinic Judaism.* 4th ed. 1980.

Dawson, John C. "The Religion of Democracy in Early Twentieth-Century America." *Journal of Church and State* 27(1985): 47.

Donagan, Alan. *The Theory of Morality.* 1977.

Drinker, Henry. *See* Trollope.

Dunlap, Mary Montgomery. "The Achievement of Gavin Stevens." Ph.D. diss., University of South Carolina, 1970. Lists and discusses novels and stories in which Stevens appears.

Dworkin, Gerald. "Autonomy and Behavior Control." Hastings Center Report, Feb. 1976, 23.

——. "Moral Autonomy." In Englehardt and Callahan.

Ebeling, Gerhard. *Luther: An Introduction to His Thought.* Wilson trans. 1977.

Edman, V. Raymond. *Finney Lives On.* 1951. *See also Great Gospel Sermons.* Includes several of Finney's revival sermons.

Eliot, George. *Middlemarch.* 1871. Penguin ed., with notes by W. J. Harvey. 1965.

Elkins, James R. "The Legal Persona: An Essay on the Professional Mask." *Virginia Law Review* 64(1978): 735.

——. "A Counseling Model for Lawyering in Divorce Cases." *Notre Dame Lawyer* 53(1977): 229.

——. Review of *Legal Interviewing and Counseling,* by Thomas L. Shaffer. *Vanderbilt Law Review* 30(1977): 923.

——. "On the Emergence of Narrative Jurisprudence." *Legal Studies Forum* 9(1985): 123. *See also* Shaffer.

Emerson, Ralph Waldo. *See* Cole, Whicher.

Englehardt, H. T., Jr., and Daniel Callahan, eds. *Morals, Science, and Sociality.* 1978.

Epstein, Isidore. *Judaism.* 1959.

Erling, Bernard. "Discipleship at the United Nations: Hammarskjold's Religious Commitment." *The Christian Century* 98(1981): 902.

Evans, Carl D. "The Church's False Witness against Judaism." *Christian Century* 98(1982): 530.

Fingarette, Herbert. "The Meaning of Law in the Book of Job." *Hastings Law Journal* 28(1978): 1581.

——. *Self Deception.* 1969.

Fiorenza, Elisabeth Schussler. *In Memory of Her: A Feminist Theological Reconstruction of Christian Origins.* 1985.

Fletcher, Joseph. *Situation Ethics.* 1966.

Flood, Charles B. *Lee: The Last Years.* 1981.

Foote, Horton. Screenplay of *To Kill a Mockingbird.* Foreword by Harper Lee. 1964.

Fortas, Abe. "Thurman Arnold and the Theatre of the Law." *Yale Law Journal* 79(1970): 988.

Fox, Richard. *Reinhold Niebuhr.* 1985.

Frank, John P. "The Legal Ethics of Louis D. Brandeis." *Stanford Law Review* 17(1965): 683. In *A.L.E.*

Frankena, William. *Ethics.* 2nd ed. 1973.

Freedman, Monroe. *Lawyers' Ethics in an Adversary System.* 1975.

——. "Personal Responsibility in a Professional System." Pope John XXIII Lecture. 27 *Catholic University Law Review* 27(1978): 191. Excerpts in *A.L.E.*

Fried, Charles. "The Lawyer as Friend: The Moral Foundations of the Lawyer-Client Relation." *Yale Law Journal* 85(1976): 1060. *See* Dauer and Leff.

Friedman, Maurice. *Martin Buber: The Life of Dialogue.* 1955.

——. *Martin Buber's Life and Work: The Middle Years, 1923–1945.* 1983. Includes story of Leo Baeck.

Frost, Robert. "The Tuft of Flowers." In *The Poetry of Robert Frost,* edited by Edward Connery Latham, 22. 1969.

Geach, Peter. *The Virtues.* 1977.

Goffman, Erving. "The Nature of Deference and Demeanor." *American Anthropologist* 58(1956): 473.

Goldberg, Michael. *Jews and Christians: Getting Our Stories Straight.* 1985.

——. *Theology and Narrative: A Critical Introduction.* 1982.

Graves, John Templeton. "Fiat Justitia, Ruit Coelum." *New Republic,* March 30, 1938, 218. On James E. Horton.

Great Gospel Sermons. 2 vols. 1949. *See also* Edman.

Green, Ronald M. "Abraham, Isaac, and the Jewish Tradition: An Ethical Reappraisal." *Journal of Religious Ethics* 10(1982): 1.

Guggenbuhl-Craig, Adolf. *Power in the Helping Professions.* Gubitz trans. 1971.

Guy, J. A. *The Public Career of Sir Thomas More.* 1980.

Hackett, Francis. *Henry the Eighth.* 1931.

Hammarskjold, Dag. *Markings.* Sjoberg and Auden trans. 1965. *See* Erling, McClendon.

Harriman, Mary Case. "Miss Fixit." *New Yorker,* Jan. 30, 1937, 21; and Feb. 6, 1937, 22. *See also* Berkman. In *A.L.E.*

Harris, Lis. *Holy Days: The World of a Hasidic Family.* 1985. Also in *New Yorker,* Sept. 16, 23, and 30, 1985.

Hauerwas, Stanley. *Against the Nations.* 1985.

——. *Character and the Christian Life: A Study in Theological Ethics.* 1975.

——. *A Community of Character.* 1981.

——. "Constancy and Forgiveness: The Novel as a School for Virtue." *Notre Dame English Journal* 15(1983): 23.

——. *The Peaceable Kingdom.* 1983.

——. *Truthfulness and Tragedy.* 1977. Includes Hauerwas-Burrell essay on Albert Speer.

——. *Vision and Virtue: Essays in Christian Ethical Reflection.* 1974. *See also* Shaffer. *On Being a Christian and a Lawyer.*

Hauerwas, Stanley, and Alasdair MacIntyre, eds. *Revisions: Changing Perspectives in Moral Philosophy.* 1983. Includes two Murdoch essays and Mouw's paper on biblical medicine.

Hazard, Geoffrey. "An Historical Perspective on the Attorney-Client Privilege." *California Law Review* 66(1978): 1061.

——. *Ethics in the Practice of Law.* 1978.

Herberg, Will. "The Social Philosophy of Karl Barth." Introduction to Karl Barth, *Community, State and Church.* 1968.

Herman, Sondra R. "Loving Courtship or the Marriage Market? The Ideal and Its Critics, 1871–1911." *American Quarterly* 25(1973): 235.

Heschel, Abraham J. *Between God and Man: An Interpretation of Judaism.* Edited by F. A. Rothschild. 1959.

Higgins, George V. *A Choice of Enemies.* 1984.

——. Interview. *Boston Magazine,* March 1981, 77.

——. *Kennedy for the Defense.* 1980.

——. *Penance for Jerry Kennedy.* 1985.

Hilfiker, David. *Healing the Wounds.* 1985.

Hodge, Charles. Review of Hoffman's *Course. Biblical Repertory and Princeton Review* 9(1837): 509.

Hoffman, David. *A Course of Legal Study.* 1817. 2 vols. 2d ed. 1836. The "Resolutions on Professional Deportment" are in vol. 2 of the second edition, at pp. 752–75.

——. *Chronicles Selected from the Originals of Cartaphilus, the Wandering Jew.* 1853–54. The first of six volumes but the only one published.

——. *Introductory Lectures and Syllabus of a Course of Lectures.* 1837. Includes Kent review.

——. *Miscellaneous Thoughts on Men and Things.* 1841.

——. *To the Trustees of the University of Maryland in Relation to the Law Chair.* 1826.

——. *Viator; or A Peep Into My Note Book.* 1841.

Holden, Pat, ed. *Women's Religious Experience.* 1983.

Holtzmann, Fanny. *See* Berkman, Harriman, North.

Horton, James E. *See* Carter, Graves, Patterson.

Houston, Charles Hamilton. *See* McNeil.

Howells, William Dean. *A Modern Instance.* 1882. Riverside ed., 1957. Excerpts in *A.L.E.*

——. *The Rise of Silas Lapham.* 1885. Signet ed., 1963.

Hubbard, B. A. F., and E. S. Karnofsky. *Plato's "Protagoras."* 1982.

Hunt, R. S. "Problems and Processes in the Legal Interview," *Illinois Bar Journal* 50(1962): 726.

Illich, Ivan. *Medical Nemesis.* 1976.

Jagerstatter, Franz. *See* Zahn.

Jeremias, Joachim. *The Parables of Jesus.* 2d rev. ed. Hooke trans. 1972.

——. "The Jewish Law Student and New York Jobs." *Yale Law Journal* [Note] 73(1964): 626.

Jones, Donald G. *See* Little.

Jones, Harry W. "The Uneasy Ethics of Partisanship." *Villanova Law Review* 23(1978): 957. In *A.L.E.*

Jones, Thomas Goode. "Code of Ethics Adopted by the Alabama Bar Association." 1887. *Alabama Reports* 118(1899): xxiii. *See* Armstrong. In *A.L.E.*

Jonsen, Albert R. *Responsibility in Modern Religious Ethics.* 1968.

Jung, Carl G. *Analytical Psychology.* 1968.

——. *On the Nature of the Psyche.* Hull trans. 1960.

——. *The Psychology of the Transference.* Hull trans. 1954.

——. *Psychological Reflections.* Jacobi ed. 1953.

Kaiser, Walter C., Jr. *Toward Old Testament Ethics.* 1983.

Kalisch, Philip A., and Beatrice J. Kalisch. *The Advance of American Nursing.* 1978.

Kaplan, Abraham. "The Jewish Argument With God." *Commentary* 70(1980): 43.

Katz, Jay. *The Silent World of Doctor and Patient.* 1984. Appendices include A.M.A. codes of medical ethics.

Kennedy, Duncan. *Legal Education and the Reproduction of Hierarchy: A Polemic against the System.* 1983. Abridged in *Journal of Legal Education* 32(1982): 591 and in *The Politics of Law: A Progressive Critique,* edited by D. Dairys. 1982.

Kennedy, Jeremiah F. *See* Higgins.

Kent, James. *See* Hoffman.

Kierkegaard, Soren. *Either/Or.* Lowrie trans. 1959.

——. *Words of Love.* Long trans. 1964.

Knapp, Bettina L. "From Hero to Horror: Louis-Ferdinand Celine, M.D." In Peschel.

Lee, Harper. *To Kill a Mockingbird.* 1960. *See* Foote.

Lee, Robert E. *See* Flood.

Letwin, Shirley Robin. *The Gentleman in Trollope: Individuality and Moral Conduct.* 1982.

Lewis, C. S. *The Four Loves.* 1960.

Lewis, Sinclair. *Arrowsmith.* 1925. Modern Library ed., 1933. Includes introduction by William Soskin.

Little, David. "Duties of Station vs. Duties of Conscience: Are There Two Moralities?" In *Private and Public Ethics,* edited by Donald G. Jones, 125. 1978.

Llewellyn, Karl. *The Bramble Bush: On Our Law and Its Study.* 1951.

Luban, David, ed. *The Good Lawyer.* 1984.

Luther, Martin. "Secular Authority: To What Extent Should It Be Obeyed?" *Works of Martin Luther,* 3: 228. Schindel trans. 1930. Also in *Martin Luther: Selections from His Writings,* edited by Dillenberger. 1961.

McGuire, John M. Review of *Yankee Lawyer: The Autobiography of Ephraim Tutt,* by Arthur Train. *Harvard Law Review* 57(1943): 258. In *A.L.E.*

MacIntyre, Alasdair. *After Virtue.* 1981. *See* Wachbroit. Excerpts in *A.L.E.*

Maimonides, Moses. *The Code of Maimonides.* [Mishneh Torah.] Hershman trans. 1949.

Mann, Thomas. *Buddenbrooks.* 1901. Lowe-Porter trans., 1984.

Manners, Miss. *See* Martin.

Maritain, Jacques. *Man and the State.* 1951.

Marius, Richard. *Thomas More.* 1984.

Marshall, Bratter, Greene, Allison, and Tucker. *See* Tivnan.

Marshall, George C. *See* Bland and Ridenour.

Martin, Judith. *Common Courtesy.* 1985.

Marty, Martin. *Righteous Empire: The Protestant Experience in America.* 1970.

Mason, Alpheus Thomas. *Brandeis: A Free Man's Life.* 1946.

Mason, Philip. *The English Gentleman: The Rise and Fall of an Ideal.* 1982.

May, William F. *Notes on the Ethics of Doctors and Lawyers.* 1977. Excerpts in *A.L.E.*

——. *The Physician's Covenant: Images of the Healer in Medical Ethics.* 1981.

McBrien, Richard. *Catholicism.* 2 vols. 1979.

McCann, Dennis P. "Hermeneutics and Ethics: The Example of Reinhold Niebuhr." *Journal of Religious Ethics* 8(1980): 27.

McClendon, James. *Biography as Theology.* 1974. Excerpts in *A.L.E.*

McKenzie, John. *The Two-Edged Sword.* Image ed. 1966.

McNeil, G. R. "Charles Hamilton Houston: Social Engineer for Human Rights." In *Black Leaders of the Twentieth Century,* edited by John Hope Franklin and August Meier, 221. 1982. Also in *A.L.E.*

McThenia, Andrew W., and Thomas L. Shaffer. "For Reconciliation." *Yale Law Journal* 94(1985): 1660.

Medina, Harold, ed. *Mr. Tutt at His Best.* 1961. *See* Train. *Saturday Evening Post* stories. Two stories, "Sweet Land of Liberty" and "In Witness Whereof," from this anthology, are also in *A.L.E.*

Meilaender, Gilbert C. *Friendship: A Study in Theological Ethics.* 1981.
——. "Is What Is Right for Me Right for All Persons Similarly Situated?" *Journal of Religious Ethics* 8(1980): 125.
——. *The Theory and Practice of Virtue.* 1984.
Milgram, Stanley. Report on experiments in obedience. *Human Relations* 18(1965): 1.
Miller, Perry. *The Life of the Mind in America.* 1965.
Mink, Louis O. *Fellowship.* 1983.
More, Thomas. *See* Bolt, Guy, Marius, Shaffer (*On Being a Christian and a Lawyer*).
Morgan, Charles. *See* Powledge.
Mouw, Richard J. "Alasdair MacIntyre on Reformation Ethics." *Journal of Religious Ethics* 13(1985): 243.
——. "Biblical Revelation and Medical Decisions." In Hauerwas and MacIntyre.
Murdoch, Iris. "Against Dryness: A Polemical Sketch." In Hauerwas and MacIntyre.
——. "On 'God' and 'Good.' " In Hauerwas and MacIntyre.
——. *The Sovereignty of Good.* 1970.
Nelson, Daniel M. "The Virtue of Humility in Judaism: A Critique of Rationalist Ethics." *Journal of Religious Ethics* 13(1985): 298.
Nemethy, Andrew. "Country Doctor." *Vermont Life,* Winter 1984, 50.
Neuberger. "Women in Judaism: The Fact and the Fiction." In Holden. *See also* Webber.
Neuhaus, Richard John. *The Naked Public Square.* 1984.
Neusner, Jacob. *The Way of Torah.* 1979.
Niebuhr, H. Richard. *The Responsible Self.* 1963.
Niebuhr, Reinhold. *The Irony of American History.* 1962.
——. *Moral Man and Immoral Society.* 1932. Scribner's ed., 1960. *See also* Fox, McCann.
Nolen, William. *The Making of a Surgeon.* 1970.
Noonan, John T. "Other People's Morals: The Lawyer's Conscience." *Tennessee Law Review* 48(1981): 227. Excerpts in A.L.E.
North, Jane. Essay on Berkman's biography of Fanny Holtzmann. *See* Berkman, Harriman. In A.L.E.
Novak, Michael. *In Praise of Cynicism (Or) When the Saints Go Marching Out.* 1977. Abridged in A.L.E.
——. "Catholics and Power." *Notre Dame Magazine,* Feb. 1980, 12. Abridged in A.L.E.
Paley, William. *See* Whately.
Panichas, George A. *The Simone Weil Reader.* 1977.
Pannenberg, Wolfhart. "Freedom and the Lutheran Reformation." *Theology Today* 38(1981): 287.

Patterson, Haywood, and Earl Conrad. *Scottsboro Boy.* 1973.

Pellegrino, Edmund D. "Percival's Medical Ethics." *Archives of Internal Medicine* 146(1986): 2265.

Pellegrino, Edmund D., and D. Thomasa, eds. *A Philosophical Basis of Medical Practice.* 1981.

Percival, Thomas. *Percival's Medical Ethics,* edited by Chauncey D. Leake. 1975. An array of codes of medical ethics, including some of those discussed in this book, is in the appendices.

Peschel, E. R., ed. *Medicine and Literature.* 1980.

Peter, Val J. "Vicarious Morality and the Law." *Creighton Law Review* 14(1981): 1379.

Peters, Thomas J., and Robert H. Waterman, Jr. *In Search of Excellence.* 1982.

Pincoffs, Edmund. "Quandary Ethics." *Mind* 80(1975): 552. Also in Hauerwas and MacIntyre.

Plato. Socratic Dialogues. In *Plato: The Collected Dialogues,* edited by Edith Hamilton and Huntington Cairns. 1961. *See also* Hubbard and Karnofsky, and White (James Boyd).

Plaut, W. Gunter, ed. *The Torah: A Modern Commentary.* 1981.

Powledge, Frederick. "Something for a Lawyer to Do." *New Yorker,* Oct. 25, 1969, 63. On Charles Morgan. Excerpts in *A.L.E.*

Redmount, Robert S. "Attorney Personalities and Some Psychological Aspects of Legal Consultation." *University of Pennsylvania Law Review* 109(1961): 972. *See also* Shaffer and Redmount.

Rodes, Robert E. *The Legal Enterprise.* 1976.

——. *Law and Liberation.* 1986.

Rodes, Robert E., and Thomas L. Shaffer. "Law for Those Who Are to Die." In *New Meanings of Death,* edited by Herman Feifel, 291. 1977.

Rogers, Carl. *Client-Centered Therapy.* 1951.

——. *On Becoming a Person.* 1961.

Rose, Phyllis. *Parallel Lives: Five Victorian Marriages.* 1984.

Rosenthal, M. L., ed. *The William Carlos Williams Reader.* 1966.

Rowley, Harold Henry. *The Servant of Jahweh.* 1952.

Ruether, Rosemary Radford. *New Woman, New Earth.* 1975.

Schnackenberg, Rudolph. *The Moral Teaching of the New Testament.* 1965.

Scholler, Heinrich. "Martin Luther on Jurisprudence—Freedom, Conscience, Law." *Valparaiso University Law Review* 15(1981): 265.

Schudson, Michael Steven. *Discovering the News: A Social History of American Newspapers.* 1978.

——. "Public, Private, and Professional Lives: The Correspondence of David Dudley Field and Samuel Bowles." *American Journal of Legal History* 21(1977): 191. In *A.L.E.*

Schwartz, Murray. "The Death and Regeneration of Ethics." In *American Bar Foundation Research Journal* (Fall 1980): 953.

——. "The Professionalism and Accountability of Lawyers." *California Law Review* 66(1978): 669.

Schweid, Eliezer. "The Authority Principle in Biblical Morality." *Journal of Religious Ethics* 8(1980): 180.

Selzer, Richard. *Mortal Lessons.* 1976.

——. *Rituals of Surgery.* 1980.

Shaffer, Thomas L. *American Legal Ethics.* 1985. Abbreviated in this volume as *A.L.E.*

——. "David Hoffman's Law School Lectures, 1822–1833." *Journal of Legal Education* 32(1982): 127.

——. *Death, Property, and Lawyers.* 1970. Updated in *Family Systems and Inheritance Patterns,* edited by Marvin Sussman and Judith Cates, 87. 1982.

——. "The Gentleman in Professional Ethics." *Queen's Law Journal* 10(1984): 1.

——. "Jurisprudence in Light of the Hebraic Faith." *Notre Dame Journal of Law, Ethics, and Public Policy* 1(1984): 77.

——. *Legal Interviewing and Counseling.* 2d ed., with James R. Elkins. 1987.

——. "The Legal Ethics of Radical Individualism." *Texas Law Review* 65 (1987): 963.

——. *On Being A Christian and A Lawyer.* 1981. Includes Hauerwas-Shaffer essay on Thomas More.

——. *The Planning and Drafting of Wills and Trusts.* 1972. 2d ed., 1979. *See also* Rodes, *The Legal Enterprise.*

Shaffer, Thomas L., and Robert S. Redmount. *Legal Interviewing and Counseling Cases.* 1980.

——. *Lawyers, Law Students, and People.* 1977.

Sharswood, George. *An Essay on Professional Ethics.* 1854. 4th ed., 1876. Also in *American Bar Association Reports* 32(1907), and in *A.L.E.*

Shaw, George Bernard *The Doctor's Dilemma.* 1909. Bretano's ed., 1928, and Penguin ed., 1975.

Shklar, Judith. *Ordinary Vices.* 1984.

Shriver, Donald, and Karl Ostrom. *Is There Hope for the City?* 1977.

Sigal, Phillip. "Reflections on Ethical Elements of Judaic Halakhah." *Duquesne Law Review* 23(1985): 863.

Simon, William. "The Ideology of Advocacy." *Wisconsin Law Review* (1978): 29.

Smith, Timothy. *Revivalism and Social Reform in Mid-Nineteenth Century America.* 1958.

Snow, C. P. *Trollope: His Life and His Art.* 1975. Lists and describes the novels.

Socrates. *See* Plato.

Sommer, R. *Personal Space.* 1969.

Sophocles. *Antigone.* In *Sophocles: The Oedipus Cycle,* edited by Dudley Fitts and Robert Fitzgerald, 183. 1977.

Soskin, William. *See* Lewis, Sinclair.

Speer, Albert. *Inside the Third Reich.* 1970. *See* Hauerwas, *Truthfulness.*

Steele, F. "Physical Settings and Organizational Development." In *Social Intervention,* edited by H. Hornstein et al. 1971.

Steinberg, Milton. *Basic Judaism.* 1947.

Steiner, Bernard C. *Life of Roger Brooke Taney.* 1922.

Story, Joseph. Review of Hoffman's *Course. North American Review,* Nov. 1817, 76.

Szasz, Thomas. *Law, Liberty, and Psychiatry: An Inquiry into the Social Uses of Mental Health Practices.* 1963.

——. *The Theology of Medicine: The Political-Philosophical Foundations of Medical Ethics.* 1977.

Taney, Roger Brooke. *See* Burt, Steiner.

Taylor, Lawrence. *A Trial of Generals.* 1981.

Thielicke, Helmut. *Theological Ethics.* Eerdmans English ed. 3 vols. 1969.

Thomas, Lewis. *The Youngest Science: Notes of a Medicine Watcher.* 1983.

Tigar, Michael. "A Lawyer for Social Change." *Center Magazine,* Dec. 1971. Excerpts in *A.L.E.*

Tillich, Paul. *Morality and Beyond.* 1963.

Tinder, Glenn. *Tolerance: Toward a New Civility.* 1976.

Tivnan, Edward. "The Death of a Law Firm." *New York Magazine,* July 26, 1982, 37. In *A.L.E.*

deTocqueville, Alexis. *Democracy in America.* 1835. Random House ed., 1945. Excerpts in *A.L.E.*

Torah. *See* Plaut.

Toulmin, Stephen. "Ethics and Equity: The Tyranny of Principles." *Gazette* 15(1981): 240.

Train, Arthur. *Yankee Lawyer: The Autobiography of Ephraim Tutt.* 1943. *See* Medina. Excerpts in *A.L.E.*

——. Review of *Yankee Lawyer: The Autobiography of Ephraim Tutt. Yale Law Journal* 52(1943): 945. Train wrote the review of his own book. Excerpts in *A.L.E.*

——. "Case Number 4—Sweet Land of Liberty." *Saturday Evening Post,* Aug. 16, 1919. Discussed in chapter 5 of this volume.

——. "In Witness Whereof." *Saturday Evening Post,* May 7, 1921. Discussed, in addition to this volume (chapter 5), in Medina. In *A.L.E.*

Trillin, Calvin. "Making Adjustments." *New Yorker,* May 28, 1984, 50.

——. "A Reporter at Large (Harvard Law School)." *New Yorker,* Mar. 26, 1984, 53.

Trollope, Anthony. *See* Snow, Letwin, Wijesinha. *Orley Farm* has been published with a preface by Henry Drinker, on Felix Graham's legal ethics (Knopf, 1950). I quote from the 1935 Oxford edition, which uses the original (1862) serialized text.

Tutt, Ephraim. *See* Train, Medina, McGuire.

Updike, John. "Personal History: At War with My Skin." *New Yorker,* Sept. 2, 1985, 39.

Vorspan, Albert. *Giants of Justice.* 1960. Excerpts in *A.L.E.*

Wachbroit, Robert. Review of *After Virtue,* 1981 ed., by Alasdair MacIntyre. *Yale Law Journal* 92(1983): 564.

——. Review of *After Virtue,* 1984 ed., by Alasdair MacIntyre. *Yale Law Journal* 92(1985): 1559. The above two reviews differ slightly.

Walker, Thomas C. *See* Boyd.

Wasserstrom, Richard. "Lawyers as Professionals: Some Moral Issues." *Human Rights* 5(1975): 1. Excerpts in *A.L.E.*

——. "Lawyers and Revolution." *University of Pittsburgh Law Review* 30(1968): 125.

Excerpts in *A.L.E.*

Watson, Andrew S. *The Lawyer in the Interviewing and Counseling Process.* 1976.

Webber, Jonathan. "Between Law and Custom: Women's Experience of Judaism." In Holden. *See also* Neuberger.

Weil, Simone. *See* Panichas.

Welter, Barbara. "The Cult of True Womanhood: 1820–1860." *American Quarterly* 18(1961): 151. Also in Pressen, Edward, ed. *The Many-Faceted Jacksonian Era,* 46. 1977.

Whately, Richard. *Paley's Moral Philosophy.* 1859. Excerpts in *A.L.E.*

Whicher, Stephen E., ed. *Selections from Ralph Waldo Emerson. See also* Cole. Includes the Divinity School Address.

White, James Boyd. "The Ethics of Argument: Plato's *Gorgias* and the Modern Lawyer." *University of Chicago Law Review* 50(1983): 849. Also in White's *When Words Lose Their Meaning.* 1984.

White, James P. Memorandum to the deans of ABA-approved law schools, QS8283–18, Jan. 24, 1983. Other reports on national law school statistics by Dean White are published annually in the *American Bar Association Journal.*

Wiesel, Elie. *A Jew Today.* 1978.

Wijesinha, Rajiva. *The Androgynous Trollope: Attitudes to Women amongst Early Victorian Novelists.* 1982.

Williams, William Carlos. *Autobiography*. 1951. *See also* Rosenthal.
Wire, Antoinette Clark. "Economics and Early Christian Voices." *Pacific Theological Review* 19(1985): 15.
Woloch, Nancy. *Women and the American Experience*. 1984.
Wyatt-Brown, Bertram. *Southern Honor: Ethics and Behavior in the Old South*. 1982.
Yoder, John Howard. *The Politics of Jesus*. 1972.
——. *The Priestly Kingdom*. 1984.
Zahn, Gordon. *In Solitary Witness: The Life and Death of Franz Jagerstatter*. 1964.

Index of Names

Real persons, living or dead, who are discussed or mentioned in this book are listed in the index of names. Those whose names appear merely in a list or in the chapter notes or bibliography are not included. Names of characters in stories, either fictional or real, appear in the index of stories.

Index of Stories

Names of characters appearing in stories are also listed in this index, with the titles of the stories, books, plays, or television series in which they appear cited in parentheses.